PRAISE FOR *When I Am Italian*

"A beautiful book. It takes us through the decades of the last century and into this one to ask what it means to be Italian long after one generation's arrival, and to consider how deep and elemental the facts of that are. This is a subtle, moving, and original piece of work—to read it is to see the world around us differently."
— Joan Silber, author of *Improvement: A Novel*

"*When I Am Italian*, Joanna Clapps Herman's exquisite new memoir, begins with her rich, cocoonlike childhood inside an extended Italian American family in Waterbury, Connecticut. With its all-encompassing rituals of food, talk, and work, her family has transposed the rhythms of southern Italy to the new world. It's only when Clapps Herman leaves home—to escape the restrictions and claim her own life—that she realizes that this part of her identity does not necessarily reflect how the rest of America sees itself. With beauty and insight, *When I Am Italian* gives us Clapps Herman's fully lived understanding of the complex interweaving of culture and finding self."
— Lisa Wilde, author of *Yo, Miss: A Graphic Look at High School*

WHEN I AM ITALIAN

To Detta –
Joanna Clapps Herman

WHEN I AM ITALIAN

Joanna Clapps Herman

excelsior editions

AN IMPRINT OF STATE UNIVERSITY OF NEW YORK PRESS

Cover image: The family at Sunday dinner. Courtesy of
the author.

Published by State University of New York Press, Albany

Excelsior Editions is an imprint of
State University of New York Press

For information, contact
State University of New York Press, Albany, NY
www.sunypress.edu

Library of Congress Cataloging-in-Publication Data

Names: Herman, Joanna Clapps, author.
Title: When I am Italian / Joanna Clapps Herman.
Description: Excelsior editions. | Albany, NY : State University of
    New York Press, Albany, [2020]
Identifiers: LCCN 2019000459| ISBN 9781438477183 (pbk. : alk.
    paper) | ISBN 9781438477190 (ebook : alk. paper)
Subjects: LCSH: Herman, Joanna Clapps. | Italian Americans—
    Biography. | Italian American women—Biography. | Italian
    Americans—Ethnic identity. | Herman, Joanna Clapps—Family.
    | Herman, Joanna Clapps—Travel—Italy. | Italian Americans—
    Connecticut—Waterbury—Social life and customs. | Waterbury
    (Conn.)—Biography.
Classification: LCC E184.I8 H47 2020 | DDC 973/.0451—dc23
LC record available at https://lccn.loc.gov/2019000459

10 9 8 7 6 5 4 3 2 1

Per Lucia, sorella di luce

CONTENTS

Move to America

Italia, sempre italia

The Grief Estate

ACKNOWLEDGMENTS

.

There are always too many people to thank and acknowledge at the conclusion of any project. But to make an attempt, I want to thank my beloved friend Myra Goldberg who read and reread these pieces too many times, always with love and encouragement. My sister, Lucia Mudd, who reads my work and is always with me when I need her, and as much as when I don't; my oldest best friend and cousin, Beatrice Avcolli, who lived through much of this with me and who found a piece, an important piece of my writing that had gone missing.

I also want to thank my Italian sisters who make my world a better place in which to read, write, think, and whom I love deeply: Edvige Giunta, Nancy Carnevale, Annie Lanzilotto, Maria Lisella, and Maria Laurino.

I thank my Italian brothers Peter Covino, George Guida, and Joseph Sciorra.

I love and thank Theresa Ellerbrock, Judy Solomon, Linda Sherwin, Wendy Dubin, Liz Rudey, Maria D'Amico, Lisa Wilde, and Sarah Marques, who are my friends, writers, and artists.

I am grateful to Katharine Bernard for editing and proofreading; my lovely stepdaughter, Donna Herman, for proofreading and editing, as well as Robert Oppedisano for editing and fine suggestions for cuts and additions.

Working with Jenn Bennett-Genthner and Michael Campochiaro has been a great pleasure. Actually more fun than I think it's supposed to be. I'm extremely grateful to both of them.

But above all I want to thank James Peltz for his enduring qualities as an editor and as a friend.

INTRODUCTION:
MANY MISSING STONES

My son, James Paul Herman, who is a neuroscientist, has explained a few basics about the brain to me. He tells me that there is so much sensory information impinging on our senses every instant that it's necessary for us to selectively prioritize only a small portion of that stimuli on which to base our moment-by-moment decisions, thoughts, and actions. We're built to respond to stimuli, but we simply can't respond to each and every bit of information that incessantly arrives at the portals of our perception.

He's also explained that memory actually works very differently than we think it does. The recollection of a past event is less like visiting a favorite painting in a museum—the viewing of an unchanging object that we can examine any time we choose; instead it is more like re-creating the painting, and in the act of remembering storing it away with new modifications. Over time, our memories accrue distortions. Although they derive from our original experiences, each time we return some aspects are amplified, others diminished; new details are added, and some lost forever. In short, memories are never accurate recordings of what we have experienced, and are further altered every time we go back to them.

These are the facts.

I point this out because writing works in a similar way to our perceptual processes. Moreover, memoir writing is inherently problematic.

To write anything it's necessary to eliminate much of what comes to mind as we work, so that we can create order out of the plethora of words, ideas, and images that swim forward as we try to fasten language to a page or screen. Then too, a writer has to create a through line, and hold her focus, which means we cannot and should not allow ourselves to go down every path that presents itself as we work.

There are many missing stones along this path. (Reading my earlier memoir, *Anarchist Bastard: Growing Up Italian in America*, will fill in some of the missing pieces, but only some). Like all memory, it's also distorted, but never willfully. I attempt to be simultaneously as truthful as I can be and still shape the narrative as a writer. Probably that's oxymoronic.

The central question underlying this book is this: can a person born outside of Italy be Italian? This question can't be answered with a simple hyphenation of Italian-American. This hyphenated identity coming from the academy, while technically correct, is for some of us (me in particular) too formal and technical. It wasn't what we called ourselves: therefore, it feels inauthentic when I say it. While I know I am American, I know, too, that I am Italian.

How do I claim such an identity when I am not able to speak the language more than primitively? The voices I heard around me: tones and cadences, the broken English, the letters from Italy being read out loud to my grandmother, the dialects that were spoken, the kinds of jokes and stories we told, the Italian and American songs, the vernacular English, even the provincial accent I carry with me are all a part of the grounding soil from which I came. It's all in the soup of vocal and written words that I call on when I write.

How do we keep all of these aspects of our identity and our questions about what identity means in perspective? An ethnic identity can embrace and give comfort and it can confine and imprison. How do we keep this clear to ourselves as we investigate these questions? If, like me, you are from one of Italy's overseas colonies, at least some of this *Italianità* will be in your skin, bones, and heart: other pieces have to be understood, considered, called to ourselves through study, travel, reading. Some of it is just longing. How do we know which pieces are which?

There are as many ways to be Italian as there are Italians, Italian Americans, Italians in Italy, Italians in diaspora the world over. Moreover, the ways of being Italian have changed radically in all of our homes, along with modern life. Still there are some things that people who have been raised in this culture share, value, and even disavow, yet engage in compulsively.

My ancestral village in America is Waterbury, Connecticut. It's in places like Waterbury, Brooklyn, the Bronx, Queens, Hoboken, Patterson, Boston, Cleveland, Chicago, Detroit, New Orleans, Pittsburgh, South Philly, Kansas

City, Baltimore, Providence, and all the other Italian neighborhoods and communities throughout America where we learned the rules and customs, the recipes and the rituals of our tribe.

It was in those places we learned to be Italian, Sicilian, southern Italian; there where we were in and out of each other's kitchens on a daily basis, helping each other, driving each other nuts, and always there for each other in times of crisis. We not only were well trained in the cultural mores, we didn't know any other way for quite a while, especially, if like me, you were raised in one of the places where relatives live cheek by jowl.

I've tried to set out the stones of the path I've taken from Waterbury out into modern life. I've written about my early life in Waterbury in my extended embracing family, about how important food and work are to people from my culture. I've written, too, about going to college, about what my young working life in New York City was like and what being a lifelong reader and eventually a writer has meant to me. I've written about my long professional life as a teacher, as well as my life with my husband and son. There are essays about travel, and what it has been like to lose people I love. Throughout these decades my original family in Waterbury and Italy have remained central to what is important to me. Each decade changed me; each experience changed me. Therefore, every essay attempts to address one or another of those varied experiences. But many stones are missing.

Therapy hasn't been a single stone on the path, it's been *the path* on which I've tread for years. Yet I haven't been able to write an essay about what a central role it's played in my life. In a sense it's a ghost piece of this collection. It's just too big and complex: the micro- and the macrodimensions of my adult psyche. Therapy has been as essential to me as family, friends, love, reading, writing, and work. It's been much more important than any formal education I've had. It helped me find my way through the labyrinth that has been my personal attempt to both continue to belong to and to be separate from the tribe I come from. Therapy has enabled me to understand what my Italian life has meant to me and how to write about this crucial material.

For now, I leave you with this: Every ethnic community initially is a liminal space on the way to America. But at the other end of such a long journey, I have come to the certainty that wherever we bury our dead inevitably becomes our home.

WHAT DOES IT MEAN
TO BE ITALIAN?

Quando sono italiana:
When I Am Italian

SUMMER MORNINGS WHILE MY COFFEE IS BREWING I SLIP MY FEET INTO the plastic slippers I keep by the door, before I go out on my terrace in my nightgown or an old, loose dress to sit. This is a luxury in New York City, wearing *una vestaglia* outside, in full view, but not in public. Half asleep, I sit and study my large pots of geraniums. The endless rain this spring has forced excessive blossoming. There are some that are dark velvety reds, a single pale Giotto pink, and two shades of coral. I gaze at my flowers and then off into the distance at the Hudson River and at Riverside Church. The Number 1 subway descends into the tunnel with a noisy clatter. I go to gather my cup and milk and coffee from the kitchen, setting them out on the Moroccan tray table, look around again, and slowly begin to drink my coffee. The *Times* is under my coffeepot so that it doesn't blow away, but I rarely read the paper out there: too breezy.

After my first cup of coffee, I stand to visit each large pot and inspect my blossoming plants. My body is relaxed under the thin fabric loosely grazing my skin; the skirt flaps in the morning breeze.

Is this blossom ready to be snapped or clipped, then stuffed down into the soil in the pot? Are there still buds under the flower waiting to unfold? This takes time and consideration. I don't act quickly. I stick my fingers in the dirt. How dry is it? Water? I go back to my coffee, sipping and gazing.

I'll spend some time going back and forth to my kitchen filling watering cans. The watering leads to the various colored petals scattering over the terrace. I might gently shake the dense ripe blossoms to loosen the ones that are ready to drop.

Then I sweep. The soft repetition of brush, brush, against the hard surface, the sound and the motion of the broom, makes a meditative moment. I seek out every crevice between pots, sweep, sweep. Sometimes I sweep more than is needed, loosen a few more petals, tweak another blossom to make room for the new buds underneath. The gathered petals create a small pool of color.

Each brush calls up in me *anime di donne italiane*, the spirits of Italian women. They flow into me with each sweep of the broom, inhabit me. Brush, hush, a whisper from woman to woman. All my Italian women are with me: Siciliane, Lucane,[1] Calabrese, Abruzzese, Napolitane, Pugliese join this convocation. They are in me, with me. Mornings, Mediterranean women sweep around their pots on their *terrazzi*, or in front of their doorways, around their plants: they bend to pick up a stray stem or stick or pebble from the ground, a bit of litter. They, too, are in their *vestaglie*. They, too, sprinkle water on plants, then throw some of the water on hard stone pavement, throw a rag down to the ground. The broom collects the rag in its bristles, then sweeps away the dark earth stains. Then they rest on their brooms, look off.

All of this is real. Something that lives in me.

Other gestures and postures transport me to this state. When I come upon women crossing their arms over their breasts, standing outside their doorways talking to their neighbors in southern Italy or Sicily, I want to stop and chat with them, pretend I live there too. When I snap the ends of string beans, mend with good small stitches, tug just so with each stitch. When I cut the bread toward my breasts instead of cutting down on a breadboard—my Italian women are with me. In me.

This archaic sense of *italianità* beckons itself to me at particular moments. Once, just steps beyond the Milano train station, about a dozen Roma children surrounded Bill, James, and me. James was a young boy. Many of the Roma were younger and tinier than James. We were in for the day from Torino. Encircling us, they touched Bill all over his body, while one small hand slipped in and out of his pocket stealing about 100 euros without him realizing it. They ran off while my husband reached into his pocket to discover the money was gone. Then this group of a dozen or so waifs dared to circle back to us to see what they have left behind. Watching them approach us again, my grandmother's shrieking dialect poured out of me, "*Chiesta ca! Ma che fai mo? Ancor' ritorn.' Ammazzatevi!*" They scattered instantly recognizing my tone, if not my words. It was the voice of an old Italian woman who's afraid of no one. No one had better dare to come near her family. It worked. I was enraged and thrilled at the same time. I know who I am at those moments in no uncertain terms. I am more than myself. I am my original self.

During the time we lived in Torino, I noticed that all the women of my mother's age dressed precisely as my mother and my aunts dressed: the same boxy rayon blouses in flowery prints were worn over sheath skirts reaching just below their knees. They all wore the same low-heeled pumps. Simple and elegant. I could and did buy almost whatever came to hand in the outdoor markets, and my mother was delighted. How had that style sailed across the ocean. It wasn't high fashion, it was simple and lovely, what older Italian women wore then, wherever they lived.

Two years ago I began obsessively searching for French bistro dishes with an orange stripe around the rim. At some point I realized this search had overtaken me, because they looked so much like the dishes that had always been on my grandmother's farm table. When I tripped into that recognition I bought even more of them. They belong to me. These dishes happen to be French bistro, but who's keeping this record? *È mio.*

All this belongs to me. Is me.

When my sister and I heard older women speaking in Portugal, Lucia turned to me. "Don't those soft *s*'s sound like Tolvese dialect?" She was so right. Didn't those women look like our aunts and grandmothers too? They wore the same long skirts, the same scarves tied to their heads as our older Tolvese relatives. Why would vernacular Portuguese sound like our dialect? *Chissa?*

When I read *Palace Walk*, the first volume of *The Cairo Trilogy* by Naguib Mahfouz, the descriptions of the coffee gatherings, with plates of sweets after school hours: the women and the children all gathered in one room every afternoon, I was stunned by recognition. This was *my* home, this was *my* family. The voice and tone of the father in that novel was identical to that of my grandfathers. I began to understand how widespread the Mediterranean culture was and is: how broad and old the culture I belong to is. Yes, this too is familiar and recognizable.

For years on my travels throughout Italy, I admired the gold necklaces on Italian women, tracing their fine Italian necks. I saved every extra penny all of one year because we were going to be in Italy that summer. I bought myself one lovely gold necklace. When I wear that necklace I am more Italian. This identification takes on a new meaning. Buying the necklace, wearing the necklace helps me assemble more of my Italianate self. These are layers I reach for, plastering onto my skin to reinforce this identification.

I study the way women dress when I travel in the Mediterranean, then buy clothes just like theirs. I study their eyeglass frames. Search for similar ones myself. My homes for decades have been filled with coffeepots, platters, silverware, duplicating the ones I've found in the Italian and French homes of family and friends, in flea markets, in home good stores.

These are things I gather to me as I travel, take home to store in my home and inside me.

I am Italian. I am Mediterranean, I reassure myself.

While Waterbury,[2] my Italian ancestral village, my Italian colony, came first, once I was firmly outside the paradigm of my origins, all my extensive travels throughout the Mediterranean, in Italy especially, the reading, studying, observing, has reinforced what I knew as my Italian self. I carefully harvest each observation, each new understanding, applying the additional layers like gold leaf onto myself.

This is invocation, is an embracing, but also, an insistence. But to whom am I insisting?

Perhaps the construction of this overlay onto my origins is not just an embrace of the larger Italian culture, but in my intensity is, at times, exaggerated. Perhaps I've even become a fabricator of the first fraudulent order.

I'm a primitive Italian speaker. I get by in Italy. Although the sounds of my dialect create an intimacy and longing when it swishes past my ears, I only have a scattered vocabulary, the dialect words we used daily alongside of our everyday English. Merely, the obvious.

I was born and raised in America, however much our daily lives were embedded in the ancient ways of southern Italian immigrants. I grew up listening to rock 'n' roll in the late '50s, as it poured through our radios; Fats Domino, Buddy Holly. I went to sock hops in high school. I wore madras plaid shirtwaist dresses with the best of them. I learned to dance the jitterbug first, then the twist, then the jerk, then I learned to move my body to the rhythms of rock and soul. Motown still thrills me. I have lived through the civil rights movement, the women's liberation movement, the sexual revolution, the assassinations of Martin Luther King Jr., John F. Kennedy, Robert Kennedy, and Malcolm X. I am embedded in our history.

I enjoy the privileges, and I am ashamed of the meanness that attends growing up at the height of the America First World Empire days.

When I'm in Italy, clearly *sono americana*. They know it, so I have to know it.

While I work always to create another deposit of this complex, layered identity, I am really only trying to say one thing. This is a confession, so I'm just going to go ahead and say it. I confess. I am American.

Just not when I'm sweeping my terrace.

WATERBURY, CONNECTICUT, MY ANCESTRAL VILLAGE

Up the Farm

"UP THE FARM, WE'RE GOING UP THE FARM. DO YOU WANT TO GO WITH US, Aunt Vicki? My mom told me to call and see you if you want to walk up with us?"

"Aunt Toni just stopped by. Let's see if she wants to go too. When are you going?" I'm standing by the phone that hangs on the wall in our kitchen. "We're going right away, I think. Mom, when are we going to go? Aunt Toni's there and Aunt Vicki wants to know."

"Tell her in about half an hour," my mother yells from her bedroom. She is almost finished cleaning in there. "Tell them the coffee's on, not to put any on and to stop in when they're ready and have a cup—if they're coming."

"Did you call Aunty Ag yet?" Aunt Vicki wants to know after I tell her what my mother said. Aunty Ag is their oldest sister. She lives next door to Aunt Vicki.

"Not yet, but I'm going to call her next. Can Linda come down as soon as she's ready?" Linda is Aunt Vicki's daughter, my age, my cousin, my playmate and constant companion.

"We'll be down as soon as we clean up." She doesn't say if Linda will come down early.

These are my mother's sisters, Aunty Ag and Aunt Vicki and Aunt Toni. They were all brought up on the farm where Grandma and Grandpa still live. Uncle Rocco, the only son, lives there too, with his wife, Aunt Bea, and their kids, and the pigs, and cows, and rabbits, and chickens, and dogs and cats, and sometimes a horse or a mule. Aunt Bea is the only sister-in-law. Everything is always the same up the farm. Except for my Aunt Bea. She's the only thing that has changed at the farm. She's not Italian.

We live "down the hill," Aunty Ag, Aunt Vicki, and us. Aunt Toni lives "over the hill." But "up the farm" is the middle of everything in our family. "Up" is up a small, gently graded slope. None of us lives more than a ten-minute walk away.

My mother told me to call the aunts. In each household, the mothers and their children wash their faces, change clothes from play to clean, and we all get ready for our walk up the farm. The men are at work, at a factory or on a construction site. We will get home before they do, so they won't come home to empty houses, empty tables, and cold stoves, but these midday hours are ours, the moms' and the kids', to spend any way we want. Taking a walk up the farm is just right for those sunny hours when the beds have been made and the furniture dusted and it's too early to start supper anyway.

My face is clean. I have on a starched, ruffled pinafore. The seams of my pinafore, stiff from the starch and iron, scratch against my belly. I don't mind on a hot day like today because I only have to wear panties and my pinafore, not even an undershirt. It feels so good to have so little on, as if I could do anything. I am waiting by the living room window. My mother and sister are still getting ready. I have on my new white sandals. My toes stick out in front and the holes in the straps seem so friendly to me.

I see my cousin, Linda, coming down the dirt sidewalk. Oh good, I think, she's coming early. Then I see the small parade behind her, her little brother Joey and my aunts and the other cousins.

"They're coming, Mommy," I yell, to hurry my house along.

"Put the cups on the table and get the cake out," my mother yells from her bedroom. She is always putting on her lipstick just when company comes. She and my sister come out of the bedrooms.

My sister is dressed the way I am. Her pinafore is a little bigger than mine, and she has red rickrack on the edges of her stiff ruffles. My mother loves rickrack. She sews it on everything, even on the *mappines*, our dishcloths.

My mother is wearing my favorite of her dresses. It has flowers all over, green and pink, with soft sleeves, like little capes, on each arm, and a full skirt. Her pink earrings match the flowers on the dress, but her lipstick stands out red, different from the other colors. Her lips seem so whole, more real than real lips. When I get big and wear lipstick, I wonder if it will make my lips look like that too.

"Don't get dirty playing," she calls to Lucia and me, as we run outside to meet our cousins to play—Gilda, Diane, and Linda, who had washed, combed their hair, and gotten ready, too. They have on ruffled skirts or cotton dresses with tiny, puffed sleeves, and sandals, or black patent leather shoes. But Gilda has red patent leather shoes. That's because she's biggest and takes tap and ballet. Only Bede, the youngest of us girls, isn't here to play now on the walk up. She is Uncle Rocky and Aunt Bea's daughter, and she lives up the farm. My aunts are all dressed up, like ladies, like my mother. Dressed like ladies, all of them, but each different, too. Aunty Ag always wears pretty necklaces and pink. Aunt Tony wears polka dots and buttons and pockets. Aunt Vicki's the youngest: she wears bangs and wide, scoop-necked dresses.

The aunts go inside for coffee. We play tag outside and show each other our somersaults and splits. But we keep running in and out of the kitchen door, pleading with them to hurry up. Finally, they get up from around the kitchen table and put their cups in the sink. One quickly washes them, another wipes the table. My mother hurries to her bedroom for her pocketbook, to get the card they will all sign to send to Aunt Antoinette in New York, and to make sure that she has the letter that came from Tolve in Italy yesterday so she can read it to everyone up the farm. Then we leave our house.

We begin our walk up the hill. The mothers walk so slowly that we play tag all the way up, get too far ahead of them, in case those dogs start barking. We can go as far ahead as they can see us, then we have to wait again—until we're past the dog and near the rock. The rock is halfway up the hill. It's the only sitting spot on the way that is shaded by trees. It's big, about as tall as Gilda, who has her red shoes on. She's the oldest, so she tells us what to do. "Let's run to the rock to wait for them there," Gilda says. "Then we won't have to be on this stupid hot road." She thinks of these things.

We run up the hill as fast as we can.

"Hey, where are you going? Don't go too far," the mothers cry from behind us.

"We're just going to the rock," we take turns yelling, as we race to see who can get there first. "We'll wait for you slowpokes there. And we'll be nice and cool and you'll be so hot," we shout, taking our tone from Gilda. This is a great rock. It's big enough to call a boulder. "This is a boulder," we tell each other. This we probably learned from Gilda, too. She knows everything. This rock is so big and fat that there's only one way to get to the top. It has one small foothold, halfway up. It's so high that you have to reach your leg up to it and wiggle your toes in and hoist yourself to the top. Sometimes you don't make it and your foot is left in the step—but you don't want a boost, you want to do it yourself. If we are all up on the top at once it gets too crowded. Then someone says, "I can jump right down." And somebody else says, "And I can jump right down without even falling!"

On the top of the rock there is a crack right down the middle. "What if this rock split right down the middle while we're sitting up here?"

"I'd jump right down to the middle of the road as soon as I heard it start to crack," Diane says. She's fast. I think to myself I better keep listening. "But what if there's an earthquake and you didn't have time to jump?"

"I'd still jump—only farther!"

"But what if it just split and you fell into the middle of the crack and you were stuck and you couldn't even get out?"

Now I see the mothers coming up around the curve in the road. The sun shines down on their thick curled hair, and on their strong arms. It slides down the folds of their full-skirted dresses. They place one foot down at a time, definitely and slowly. They don't pay attention to their slow, deliberate steps, only to what they're saying. They turn to face whoever is talking, twisting their heads sideways as they walk toward us. They look so pretty, so sunny.

"We're in the shade and you're on the hot road," we shout down to them. We're high up on the rock.

"If you weren't such slowpokes, you wouldn't have to be hot." They come closer, slowly. Linda and I jump down off the rock.

"Don't scrape your knees, one of the mothers calls, turning away from their conversation for a minute. When they finally come abreast of the rock, we shout to them, "Look at this crack in the rock. We almost fell in it. What would happen if we fell in it? Would we have to stay there forever?"

"You couldn't fall in it. It would never crack."

"But if it did, could they break it open without hurting us?"

But they are even with us now, so it's time to run the next stretch of the road, not to wait for what they'll say.

Around the next curve in the road, the farm comes into view. Linda and I start looking for Bede to see who spots her first. I look in the fields to see if she's running with her brothers. She isn't. She's not under the tree, either.

I want to call to her first, "We're here. Come down and walk with us," before Linda gets a chance to, but I can't see her. As we come closer, I try to see if Bede is anywhere on the porch.

The porch is strewn with broken, rusty wagons, wooden crates, baskets of tomatoes, and a low, weathered table, covered with more tomatoes laid out to ripen. A strange new mutt is tied to the leg of the wooden table. He's big. He lies there, jaw resting on the cement floor, eyes blinking, his back legs curled to one side, the front ones straight out on either side of his jaw. There's a dish of drying food beside him. Flies buzz onto the food. No life, only this dog and the flies. I look up to the sun porch trying to see through the screen windows and through Grandma's many plants. I see someone moving, but I can't tell who it is. Whoever it is waves to us and leaves the screened window. If it's Bede, she'll be down in a minute.

To the right is the cow field. It's the field on the edge of the lake. The cows are scattered throughout it. Some are down by the water, drinking. The fence around the cow field is made of bedsprings wired to posts, posts wired to boards, boards wired to wire. Next to the field is a brick bread oven. It's just right to play house in. There's a mulberry tree that hangs over it. We gather the berries and leaves to feed our babies. In the front of the house is a stone well with a metal arch for the well wheel. It looks like a big stone sand pail to me. Grandpa has it covered with two thick slabs of slate, since they stopped using it, we won't fall in. There is a crack between the two slabs. I worry about this crack even more than the one on the rock, but I climb up there anyway and put my eye right up to the crack to see what's down there. There's a big dark hole down there. We squeeze tiny pebbles through the crack to hear then splash down below.

"You gonna falla down and die," Grandpa always yells when he finds us up there, though the slabs weigh two hundred pounds apiece. The well is in the middle of an area paved with big, irregular flat stones. The bottom half of the house is made of these stones, too.

"How did these rocks get here?" we ask Grandpa, over and over.

"A big giant came and bring 'em to me," he answers.

"Oh, come on, Grandpa. There's no such thing as giants."

"Yes, there is. How you think they gotta here? You think I could carry them all by myself? He lives down in the well and he gonna get you if you go up on top. I only let 'em out *quando* I need 'em."

"Let's see him."

"No, no. Oh, I can no do that. He's gonna eat you all up." Inset in the rocks on the lower part of the house are arched, leaded windows, and a heavy arched wooden doorway leads into the cellar. I don't like to go in this way. It's dark and damp in there. One room down there is the wine cellar. That part has a dirt floor and rocks from the earth for walls. It smells like wine and it's musty. Grandpa's barrels are lined up purple-brown. How anyone can drink what comes out of these old barrels. The cheeses that Grandma makes and the hams that she prepares, all covered with black pepper, hang from a beam over the barrels. The pepper makes the hams look dirty to me. The strong smell of this room makes me think that this is where the giant lives. The cellar pantry is another room down here.

That's where hundreds of glass jars are up on the creaky wood shelves. The jars of tomatoes are filled with red, wet globs, pressing against the glass. Little yellow dots, the seeds, are stuck inside, too, and limp pieces of green peek between the red globs. It's too damp, too smelly, and spiderwebs dress the jars. It's old down here and the stairs creak when we walk up and down to the kitchen.

So I'm glad Bede comes down the other way. She jumps down from the third step. "Hi!" she yells, "Can you stay?" The all-important question is how long can we play together. It is never enough; though we meet almost daily, we always want more of each other.

We turn to our mothers, "Can we stay long? Please, please! Can we stay all afternoon?"

"We'll stay about an hour."

"How long is that? Is that a long time?"

"Yes."

"Is it a long, long time?"

"Oh, don't waste your time asking all these questions. Go upstairs and say hello to everyone, and don't forget to kiss Grandma and Grandpa." We run up the stone steps, reaching for the rim of each large stone flowerpot cemented into the side of the steps, until we're at the top. There are three of them, huge, decorated all over with stones stuck into the sides. The pots overflow with geraniums. Grandma loves flowers. They are the one indulgence of her life. As we run into the kitchen through the small porch, Grandma shushes us. She sits in the big, soft chair in the middle of the kitchen. It's hers when it's not Grandpa's, and it's Uncle Rocco's when it's not hers. But Grandpa is now taking his midday nap on the couch next to her. If we wake Grandpa, he'll yell, and when Grandpa yells, everyone's afraid, even Grandma.

We go to Grandma, one by one, to kiss her. She smells like the garlic and basil in the tomato jars. She always takes my hair and pushes it behind my ears when I kiss her. "Get 'em outa you eyes," she always says. I always pull it right back as soon as she does it. It feels funny.

Grandpa is opening his eyes now. He doesn't yell, so I say, "Hello, Grandpa," and go over to see if he wants me to kiss him. He doesn't seem mad, so I do what my mother told me to do. His cheek is scratchy and he smells like Grandpa, but different too. He smells sleepy.

"Your mothers are here, too?" he asks frowning.

"They're coming up the stairs." I'm glad to be able to tell him what he wants to know. I hear the screen door slam—flimsy, then hard—out on the small porch.

"Hi, Papa," they call.

We can go, now that they're here. We pass them on the porch. Mommy bends down to my sister and me and whispers, "Did you kiss Grandma and Grandpa?"

"Yes, yes, we just did," we answer, indignantly.

I turn to my sister, Lucia. "She thinks they're going to die if we don't kiss them." She's so silly. Out the door we go. Her voice follows us outside. "Okay, make sure you stay close enough so you can hear us when we call you. We can't let Daddy find an empty house."

What Crawls around Inside Us

ON THE THIRD-FLOOR APARTMENT WHERE WE LIVE UNTIL I AM SIX, THERE is a large back porch that has a clothesline stringing the house to the telephone pole at the end of the yard. My mother hangs our wash off that back porch several times a week. The creak of our rocking horse sitting on the back porch accompanies the quiet breezes from the trees. This is where we often play, so that my mother can keep track of us from the kitchen as she goes about her housework. But today I am downstairs in the backyard of this three-story, wood-frame house where my family lives in the attic "rent" owned by our *paesans*, the Pagano family. "Be quiet now. Don't make the landlord mad. Don't kick the stairs. The landlady will get mad." Mr. and Mrs. Pagano are small benevolent people who welcomed us into their home, who gave us cookies, who never raised their voices to anyone. Still, the invocation of their titles, landlady, landlord, terrifies me.

At the back end of the yard, down the path that runs under the grape arbor are the garbage cans, right next to the old rusty oil barrel where garbage is burned. It stinks, *pee-ew*, a bad smell.

Lucia must have been at school in her kindergarten because I was by myself in the front yard. I never left my sister's side if she was nearby. I might have been making piles of different leaves, twigs, and pebbles into a grocery store, when I heard a rough old *arugha* truck horn blasting into our tree-lined street. Who was this?

For a minute I couldn't see past the man sitting in the passenger seat of the beaten-up old truck. Even when I did, I was confused by what Grandpa was doing here in front of our house on Ward Street. He only comes to our house for parties when he's all cleaned up with Grandma.

"Giovanna," he called to me, "*Viene ca.*" He must have just finished his garbage collecting route and stopped to say hello. My mother would have recognized the horn of her father's truck. Otherwise why would she have come out to the tiny front porch that we never use to lean over and shout, "Papa, hi," with delight and surprise? She adored her father; she was a favorite of his. She had a small cotton kerchief tied around her hair to keep it off her face and to protect it from the dusting she's been doing. "Go to Grandpa," she laughed and encouraged me from the third floor. I hesitated. The truck was big, banged up and dirty. It was confusing to see Grandpa in his truck on Ward Street. That belonged up the farm where the pigs were. My grandfather got out of the truck and came to just outside the front gate. He wanted to pick me up and kiss me. He had on old dirty clothes. "Go," my mother laughed, "Jo." His face was scratchy.

"Hi Pete," my mother shouted to his hired hand, Pete Capozzi. "Com'on up. I'll make you both a cup of coffee." These men that my grandfather hired to help on the farm had long since sunk into the misery of the stench of booze and the pig manure from my grandfather's farm. Now Pete and my grandfather stretched their necks up toward her, smiled, and talked to my mother. They can't come up right now for coffee.

"Ma, Pete has something for Giovanna. But she won't go to him," Grandpa said to my mother. "*Viene ca,*" he gestured to me to join him at the door of the truck. Pete with a broad smile had stretched his hand out of the truck window—there's something in his dirty hand with the black under his fingernails that he wanted to give me. He takes it back and wipes it with a dirty white hanky. I looked up at mother, "Go ahead Jojo. Pete has something for you." I didn't want to go over to the smelly truck. They were all laughing.

But Grandpa he might get mad. "Giovanna, com'on 'a Pete," Grandpa said. I knew I shouldn't make my grandfather angry. There's a large coin in Pete's hand, which he reached down to hand to me.

My mother had repeated several times from above me, "Take it. Tell Pete, 'Thank you.'" I knew she was saying that I was going to hurt Pete's feelings if I didn't accept his gift. I made myself go over to the truck door and stretched my hand up to his filthy one. All three of the grownups were laughing in delight. He put the dirty coin in my hand. It was a half dollar. This was a huge amount of money for a small child in Waterbury, Connecticut in the late forties. I could barely bring myself to say what I knew I must say. Then I stood looking down at my dirty bounty. I said, "Thank you to Pete," looking down at the cracked sidewalk.

A half dollar, with the angel figure on the back of the coin. I would be able to buy a lot of candy with that filthy money that came from Pete's stinky pocket. Once I had the fifty cents in my hand I stood there frozen with misery. Then I ran down ran to the end of the path where the garbage cans were and placed it very carefully on the top of an old rusting barrel sitting next to the garbage cans. I put the coin in a watery dent near the edge of the barrel and ran down the path and up the three flights of wood stairs to my mother.

Later I went and to see if it was still there. I was surprised that so much money was still sitting there. It felt *schifoso* when I held it in my hand. But I couldn't leave it there.

My mother had us kneel down next to our bed to say our nighttime prayers before we went to sleep. But on Thursday nights when the stores were open late downtown was mother's night out. My mother and her sisters went downtown to go shopping and to see a movie. My father allowed us to use all the living room furniture pillows to build houses. After we played building houses in the living room and it was time for us to go to bed, my father, who had been reading quietly all this time, would tell us solemnly, "Put your night clothes on now girls, it's time for the *Inner Sanctum*." Nightclothes and Inner Sanctum. It seemed so funny that he called our nightgowns, nightclothes, like a word from a long time ago. *Inner Sanctum*, on the other hand, was an exciting scary radio show we listened to with my father every Thursday night. We crawled in our parents' bed with him. He was in the middle and he had an arm around each of us.

We squirmed closer to our father. We were thrilled to be hearing a scary radio show, safely snuggled next to him. Then the show began with the sound of a squeaking door opening onto chilling mysteries. Then came the haunting, insinuating voice of the narrator. "Oh, hello. There you are. I thought you might have forgotten our appointment."

Housing Memory

THERE IS A SMALL WHITE HOUSE THAT HAS INHABITED THE EDGE OF MY consciousness for so long that I can't remember when it began to make itself present. Though its origins are pure Waterbury, the North End, North Main Street where I was raised, it came to haunt me long after I left home. Sometimes this house recedes from memory for years; then at unpredictable times, it returns, either in dreams, or more often simply hovering at the border of memory—a premonition or a warning.

That white house sat on an odd triangle of land made by the fork in the road at the intersection of North Main Street and Chase Avenue. Hill Street Extension created the third short side. It's that bit of street that cut this triangle off from the larger parcel of land it was originally part of. It's a scrap of land left over from when Waterbury grew. It was just left there, orphaned.

This triangle is the result of a forgotten history, when this part of Waterbury was called Piersallville. It's from another time. Even in my dreams and memories, the white house isn't firmly affixed to its scruffy triangle of land; it's as if a storm blew it there once, and the people who owned it forgot to pick it up and take it back to where it belonged.

I seem to be the only one who remembers that white house, even though everyone I know in Waterbury knows the triangle of land.

But all of us remember the Scoville house. The Scoville house had its own peculiar distinction. The Scoville family lived on the corner of North Main

Street, just across the street from our bus stop, so the corner opposite from that triangle.

The Scoville house was dark and in permanent disrepair, as if unmoored from civilization. There were more dogs and cats than you could count. Other animals too. There were chickens; I heard a cock crow every morning. There was a pony out back in the barn. All of the other animals had the run of the yard and the house. There may have been goats too.

So it stunk. A rank animal smell emanated from the house out into the unkempt, debris-strewn yard and into our street. We walked past it quickly, to get past its animal reek on the way to the stop where we waited for the bus to school. The smell behind us, we jabbered, argued, and fooled around while we waited. The corner belonged to all of us from this neighborhood.

The three oldest cousins of the Becce family were the Scarpa kids, who lived two houses away from the Scoville house. Gene, Bob, and Gilda are my Auntie Ag and Uncle Gene's first three children. Each of them delivered newspapers in our neighborhood—to the Scoville's too. The Scoville house was *schifosa*, but not mysterious, not like the white house.

Gilda remembers that although Mrs. Kellogg owned the house, it was her sister, Mrs. Scoville, who lived there with her husband and their only daughter. "I never went in the house when I had to collect money for the paper," Gilda says. "I'd stand on the porch (Do you remember that beaten-up porch?) and their dogs (They had so many!) would start barking and barking. I could tell you so many stories about dogs on that newspaper route. They would open the door just a little and smile at me and stick their hands out of the door with the money—it was always change and it would always be hot. They'd give me hot coins. They kept the money on the wood stove."

"They had a small pony in a little barn out in back called Lucky. My mother and I would walk over to feed him.

"He was standing there in manure up to his ankles. They never cleaned out that barn. And he was blind. 'But why is he called Lucky?,' I asked my mother. He didn't seem so Lucky to me. I was only about four years old then."

The Scovilles' daughter died when she was sixteen years old. Gilda tells me that her mother, my Auntie Ag, said the daughter was very pretty. "I don't know if it was all the dogs or what. They found lots of hair in her lungs when they operated on her," she remembers her mother saying.

The hair found in her lungs could have been a malignant teratoma tumor, which grows slowly in children over time, genetic cells gone awry. Sometimes these growths include teeth, hair, even bone. But our family blamed the Scoville girl's death on her dirty, uncivilized home. A beautiful teenager who grows up there dies with hair in her lungs. It all seemed to fit.

"Miss Kellogg, Mrs. Scoville's sister, who owned that house, would come down to use our phone when she was visiting her sister," Gilda continues. "They didn't have a phone. She smelled so bad my mother had to open all the windows after she left. That whole family smelled. She lived on a farm, and I guess they were all used to living with animals like that. Miss Kellogg was a very smart woman. She had a job as a stenographer for the court. She went to work smelling like that. But they kept her because she knew the law better than anyone.

"My father took me to visit Miss Kellogg up at her farm in Wolcott, and she had the most beautiful pear trees and apple trees. We could have as many apples and pears as we wanted. My brothers and I were the only kids on the street at that time, so everyone was really nice to us.

"Across the street from the Scoville's on the corner there was a mansion with maids and stables. The maids wore those black uniforms with white aprons and white caps like you see in the movies. They'd be out back beating the rugs.

"They kept horses. I remember the maids. There was a woman with very blue eyes. 'Can you see out of those eyes?' I asked her. I wasn't sure that they worked. They didn't look like the eyes in our family. We all had dark eyes.

"There was a black caretaker. His name was Mr. Porter, a big guy with gold teeth. He was in charge of the horses. My brothers used to ride the horses all the time. I went up by myself at four; I was allowed to go all over the neighborhood by myself. I told him, 'I want to ride a horse.'

" 'Okay,' he said, and he put me up on top of the horse and walked me around on the horse. That was a big day for me."

Gilda's older brother Gene Scarpa is the firstborn grandchild of the Becce family.

He's a tall handsome man, full of charm and generous smiles. He knows a lot about our family.

"My sister's got it all wrong," Gene says. "There was no mansion there. There were stables on the corner where they kept horses—there had been a large horse farm there. But only the stable was left. People boarded their horses there, but you could also rent other horses that they kept there, and ride on a dirt trail behind where the woods were. My brother Bob and I used to go riding all the time on that trail. It was so beautiful. That was before the shopping plaza came in and changed everything. Modern life."

Gene tells me that the triangle of land was once a part of horse farm, which is why there was a horse stable there. Once you crossed the street away from the bus stop and that triangle of land, you were on the short stretch of North Main Street—before it turns into Bucks Hill Road—where our families lived.

Although every other house in our neighborhood was neatly groomed and painted regularly, yards mowed, raked, shoveled, the Scoville house was still a part of the neighborhood. We hurried past the smell, but we accepted the house as a part of our world. No one ever called the health department or social services. The '50s still had a connection to an older, more disorderly world, where troubles and chaos weren't always boxed up or sent out of sight.

In 1950, my family left our third-floor rent in the Pagano's house at 56 Ward Street and moved to 2279 North Main Street, into "the new house." The new house was built from a plan my father found in the *Waterbury Republican American*. The plan had a kitchen, a living room, two bedrooms, one bathroom, a front porch, and a garage; although modest in dimensions, it was a grand undertaking for us. For two years, everything we did was about the new house. My father sent for the plan, then hired a Dutch architect to modify it a bit, bought the lot, and then my parents began building. They did as much of the work as they could themselves. My father built us a small playhouse out of the cinderblocks—until he needed them for the cellar. We'd go up in the evening after my father came home from work and on weekends. Both of my parents did the masonry work, setting the cinderblocks for the cellar. My mother painted the cellar walls with black tar. My father built out the floor over the cellar. When the floor over the cellar was finished, it was a celebration. My father acted as contractor, hiring men he knew from years of working in construction. He oversaw the framing, the plumbing, the electrical, and the rest of our new house, each job in turn.

We were always excited to go up there because our house was being built just a couple of houses down from our cousins. Each work session, each visit just to see how it was coming was a chance to anticipate living near our family. My cousins would come down and play with us on the lot. My aunts and uncles would stop by. We'd go up on Sundays just to take a ride and look at the house. We picnicked on the construction site, ran around in the dust and mud, Lucia and I helping with the small tasks. We were going to live in the new house that we had watched being built, close to our cousins. We'd be going to a new school. Everything in our lives revolved around the new house.

Once, when the framing was completed, my father showed us the part of the house that was going to be our bedroom. Lucia remembers that we lay down on the floor where we had mentally placed the bed. Then, she tells, as we lay there, first we pretended to be reading in bed. Then, because we knew we weren't allowed to read after we went to bed, we pretended we had pulled the blankets over our head and were reading by flashlights under the covers. Everything would be possible in the new house.

I remember that when the house was completed and we were going to move in the next day, my mother teased us and said, "It's finished now. Would you like to stay here tonight?"

"Yes, yes," Lucia and I screamed in delight, and it was clear at first that our parents wanted to as much as we did. The idea hung there in the air for a minute. It was real for that small moment.

"But we really don't have anywhere to sleep," my mother said. We don't have beds, or blankets or pillows. After tomorrow we'll always live here." My father looked on in agreement, a sweet smile on his face that said, she's right but wouldn't it have been fun?

Neither Lucia nor I have any memory of moving day. Only all of the days we imagined living there all that long time it was being built.

It was a ranch house—slender and horizontal—instead of substantial and vertical like the other houses we knew intimately, that our families lived in. It was modest, but that was not how we saw it. It was modern. Our own house. Brand new. Everything about this thrilled us.

The house was in a neighborhood with old, large, elegant Victorians nearby; some members of our families lived in slightly smaller versions of these beautiful old homes. In the early '50s all kinds of houses were being built in what had been nineteenth-century neighborhoods, on lots that had been fields and woods. Our house, at 2279 North Main Street was just down the street from where two of my mother's sisters and their families lived. The rest of my mother's family was very nearby. We were where we belonged. Among our own. Even the Scoville house was a part of our world; it was just ugly, *schifoso*. Not scary.

But the white house is different. No one seems to remember it but me. I called my cousins. They gave me names of other people to talk to. No one remembered it. I decided to go to Waterbury to do some research. In the mornings I would start out at my favorite place in Waterbury, a bookstore café called The John Bale Book Company. Someone there always had a new idea or suggestion.

Everyone helped me, gave me advice, and did research with me. Ruth Glasser, a friend and a professor at the University of Connecticut, took me to City Hall where we looked through land records and property cards for hours. Anita Bologna at the Silas Bronson Library helped me look through Waterbury city directories for an address of the white house or for one next to it. I was getting somewhere.

This became a community project, now. The next day Ruth helped me get in touch with Michael Dooling at the Mattatuck Museum, who helped me look through a photography collection of many city houses filed by street addresses that went very far back. No soap. We looked at Sanborn Insurance Maps from 1921 to 1950 but they didn't include the stretch of North Main Street that I was looking for.

Danny Gaeta, who owns The John Bale Book Company with his wife Edith Reynolds, thought he had a book that might be helpful. John Bale's bookstore is a nexus of everything and everyone in Waterbury. It is one of my favorite places to spend time, in or out of Waterbury. It has a great collection of secondhand books, a wonderful café, a table for book clubs to meet. A second floor filled with treasures, maps, rare books, and a tearoom. I always start my days in Waterbury there. The next morning, Dan brought me an oversized gold-lettered volume on Waterbury from 1896. Its maps were elegant and clean, each street clearly drawn on a fairly large scale. Seemingly each building was accounted for. The book had a detailed key to every structure built in Waterbury up to its publication date. We turned pages as we traveled up North Main Street. But the pages stopped at Tudor Street, maybe less than a mile short of where I was looking. Apparently my neighborhood was still outside what was considered central Waterbury in 1896.

If only there was some Waterbury atlas that went up to 1920, say. But, no, there was none. I would have to give up. All the kindness and help in the world from friends and strangers wasn't bearing results.

I began to think that the white house was a dream image I had created after I left Waterbury.

Real or imagined, the small white house had a dilapidated feeling to it, as if no one ever took care of it. Although the Scoville house was truly a product of profound neglect, it was a part of our ordinary lives. If the Scoville family was odd, eccentric (perhaps even, as we used to say, not all there), they still were real, a part of the world I grew up in and knew. They were our odd ones. They belonged to us.

The white house had a ghostly quality, one of grief, or loss, even a sense of disconnection from reality. I thought transients may have lived there for short periods of time. Or it could be that all I am remembering or imagining is the desolation of poverty. Who knows?

I kept on asking anyone who had anything to do with that neighborhood, every aunt and cousin Lucia and I visited in those few days. When we had dinner with my younger cousin, Vicki Jean, who also waited on that corner for twelve years for the bus to school, she said, "No, I don't remember a house like that." Later on during dinner she cocked her head and said thoughtfully, "You know what? You should ask my brother Lewis. He was a newspaper boy for a long time on our street. And he has a phenomenal memory."

One more person. One more question. *Perch' no?*

A few days later I called Lewis out in Northern California. "Oh, yeah," he said, "if I think back to what you are asking me about, I'm pretty sure I know which house you mean. It had a front porch? Right?" A porch came into focus. Had it been attached to the house of my memory? After Lewis asks that I'm sure it had been. Maybe. "Yes, that's right," I said.

"And, yeah, it was down from where the gas station is now?"

Finally, someone who remembered it.

"Yes, yes, that was the one!" I said.

How is it that Lewis Semprini and I are the only two people from our family who remember that house? Either my memory helped him remember or my delusion helped him create one of his own. I'd like to think we both remember it.

"Do you remember that there were always poor people living there? Always a few bedraggled kids in the yard? How come we didn't know them?"

"Who knows? I think it was the family that owned the gas station that lived there some of the time. But I never delivered the newspaper to them. They never subscribed. The kids I saw outside that house didn't seem to be looked after. We didn't know them and we knew everyone."

The house was the limit of my world. It was separate from everything that was home to me, everything that was mine and ours, just beyond where I most belonged.

I was going to have to travel beyond that point to get out into the larger world. It must have begun to make its appearance in my unconscious life, as I had to face difficult new territories: probably at times when I had to grow beyond my original self.

These are the things that crawl around inside us, hiking and trekking our interior terrains of hills and streets and smells and unkempt white houses that were there or were not there, that belong and don't belong but that stay with us either way.

Blue

IT WAS ABOUT THAT TIME THAT I BEGAN MY SEARCH. I WAS TEN, I THINK. I was standing out on the back lawn, on a hot summer afternoon—one foot shoved forward, a slab of hair hanging in my face. I was looking down at the grass. This picture slides up from the back files to claim the beginning of my search. I know it was on a day like that.

The search didn't really, actually, begin. It was just one of those summer thoughts that bounced around my brain because the other kids couldn't play with me, because my mother was taking a nap, because it was so hot I didn't know what to do.

I was out in the backyard, I kicked the grass, and the idea shimmered into existence in the heat of the afternoon. It didn't occur to me. I just looked down at the spot I had kicked, where there had been green and now there was brown.

I was shocked by what I had done to the lawn that was a source of Saturday pride to my father. I had ripped the green fabric that he worked so carefully, smoothing into perfection this whole of green silk. He cursed the dandelions, stared seriously at the sky when it didn't bring him rain. So I knew that this making a rent in his work was a matter of some weight. I had made a brown mark on his perfection.

I got down on my knees to tuck the clod back into the brown hole. I patted it gently back in place. And I noticed how brown dirt showed through the fine green blades. I had never noticed this before.

I perched myself in a crouch above the grass to see at what point the brown stopped showing through. The blades were strokes of many greens. The grass was yellow too, blue, had edges of red. And still the grass was set against mottled browns. The brown earth was persistent. The grass was color. It wouldn't go back to grass. There it was. It wasn't what it had seemed to be.

It was the kind of shock a child has the first time she realizes that all the blue on a map means that there's so much more water than earth on earth, and the solid ground beneath her small feet is suddenly no longer so solid, so absolute. Or the same when she finds out that above and beyond those hard, tiled walls of the Holland Tunnel, on the way to see Uncle Joe and Aunt Mena, is the hard water of a rushing river, only pushed back for a time by human labor. Those walls can't last forever, a child realizes with greater clarity than the adults she rides with.

And abruptly the world changed, and what was as sure as a mother's held hand was suddenly as elusive as the idea of God. I was just then trying with such difficulty to come to understand each Sunday at St. Lucy's Church, in the basement after the nine o'clock children's mass, where we learned that God could see anything, all the time, and was in everything, and indeed was life itself. It was too hard to see. I needed a picture.

I could only see an old man floating high up in heaven, resting on a cloud or alighting on the top of the tallest tree. But that God wasn't being life itself. I didn't doubt what was told to me, but no matter how hard I pushed back the borders inside my head to see space in all directions, not stopping ever, God going everywhere all at once, without end, no matter how I prayed to believe, I couldn't picture it. Him.

This was a far simpler shock than all that. A small one. It was just that I had always known that grass was green, that my father's grass was especially green, and I had just found out that the green was far from entirely green in the way that I had, up until then, held it in my head.

I looked up across the lawn and saw that from some distance it was green, familiar. And here's the first, fine-spun wisp of my search, when my idea broke loose from hundreds of other passing thoughts, indefinite, involuntary, without shadows, but there, simple, frail. A child's idea.

So simple, so frail, such a child's thought that I hesitate to tell it. Without the heat of that afternoon.

Was there any place, I wondered, standing out there in the backyard with my hands in my pockets, staring off at the hot summer grass, where I could look straight ahead and see all grass, all green, nothing but whole green grass?

Was there any place where I could look straight ahead and see all of any one color, just it, unbroken, unshadowed, in front of my eyes? Whole?

I went, then, on that afternoon, to my mother's porch, which commanded a wider view of my father's lawn, waiting to find if, when all the green was joined. It joined gently back into a sea of green, but so too did my mother's laundry on the line, a neighbor's roof and trees at every edge, join in the demand for space in my vision.

I tried pure sand next. Utterly plain beige, it beckoned me from across the hot, green grass at the outer edge of the lawn. I crossed and went down on my knees. The beige broke into tiny spots of deepest reds, hard purples, gleaming whites. I was amazed at this plain deception. At least if the hues had been shades of brown, but they were as rich and varied as an oriental carpet. My sand was flawed.

There were other experiments that day, either too silly or too complicated to explain. I would have to tell you about my family, church, and school, and I really want to tell you about looking for one color. There is, though, one from that first day I will recount, because it was the most sensible, the most obvious, and ultimately the most disappointing, when it too fell into reality. I am talking about looking straight up at the sky.

By that point in the afternoon I had flattened my nose to the side of our pale-green house—so many cracks in the paint—and I had climbed my way to the top of our tallest tree—the sky all branch broken, telephone wires everywhere. I crouched, then stood, and twisted my body into places and positions to try to see all, but only one thing.

It must have been during those acrobatics when I noticed even more than my father's lawn, what there was most of, was sky. I had to get to a place that would allow me to see just it. I went to the center of the wide, flat lawn and stretched myself as flat as I could against its damp green skin and looked up.

It was blue, violently blue, with no luscious or frail clouds trailing across its hard surface. The only way I can describe it to you is to say it the way my mother once told me about a new blue dress she'd bought. "Blue, you know, that blue that when someone says 'blue' that's the blue you think of." So it was that blue, my mother's blue, up there. But when I lay down on my father's lawn, and looked up at my mother's blue, and asked myself if I had found the spot from which to see only blue in front of my eyes, I had to admit that the red chimney crept into one corner, the clothes line cut across another edge, and the trees laced my toes.

I think here we have the actual moment when the afternoon's hot fragile spin must have idled from clear frustration and lodged itself, utterly, in my young brain.

Had I been able, on that afternoon, to get my father's ladder from the side of the house where it stood, and carried it to lean against the roof's edge; had I been daring enough, without permission, to climb the ladder to the roof and lain flat at the peak of the roof's point, my spine against the house's own; and had I looked straight up into all that blue that would have been directly above me and seen nothing but it, I would have no doubt looked at it intensely for several minutes, felt the roof's peak at my back, clambered down, replaced the ladder, or left it leaning against the house's red side, and ambled off to figure out how else to waste the afternoon away. I would have done it and the glow of that day would have died the death of the easily attained.

But since I dared not consider such a bold act as getting my father's ladder, climbing it, and lying on my back in order to see my sky, since I lay instead on the grass looking up, disappointed at my unholy sky, in an unholy universe that refused to yield its blueness to me, the idle afternoon's fancy was thwarted, and collapsed into an idea. An idea that I could carry it around to try on other warm afternoons, other cool nights, other dawns.

As an idea it became a quiet, steady obsession.

Because I was more obedient than disobedient, more ordinary than extraordinary, because I wouldn't think of doing something as bold as taking my father's ladder from its place and putting it where I needed it, when I knew it would make him mad, the afternoon's meandering broke into pieces that would not fit into the one piece that I looked for, first whimsically, then persistently, but broke instead into those elusive fragments called thought. So I entered quietly with dirty fingernails, plaid shorts, into a search for God.

The truth is that the memory is vague and only included being out on the lawn and wanting to see one color. I am not amazed that I went on a search for God and called it color: color and God were what my world was made of. I am amazed that I went on that search almost indifferent to the results of my quest. I went with confidence about my search from a point of view, a place in the world from which to see the uninterrupted sky.

The search must have stopped that first day with my mother waking from her nap, coming to the kitchen window that overlooked the backyard, and yelling out, "What are you standing there like that for, doing nothing?" She didn't think much of people who wasted their time. She mended clothes in the car on the way to my grandmother's, crocheted when her sisters came to visit, and had a nail file ready by the door while she waited for my father to back the car out of the garage.

"Come in," she yelled, "I need you."

And I am certain that when I went in she said, "Why didn't you do the ironing?"

"Because you were sleeping and everyone else is out. Why should I be the only one working?"

"Because it's your job. You can't play until it's finished." I walked slowly to the cupboard where the ironing board was kept. "Not now. I need something from the store." What she said was just to keep me in line. "Daddy will be home from work. We need milk and bread, a large loaf of Spinelli's, two quarts of homogenized."

I had been hollered at. My sister was swimming, or somewhere with boys. Hadn't taken me. I was supposed to iron.

Three days later, I insisted that my thirteen-year-old sister take me with her when she went swimming in the lake where she would "meet those stupid guys. I'll tell Mom if you don't take me."

So I floated on my back, farther out than I was allowed to go, and whatever was left in my mind of that hot still afternoon on the lawn slipped to the surface of the water with me. I might have a good view from the upholding waters. But instead, the lifeguard's chair rolled into view beyond my feet, and I too, apparently, came into his view because he screeched his whistle to say that I had to swim back to the raft, the limit of where we were permitted to swim on that large lake.

When I tried later again that day to see my sky from the raft in the center of the lake, one of the eighth-grade boys ran dripping across my face with a great laugh, then pushed me in because I was Lucia's little sister and a fifth grader. I did not see it that day either. My blue sky. Not that summer.

The hot days closed into fall, and the idea drifted with me occasionally, and I went back to Webster School and sat in the fifth-grade classroom of Mrs. McCann.

"Michael Simpson, you who threw that spitball. I know it was you."

And quiet Michael tried to convince her that it was not he.

"I know it was. You might as well confess. You have five minutes before you'll be taken to the principal's office for a strapping." Four minutes later when he confessed, she smiled mightily. "I knew I was right."

I looked out of the window, wishing the sky were closer. I knew that it wasn't Michael.

"Principal, that's "*pal*," not "*ple*." You can remember that easily, because the principal is your pal." Mrs. McCann—I can say that I went back that fall to her class and wished I could be almost anywhere else.

We went to St. Lucy's for religious instruction, for catechism, on released time each Monday at two o'clock. We were released into the hands of the nuns so that they could release us to God. Sister St. Mary Michael was exactly what a nun was supposed to be, according to us. She was gentle, reserved, kind. One of the few. But that fall she asked us the hardest question we'd ever been asked.

"If God is perfect and He made everything that is on this earth, why did He make sin?"

The class was silent. Then my heart began to beat hard in me. I wanted to be the one to answer. I knew with dread when this happened that my voice would tighten and crack, that I would want to cry, but that I couldn't stop myself from raising my hand, opening my mouth, and emitting whatever strained words pushed out. Between the lurches of my heart I wondered what I would say. Sister St. Mary looked to me. "Yes?" she inquired. I rose from my chair.

"Well, God was perfect at first," I said, "and He was everywhere, all quiet and perfect and the whole universe was one thing, God"—the story began itself—"but one day as God was lying there, everywhere, He looked at all the light He had shone in all directions and thought 'how beautiful,' and that thought took up some of his space. And it made a shape, a crack in his perfection where the thought started. And that was the first time He wasn't perfect." I had warmed to my tale.

"So He took that crack and decided to make it into something, like a tree, a perfect tree." My voice was still strained but now I was driven certainly down my path. Sister St. Mary Michael looked plainly at me; I looked wildly away and went on.

"But as He looked at the tree He had made, He had another thought, 'Isn't that lovely,' because it was, and so another spot came from that thought, so He had to make something else. So He did. And that's how He made everything and that's how He's in everything." Now I raced to my conclusion. "And once He started things, He had to make everything there was to make, so He had to make sins, too. So He did. They make very dark spots, but because God made them, they're still sort of perfect, perfectly bad."

It wasn't right to make up stories about God. Not in catechism. Not in front of a bride of God.

Sister St. Mary looked at me with a quiet look. "That's fine," she said, "that's an interesting way to think about this." My heart was thudding and I sat down. It beat right through the end of class. I loved Sister St. Mary even more after that, but the next year she went back to her cloister where, we whispered to each other, the nuns couldn't talk to anybody, not even each other. And that was the last time I thought I was smart.

I drifted through that fall, sweeping down the long hill behind my father's house on my bike, looking up at the sky as I rode to see if I could see only sky that way. I went to the store for my mother, ran to kiss my father when he came home from work. "Is supper ready?" he wanted to know each night. I fought with my sister because she never thought it was her turn to do the dishes. And I went to Webster Grammar School and looked out the windows of Mrs. McCann's fifth-grade class, longing always to be out there among the trees reaching up to the sky. And fall turned into cool days, then into cold ones.

We raked the leaves and carefully laid them around the rose bushes and chrysanthemums to keep them warm for winter, and laid the rakes down in the cellar. And winter came.

It was in that season that I finally gave up. It was a vague idea all along and I had carried it between my breath and two seasons. But if it couldn't be done in the heat of summer, or the clarity of fall, it would not be done in the cold of winter.

Walking one wet gray day to buy cigarettes for my father, I looked at that gray clearly for the first time. I had been yelled at before I left for the store. The day matched my mood. I thought to myself: so this the only real season, cold gray without those garish lies, sun, leaves, snow. It scared me so that I was sure that I finally understood the truth about life. Without noticing, my idea of looking for blue died a damp cold death that day, and I brought the cigarettes home to my father and went to help in the kitchen with supper.

That was when I began to do better in Mrs. McCann's class, though I hated her still, and concentrated on how to do long division, and didn't bother to moon out the windows where there was nothing much more than wet and cold. I did well and won the math bee, where you added fast in your head and shouted out the answer, and I shouted loud, and I got better grades. That may have been, too, when I began to cut catechism.

So now you can see why that shimmering summer day was so wide with promise. That is childhood for you.

Winter came in gray and cold. The lake where we swam in the summer became a wide cold floor where we skated. We waited for the wind to sweep the snow from the ice with long, cold, breaths and leave it to us. Then the whole family, uncles, aunts, cousins, called each other on the phone on winter Sundays. "We're going skating. Meet you at the lake." Then my mother dug deep in the cellar for her dusty skates, we all borrowed my father's huge wool sweaters, and shouted to each other: hurry, hurry, hurry.

It was a wide heaven. We skated from long border to long border in hand-held ropes; racing, we did the whip, no lifeguard's whistles blowing here. We called out places to skate to one another in high-pitched glee, places in summer we couldn't even see.

Then we'd shout, "Out to the island, out there, race you," and be there in flashes of seconds. In summer, the island had lain quietly green, never a sound, distant, illusory. In winter, it was so easily ours. I'd sit stunned at the rocky edge and dream of long summer strokes, sliding my blades forward and back. And the long Sunday afternoon swept into cool sweeps. The edges were there but they were wide sweeps away.

I felt such deep, cool gray inside my young limbs that I skated away from the others for a while to have the cool inside to myself. I skated the wide slow edge of the lake by myself, each bladed swoop soothing me more. Then fast, I swept myself into the empty middle of that frozen world, and knelt to tighten my loosening laces before I returned to my wintery pleasure.

The gray ice and the day pleased me so, that from happiness, I sat down on the cold floor and looked at the others, far from me, who seemed to have been thrown gently down across the frozen water by a soft gray wind. I lay myself down and rested in the frozen calm. And up, high in front of my eyes, I found it. A calm, cold, gray sky, all gray, all sky, no edges of trees, no edges of mistake. And it seemed right to find one color, winter gray, finally on the ice.

What We Remember

MY FATHER IS SLAMMING THE DOOR BETWEEN THE KITCHEN AND THE garage so hard it bounces. Then, the car door goes off like a shot. He's going down the street. That's what we call it: The North End Social Club, where the boys play gin rummy or *scop'* and *briscula'* (*scopa, briscula*), cook, and watch television, after it invades the '50s. Sometimes the cops pound on the door of the club—shouting "Police!," so the neighbors'll be sure to hear. "This way the boys who have recently gotten out of the can have time to climb out the back window, so the cops won't have to pinch them for breaking parole," my father explains with deep affection for us, his friends, his life down the street.

After the ruckus, the cops, sitting down to a plate of macaroni with sausage and meatballs, tell the boys about the complaint one of the club's nosey neighbors made, saying there was too much noise coming from the club, or explain, like the regular guys they are, that they're sorry they are going to have to take Crazy Mo' in this time. His wife has filed against him again. Otherwise they'd have to pinch Dirty Mo and Other Mo too.

"They're good guys, the cops," my father explains to us in his deep, soft voice. "They don't want to make trouble." He likes to bring his girls, my sister Lucia and me, in on the goings on at the club. Explain the ways of his world to us.

But tonight, my mother stands, hair curled, lipstick on, her back arched in a fury against the stove. She's just scrubbed away the spills of dinner.

The hum of late summer heat comes in through the windows over the sink.

"He's always going down to that club. He's supposed to be taking us for a ride. It's a beautiful summer night," her glinting eyes swing over to where Lucia and I have landed, beside the stove, after we ran in from the yard. We'd been playing in the hot sinking glow when we heard their voices roar, then hiss.

"Peter, why do you get like this? Who'd you loan money to this time? Tell me. Oh, you make me so mad."

Our father stands there furious, helpful. She's got him dead to right. But that doesn't change much between them.

The avocado-green stove is a wall Lucia and I stand near for protection. There's a ribbon of hot summer air between us.

My mother glares.

She turns to us next. "You should be saying, 'Daddy, take us for a ride. Take us to the drive-in,'" my mother flings at us. She'd like to give somebody a slap.

Going for a ride and buying ice cream isn't enough to make sitting in the backseat with the two of them in the front, livid and mute with one another, worth it.

My parents are mad for each other both with wild love and terrible fights. But tonight my mother's fury is descending to a new depth.

Her words fall around us like dead leaves. Our eyes blink into the sunset in the windows behind the trees, while we wait for her to come to what we'd rather do anyway: spend the long summer nights with my mother's sisters and their kids, while all the husbands are somewhere else: Dad at the club, Uncle Rocco dressing up to go out with his friends, Uncle Gene eating ice cream, Uncle Al down at the Waterbury *Republican* plant working the night shift, and Uncle Joe in his chair asleep, dirt under his fingernails, dreaming about the neat rows of tomatoes and peppers in his garden—leaving the women and kids to walk each other back and forth on the dirt sidewalks late into the night, gossiping, *a che murmurade?* (who shall we whisper about?), our neighbors, the lousy coffee Mrs. S. served without an "and," which husband was beating his wife.

"It's getting late, we'd better walk you home," we'd say, walking up and down under the dusty trees to pull the night into longer and longer stretches, so we'd have time for another story, another cartwheel.

My mother had recently found out that she'd had a hysterectomy many months earlier, about which she was not informed until long after it was done by our beloved Dr. Lombardi, who drives from house to house to take care of us. She never questioned why it took months to recover from a D and C while she lived at my grandfather's house, and Lucia and I each stay at cousins' houses. Or why Dr. Lombardi didn't tell her until very recently.

But tonight my mother's fury has a new hysteria to it. It's as if a *taranta* has taken its bite on her.

She has never been this mad, this despairing before when they fight.

There's a frenzy, a wild overtaking of her.

She begins to screech, high pitched, a shrill wail, it rises as a siren, piercing the summer night, piercing our ears and skin. She flings herself down onto the kitchen floor, yanking the blue-and-green stripes of her dress up over her head as she falls into writhing and wailing on the linoleum.

She's exposing herself: the wrong side of the fabric is over her head, her pale legs, and her underwear showing. She shouldn't do that.

The sight sears, then seals in my brain.

I ask my sister Lucia, thirty years later sitting at her kitchen table in Cambridge, Massachusetts, if she remembers that night—my mother pulling her dress up over her head and throwing herself to the floor, the unholy shrieking, me frozen by the avocado stove, waiting for the screaming to stop.

"Remember?" she answers me incredulously. She shakes her head, quiet, sad.

We are drinking my father's favorite cold drink—large glasses of ice tea. The large heavy glass goes down to the tabletop.

Then she describes to me in exquisite detail what happens next.

"Yes, I remember that night. I was so terrified. Dad said he was going to leave us.

"He was screaming, 'Get up, Rose. Stop that, right now. Get up off the floor, or I'm leaving you.'

"But she wouldn't stop crying, screaming. She wouldn't get up. He was standing over her."

My father's mother had been institutionalized by the time he was five. All he remembered about his mother was her bathing him in dirty water when he was very small. "I knew what my mother was doing wasn't right, even then," he explained to his daughters much later on.

"I kept trying to get Mom to get up too. But she wouldn't move," Lucia continues at her kitchen table, "I was terrified that Dad was going to leave us.

" 'I'm leaving,' he screamed."

That must have been when he walked out the door and slammed it. That was when we heard the car begin to whine backward down the driveway.

"I ran after him." Lucia's hands are wrapped around the faceted glass. Tears are rolling down the soft skin of my sister's face.

"Went down the driveway after him, 'Don't leave. Please don't leave us!'

"When he saw me he stopped the car and got out. Put his hand on my shoulder, looked at me. 'I would never leave you girls.'

" 'Never.' Was what he said."

My sister, all those years later, lifts her amber tea to her lips, her eyes liquid, releases her memories, the rasping scrape of crickets outside the window, the quivering air of that summer night, into her kitchen.

We don't talk that night at my sister's table about *pizzica taranta*, the tarantula's bite that leads to frenzied dancing that goes on for days to release female hysteria in southern Italy where our family is from. We don't know any of this yet. We are not thinking of the way the older women in our family let out an ancient, shrill funeral keening against the cruel fates. We won't make these connections until decades later.

In Cambridge, in my sister's kitchen, we are just two American daughters reassembling a devastation from our Italian past without yet knowing its name.

Go Fish

IT WAS STILL QUIET, JUST THE WAY MY FATHER LIKED IT. NOT EVEN THE birds had started yet. Just him and the quiet, so he could go about his business; no one to interfere.

My mother was asleep beside him. She had gone into their bedroom a couple of hours earlier. They divided the night between them. She stayed up until two or three; he got up about five. She had the apartment to herself at night. He had the world to himself in the morning.

He kissed her gently on the cheek. Then got up as quietly as he could, to go into the kitchen. This was when he was happiest. Making his coffee, reading the newspaper my mother had left on the table for him when she went to bed. He made his coffee, put his teeth in, put on his old clothes. Then he sat and drank his coffee slowly and read the obituaries.

My father told me that he had tried to explain to my mother many times how he felt. How good it felt now. That it took so little to make him happy. His coffee, the newspaper, the apartment, the small back porch. Just right. No lawn to take care of, no mortgage.

I heard him more than once on long slow walks we'd take together upstate at twilight, or on long rides on the backcountry roads of Connecticut we'd take when I went to visit. I knew his mornings and the sweetness they held for him.

He knew that after his heart attack my mother didn't want to leave the street where her sisters lived. The apartment they moved to was further from her mother, my grandmother. She had to drive to see her family now, call ahead. She couldn't just walk down the street like before. "She's a good person, your mother, but she makes herself so crazy, running around, leaving no stone unturned. *Nothing needs must do* (was an old-fashioned expression he used to mean there's no other way for her), but she has to, has to, buy a present for her hairdresser's new grandchild. I mean . . . but we love her. God knows we love her."

My father loved their new apartment. It was just what they needed. My mother always made everything nice, lots of ruffles, always dusting, our house pretty and clean. "If only she didn't have to have so many *seating devices* in the house. Ones we never, I mean never, use. Oh well," he'd look off in resignation at those moments.

"She's still so pretty, even now. Not like when she was a girl; she had been desperately pretty then, like a Hollywood picture, with that smile. The prettiest girl in town in my book," he declared. "Outshines them all at St. Michael's dances, in my book."

So I knew how precious these mornings were to him. I knew that he thought things like: We did all right. Raised our girls. Sent them to college. Both married now and raising kids of their own. Not bad at all.

No one he knew had died yesterday. He put on his old work jacket and got ready to start his rounds. He walked down the small set of steps at the front of the four small red-brick apartment buildings, and started picking up scraps of paper. Those kids next door, they didn't think. Kids are like that, never thinking. But when I think about it, me and Ernie, Charlie, and Abbie, god we were really terrible, sticking our filthy hands into the ice cream bins, then running out the door. I can still see the five streaks across the tub of vanilla when we went back to the candy store. Yeah, nonchalantly lifting the freezer cover. We were wild. Climbing those telephone poles, live wires all over the place. Lucky we didn't kill ourselves.

He told me about his routine often, with such pleasure and pride. He'd walk down the street. It was still dark, but one bird was beginning to chirp in that steady monotonous way. The air was damp. But he felt warm in his jacket with the hot coffee still in him. His face was cool and awake from the damp air.

First he'd do the woods behind the school where the kids went to drink beer at night. They always left a load. He always picked up the empties there first. I knew how each of these parts of his morning routine went.

The grass was wet. Good thing he had on his heavy shoes, he'd be thinking. $19.95 at Caldor's, a bargain. He knew my mother hated them. Said they were ugly. But my father knew that she was just mad he had paid so little for them. Why did she have to shop all the time? They did all right. They were doing just fine. It was almost as if she didn't want them to be okay financially. Always another gift, for the neighbor's child. She didn't know where to stop.

He had reached the clearing where he could see them scattered everywhere. He pulled a plastic bag from his back pocket. And bent down to gather the beer cans. Each one registered a nickel in his head.

One of my father's complaints about my mother was about her need to spend money all the time. He'd say, "That's the difference between us. I'm running around picking up beer cans to turn in, and she can't spend money fast enough." But this collecting was for James, the little guy [my son]. The way he whipped around on those little legs of his, built just like his father. Priceless, that James was truly priceless. I love them all. But I've got to make sure Jo and Bill have the money for college for James."

Next, I know my father might go into the bushes where he'd find another three cans. One was squashed. He'd use that new tool he had made at home to straighten them out. There was only one guy down at the A&P who would take any can in any shape, but his schedule was always changing. Had to catch him just right. Most of the other guys were pretty picky. My father put the crushed and rusted ones saved for the A&P in the storage closet.

What did he have to do with his time anyway? He could do whatever he wanted. Why not this? For James. Let's see: the account was up to about ten grand. What with the last dividend check and all the scrap I've been picking up from the side of the road. Let's see, I got a fin for that piece of brass, a tenski for the pair of hubcaps. My father kept a running account taped to the inside of the broom closet door, for his own satisfaction. He'd show me the list occasionally. How it was adding up. We'll get there baby, he would say to the air. He adored all four of his grandchildren. Pete and repeat, he called his firstborn grandchild. Woodie man, he called his second grandson, Lucia's second son. Anna, Lucia's youngest, was Little Chicken. He called my son, James, *Terramod'* (*terramoto*, an earthquake). He knew my sister and her husband wouldn't have any problem putting those three grandchildren through school. But he was worried about Bill and me paying for college for James. He wanted James to have a good life.

That boy's going to be okay. All boy, so much energy, whipping around, whipping around. He doesn't know what to do with all the energy he has.

"Tell Grandpa how does the owl go?"

"Hoo-hoo," James always answered on cue. Sometimes I'd find my father laughing his head off. He'd been picturing James imitating an owl.

He had twenty cans. That's a buck right there. They add up. If only I could get Rose to see that. He made his rounds through the fields, in the woods, behind the shopping plaza near the exit at the drive-in. It had taken him a while before he realized the kinds of places people were likely to toss their empties. Near the entrance to Route 84, for instance. It figured people wanted to clean out their cars before they got on the highway. My father liked outsmarting them like that. But the clearing, that was his gold mine. No one but him went there to collect. But one time, after he and my mother came to see us, to see James, the field was empty when he got home. Someone else had discovered his turf. That week he had had to set the alarm for four to reclaim his territory. He showed 'em.

It was six now. He carried the bag back to the apartment. Put a load in the trunk of his car. The trunk was almost completely full. That's enough for this morning. He'd have to make a delivery today. One of those places where they didn't mind a big load. "We'll get there, baby."

He washed his hands downstairs in the basement and headed down to Moe's.

Moe was my father's friend. What a bum, my father always said about his buddy. Never did a square day's work in his life. Got to get him out today. Missed work again yesterday. I knew when Toady said he was going down to Jai Lai that was the end of it for Moe. He's just aching to get fired again.

Moe was asleep when my father got to his apartment. So he'd start the coffee, rinse out two cups from the sink filled with dirty dishes, put the box of chocolate covered donuts he had picked up along the way on the table.

"Hey, Moe Baby. Time to get up." Moe looked like he looked every morning. Like he wouldn't make it through the day. Once small and scrappy, he had been eroded by years of smoking cigarettes, drinking booze, and hanging around the track.

"Feel like hell this morning. Played cards until three."

"I keep telling you, you've got to quit this life. Give up those damn cigarettes. Nine years for me now since my heart attack. All right, have a cup of coffee and a donut."

Moe lit his first cigarette for the day, inhaled deeply. Then he went to spit in the sink.

"We'll get there, kid. I picked up a couple of bucks for James. Let's see the count was, he reached into his jacket pocket . . . three dollars and sixty-five cents. Not a bad morning's take."

"Jesus, I feel like hell. Don't know if I can make it in, Pete."

"Have a donut. You'll feel better." He would get Moe to work, but Moe was going to be late again.

"Pete, have you got a tenner on you. My son called. He needs a new fan belt. I'm in tap city. Took a bath last night."

I knew my father would pull out two fives. "All right Moe baby. It's all right."

He got Moe off about fifteen minutes late. Delivered him straight to the door to make sure he went to work. It was almost eight by now. The barbershop would just be opening, all the morning papers would be there. Joe, the owner of the barbershop, was a good guy, appreciated a little company, liked to shoot the breeze.

"Hey, Joey baby," my father would say bringing a hot cup of coffee and a few of the leftover donuts. "How's the world skinning your potatoes today?"

Joe might have an early morning cut and shave in the chair, so my father would settle in quickly to his usual spot by the window to read the papers. He turned first to the stock pages to see how the investments he made for James were doing. Have to stay on top of these things. The sun would gradually creep up over his shoulders as two or three of the usual men came in. They all knew my father and my father knew all of them. They had been playing cards for years at the social club down the street.

At nine o'clock he said what he'd say every day. "Well, I guess I'd better go get Rosie off the ground. Hang in there, Joey baby. See you tomorrow."

The sun might be coming up strong now. It might be a beautiful day. Later, my father would make a stop at the A&P, drop Rosie at the hairdressers, cook dinner. Maybe they'd take a ride over to Caldor's. It would be a perfect day.

Those mornings, he'd go into the apartment quietly, make a fresh pot of coffee. Put all of his wife's vitamins on the table, lay out the newspaper he'd bought for her because it had all the coupons she liked to clip. He'd carry a cup of lemon juice and honey that he'd fixed for her into the bedroom. He'd sit on the edge of the bed and just watch her sleeping for a while. Her hair would be wrapped in a pink chiffon scarf to keep it in place. She'd look so nice and quiet at those moments, not frantic the way she was so much of the day, just sleeping so peacefully. He hated to wake her up, but he had to get her going or she'd get even more screwed up than usual with her schedule, sleeping until noon, up until four or five in the morning.

He leaned over to kiss her. "Rosie, it's nine thirty. Coffee's made."

"Oh God," she'd say groggily. "I've got to get going. I have so much to do. Why didn't you get me up earlier?" Not even awake and already she would be off and running, all duties and errands. God, how she drives herself crazy."

"What a poor lost soul," my father always said at a moment like this, "Poor lost soul." He'd shake his head.

But then he wouldn't care. He'd take off his shoes, unbuckle his pants, lean back against the pillows.

All those years, struggling, racing, working, thinking he had to set the world on fire, killing himself for a buck. Jesus, this felt good. When he was young he kept wanting something to happen, something that would change his life. But he told me so many times, he knew better in the later years, it was going to stay the same and that was the beauty of it.

"Go fish, world," he always said out loud every morning. "Go fish." Then he'd close his eyes and go to sleep.

FOOD, FOOD, FOOD,
AND HARD WORK

Creature Life

CREATURELY LIFE HUNG SO HEAVY WHERE I CAME UP, EVEN OUR BOOKS crawled on bellies and knees, pulling us with long arms into their murky ponds and lakes, their continents. Our dogs were dusty with dirt and dead leaves. The bees stung sharp on our fat kid limbs. Our grandmother's skin was slack, smelled of garlic and Ivory soap, her apron wet from sink and stove where string beans simmered. The babies were *pisciat',*[3] the nights were long, the skin between us so moist and soluble we passed back and forth into each other, not to lose our place in either. Even my father's truck clanging up the driveway heavy with iron, was more animal than vehicle.

This dense soil of women, children, and the earth itself—my mother, our aunts, and my girl cousins, the regular pouring forth of babies, his bodied life, was never something we looked at or knew, it was our bones, our skin, it *was* the fecund quick and ordinary.

The ordinary rivets my attention still: casually piling newspapers on one arm, grabbed from the floor around our chairs, hurrying to write *nails or hook,* before I forget them on the list, racing to buy the onions in the red net bag so I can throw them diced into the olive oil to start dinner, so immediate, this electric spark of being easily, vitally alive.

My other core, writing, requires me to leave my body and the world to walk on air, on nothingness, until I've conjured enough dirt so that I can deposit it under my feet to hold me up for the impossible work of creating a new continent. Then it's a joy, but before that often fear and flailing.

Life lived on the breath, each current as it hits my skin, moving life from the air around me, through me, into and out of me again, I am in a river. When I'm struggling to enter my writing I get wistful, wishing I could spend my time just on the immediate—the errand, the chore, the mend, the phone call—and not have to reach out to some wider world that really doesn't invite me in. Each day it's a long hike into that larger world, asking again for space so reluctantly given. For long stretches, the ordinary suits me fine. Sometimes I wish I didn't have such longing for this ineffable, impermanent other outside, but in the world I live in now, the ordinary is *manca*, less, not enough anymore. The ordinary is now the work of housekeepers, nannies, the people who do our laundry, bake cookies, man our doors. In Waterbury it was a proud ordinary life: hard, urgent, and unquestioned.

Our days centered between the kitchen, the stove and sink, and table. There was tremendous knowledge and skill and respect for domestic life, care of home-garden-babies-food, womanly skills. Our talk about food was constant. "Rocky brought home a deer last week and I had to cook it right away, as soon as he butchered it. I had no idea he was going hunting that morning."

"How many cloves of garlic did you use?"

Men provided and women prepared, their tasks entwined. Husbands were deeply proud of their wives' cooking and domestic skills. When a new bride came into the family there would be the requisite teasing about her cooking skill, not to diminish her but to remind her, and everyone else, how important it was. "Can you cook a *minestra* as good as your mother-in-law?" Cooking was part of our days. It was never professional, artistic, or ambitious.

Being in a kitchen, washing greens coated with dirt from the garden, puncturing the can of tomatoes and pressing down hard on the can opener to make the hard tight twists against the metal, while women with children and babies on laps or at their feet sit at the table drinking coffee and fingering their *mappin'* while they nurse their latest worry means I am deeply at home. I was born at a time when the babies born in our family were all girls—six of us born within a space of four years. By the time we were conscious beings, we had two older male cousins. Gene and Bobby were seven and eight, and seemed so sophisticated, so utterly outside our sphere of tables and babies, in an impossible world, racing their hand-made box cars down the streets of long dangerous hills.

Behind us came other cousins, this time six boys. As soon as they could, they shook our sticky hands off (we had been in charge of them while they were tiny) and ran away disappearing in the woods and playing cops and robbers, good guys and bad guys. All of us ran wild in the woods, across fields and around lakes, but we girls had to come inside to help our mothers, to help clean and cook dinner, take care of the babies, initiated to our future responsibilities to home, kids, domestic centrality. So we also played passionately at being mothers and, sometimes, secretaries, distant and glamorous, and teachers, the only women, other than our nuns, we knew well outside the home.

THE IRONY OF PATRIARCHY

The men were a powerful force in the house, too. Their absolutely patriarchal presence was grounded in hierarchy. I'm your older brother! You have to listen to me. Grandpa's coming, get the wine on the table now before he comes upstairs. Each rank and station assigned and asserted, each rung firm and clear. Men over women, boys more important than girls, older over younger. So the eldest male of the family had a strong status. The oldest male child had great status and power even if he was the youngest sibling. All this was fixed and true, as it always had been.

The eldest woman was accorded her status, which was also always aligned with birth order. In some sense she was in charge of upholding these hierarchical rules—get your brother a plate of food; don't you see he's sitting there? So too did we all. The young girls took pride in upholding these values. I'll get that for you. Don't move. It seemed an honor to take on this role fully. "You aren't behaving in a lady-like fashion." "It's the girl's job to do this." "Be a good girl and go and get your cousin a plate of food and bring it to him." This was everyday talk. Girls shouldn't do that. Boys won't like you if you do that. This is our life in the '40s and '50s and even the early '60s.

The limits: How far was a young woman allowed to go from the home unsupervised? Each daughter was needed to support the family. My oldest aunt wanted to be a nurse, but she was made to leave school after the eighth grade to work and bring money into the household. My mother desperately wanted to go to college, but that was out of the question. It was also true for my father.

Women's lives had unfair and terrible limits: for some there was horrible violence. There was very limited access to education, limited access to the world at large, to jobs, travel, money. Yet there has been something overlooked in our backward glance. What their lives had in abundance—full and important lives.

Although we lived in this patriarchal Italian world, in its absolute rank and order, this didn't diminish the women in our family. Simultaneously, paradoxically, they were strong, smart, hard-working, opinionated, full of their own authority, certain of their value. They had a vast panoply of highly developed skills. And they knew it. Not self-consciously, but with an in-the-gut sense, something our backward glances often overlook.

Some women "wore the pants in the family." Some were equal partners, even as they maintained the rules of our own patriarchy. They were the core of our tribe, since the essence of who we were was family and home.

At first I thought this is the way all Italian women were taught to think of themselves, then I thought it might be just working-class Italian women, then I thought something "Mediterranean." Once I began to talk to my friends of every stripe and class about this we discovered our mothers were nobody's fools. They knew who they were.

When later on I heard the prefeminist commonplace that women were so catty with each other, or so competitive, that they never made the kinds of bonds men made, I felt this was a life I didn't know about or understand. We women were openly hard on each other, we fought with each other, and we loved each other crazily.

Women are still at the vital center of my being. I have always been surrounded by smart, beautiful, and hard-working women: grandmothers, mother, aunts, sister, and cousins. And friends too. These women are at the center of the way I see the world.

My Mother's Letter to Her Sister

ONCE, MY MOTHER'S OLDER SISTER, AG, WENT TO VISIT AN AUNT AND UNCLE in New York City for about a week. This was a very unusual event. My mother, as the second eldest girl, wrote to her sister regularly, even though she wasn't away for very long. This letter gives a vivid sense of how their daily lives went on the farm while they were girls in a way that I could never capture. So here are my mother's words, my mother's letter to her sister.

Chestnut Hill Road

September, 1931

Dear Ag,

Have received your loving letter today. We are all feeling fine—hope you are well and that your eye is okay. You sound like you're having a good time. Let's hope so. Nothing extra in the time you're having. Ha, ha! How would you like something extra like we're having out here. You know, upon our idle fingers, Papa placed the sheep's wool to be washed and the darned thing couldn't be dirtier.

No! I'm not coming to the wedding. Of course, not. Mama desires not, and not it is. Am I sore? Oh boy! Of course, I was boiling, so I did so much work and scrubbing to get the heat out of me that this morning I was so tired I got up at eight o'clock. Just in time for a lecture.

Of course, I can't say I went to the Roxy or Bronx Park or Encore Theater but here's where I went. Monday I went down to the shoemakers to bring my shoes and down to Betty's house to bring the machine for Macaroni. She asked for it Sunday but forgot to take it home. You know Eddie must taste those Macaroni before he goes to college. Of course, we had dinner there and then she came home with us. And did she work. She helped pick and clean 20 baskets of tomatoes. I got her story. It's swell. She wants me to go down her house and show her how to do the Macaroni tomorrow but tomorrow is Grace's shower and Ma must go down and buy something for her. I don't know who is going down tomorrow night. Grace and Tony brought over the invitation Sunday. Mary D. didn't come over Sunday on account of Carmen being sick. Betty came and took the loneliness out of us. Schools don't open until further notice—the old fools, I could bite their ears off. I'd like to make them come here and pick tomatoes and see how they like it.

No trouble with the hired men—only one left us without notice. You know, the Polish guy. It's a good thing he went. He used to scare the life out of me with that mug of his. Gosh!

Went down after your pay and you got seventeen bucks, and I spent it all!! And when I came home, I came in a taxi and when Mama saw me she killed me. Boo-hoo. Applesauce.

And another thing you have written this phrase, "Do what Mama says" more times than I have hair. Please use up paper saying something new not ancient history. Because I work myself dead every day.

Well it's nighttime now and the end of a perfect day. Of course it's ending with rain. Shedding tears for me I suppose

Mama and Papa, Roccie, Ant & Toots ask me to send millions of kisses to you. Regards to all from all.

Your loving sis, Row . . .

P.S. Please let us know where you are parked now.

P.P.S. Don't mind what I wrote because it just was a writing fit. Toodle Doo.

Hard Work and Good Food

"HARD WORK AND GOOD FOOD MAKES FOR A LONG LIFE," AUNT TONI always said. She lived until 101. She was a strong woman—body strong, strong mind, and *faccia dost'* (thick headed) too. After she retired, when she was bored and didn't have anything else to do, she gardened, cooked, canned, made sausage, cheese, and liquors. "I have to keep busy," she'd say, laughing at herself. "It's better if I'm busy, then I don't worry so much." She kept her garden until she was 98 years old.

Work soothed our family. When we weren't gardening, harvesting, canning, preserving, cooking, serving, or eating food; when we weren't building, scrubbing, or fixing or making something, we gathered at one of our tables and talked. And talked. And talked.

My mother and her sisters told and retold the stories of their punishing childhoods. This talk around the table was a recitation, an incantatory invocation for reprieve, pleading their case to the fates and gods, telling us, and each other, again and again.

"I felt so sorry for Mama. Papa would get so angry so fast."

"Didn't he see how hard she was always working for him, to please him?"

"Bringing in the water, collecting the wood to build the fire, picking the vegetables in the blazing sun."

"We never stopped."

"Never."

It was as if dressing these wounds in words would finally heal them in their young bodies.

There was plenty to celebrate, family and friends gathering, the companionship and love between sisters and their brother; being together, being young and being stunningly beautiful. It wasn't all pain. But it was too much work, too much criticism; too many hands swinging at them.

My grandfather and grandmother bought the farm with Zia Mack and Zi' Pasquale in 1912. They "went in together." They bought small pieces of land from a Mrs. Piersall, a little at a time as they had the money. First, they bought the house, then the land around it, piece by piece. There might not even have been real floors when they first bought it. The kitchen was in the basement. The root cellar was there. They cooked in the fireplace. There was no running water. Then Grandpa and Zi' Pasquale fought and Grandpa bought Zi' Pasquale out. When Mrs. Piersall moved to Florida, she tried to talk my grandfather into buying the rest of her land. "Send me the money when you have it." But my grandfather wanted only to buy the land he had money for. He would have owned a major part of Waterbury had he taken her up on her offer.

When they bought the farm, my grandfather had an artesian well built near the slaughterhouse. The oven used to be in a kind of woodshed next to the house, but they couldn't get insurance with the oven so close to the house, so they had to build a new one down by the road, away from the house.

One year they had so many tomatoes, Grandpa tried to sell large baskets of tomatoes for ten cents a basket, but people were so poor at that time they wouldn't buy them. It was the Depression—what they didn't eat, they canned. And they'd make 'u conserva too.

They had a German midwife come to the house when my grandmother was due to give birth—all the children were born on the farm (except for Ag, who was born in Italy). My mother told me it was said in this way: "She brought Vittoria out."

The house was built in 1837 as a country club, and was a fully functioning farm until 1978. It's still completely intact, all the land, and the well, and the oven are still there, if not in use. My Uncle Rocky had cows on the farm for half of the year until the end.

There was still a huge kitchen garden until my uncle got sick and died a few years ago. In August, my uncle always sent me home with huge bags of tomatoes, zucchini, mint, corn, greens, beets. Aunt Bea and Uncle Rocco canned their raspberries and the pears from their trees when they were well into their nineties.

The pigs are no longer on the farm. And there are old, rusted-out farm machines stranded in some of the fields. But the land, and the lakes, and the oven, and the well are still there.

In the following stories, told in their own words, my mother and my Aunt Toni give a sense of what daily life was like for my mother and her family living on the farm in Waterbury, Connecticut, in the early part of the twentieth century, right up to and including World War II.

Making 'u conserva (tomato paste)

"Take tomatoes and cook them down. We'd put them through a sieve and we squeezed them through to take out the skin and seeds. Then we'd spread what was left out on a sheet, cover this with cheesecloth. You had boards across the porch so the spread of tomatoes was up off the ground. You'd kind of turn the tomatoes once in a while and the sun would dry them. Gradually it would become a thick paste. Afterward we'd put them in a crock and cover the conserva with oil so it would keep. Mama would put a few spoons of that into her sauce. It made her sauce good. She'd use 'u conserva in different dishes. They did that." [Told by my Aunt Toni, Antoinette Becce Padula]

The Oven

We made the dough the night before we baked our bread for the week on Saturday. My father bought hundred pound bags of flour for my mother to use. She filled the cong', the big pan, with flour, one part whole wheat and two parts white flour and a little semolina. We put the cong' up on a stool. The cong' was a little less than a yard across, about thirty inches. It was wider at the top, and tapered down a little toward the bottom. All the girls took turns helping her. She'd make a well in the center of the flour and pour tepid water in. She had already heated the water. It couldn't be too hot or too cold. She slowly crumbled yeast into the water until it all was dissolved. She used only one yeast cake. (That was all she needed because we left the dough overnight and in the morning the bread was up.) Then she'd pull a little flour into the well of water, a little bit at a time, slowly incorporating the flour until it was all mixed together.

Or sometimes she'd supervise one of us girls and we'd do this work while she added what else the dough needed. A handful of salt, for example. And maybe a little semolina. If the dough was dry, she'd add a little more tepid water. Whoever was working the dough would pull up a bit at a time and knead it down in the pan. You'd walk around the outside of the pan to get all the flour mixed into the well of water and to knead until Mama was pleased with the consistency.

Then we covered the pan with linen cloths. Over those we put blankets, any flannel blankets around, to keep the heat in to make the dough rise.

We did this on Friday night just before we went to bed. In the morning, my mother would make us make fried dough for breakfast. We'd dip the fried pieces in sugar and that was our breakfast on Saturday. After breakfast we made our bread for the coming week.

Now with the oven. You had to build the fire. We'd go out to collect wood to start the fire. You had to build it very carefully. First you put two large logs down, then you put two other big ones across, this way and that way across, like tick-tack-toe. You kept the middle clear; you built up from the biggest pieces on the bottom, to the smallest on the top, so that the largest logs would burn slowly. In the center, you put the kindling and the paper to start the fire. Once you built that fire, you had to keep watching that oven constantly. When the sides of the oven turned kind of grey, then it was practically ready to start the baking.

When the charcoal was red, that meant the oven was ready, and we'd bank the ashes over to the right. The embers were golden. Mama would take a handful of flour and throw it in the middle and see if it charred. If it turned brown too quickly, that meant that the oven was still too hot and we had to wait a little longer before we put anything in.

We had oiled the pans after breakfast and in them spread the dough for fugazz' *and* apizz' *(focaccia and pizza). Bread got fixed in the pans in the morning when we got up.*

The first thing you put in the oven—this was very important—once it was ready, was the fugazz' *because it needed the hottest fire. We'd put oil, salt, pepper, crushed red pepper, garlic, oregano, and maybe a little basil on it. After that, the* apizz' *would go in. On that we put my mother's canned tomatoes and her homemade cheese. Sometimes she put a layer of dough, then a layer of cheese, then another layer of dough with her tomatoes and the rest, whatever she felt like doing. We ate the pizza for lunch on Saturday.*

You would have three big pans with two round loaves in each. They were big. Maybe fifteen inches across, enough for the whole week.

She'd take a mappin' *and make a ring on top of her head and balance one pan up there. She carried two other pans at the same time; one in each arm, all the way down the long stone steps from the kitchen to the oven. She held herself so straight. What balance she had.*

Before we put the bread in the oven, we'd come down with a knife, and make slices down both sides of the loaves and in front and back, and leave room for the bread to grow. That was the last thing to do before it went into the oven. The oven would bake your bread. You had to be very careful that you did everything just right so the bread would come out good. Those cuts were important to let the dough rise up more as it was baking.

My mother would hold the round loaf in the crook of her arm and cut it, pulling the knife toward her. It was out of this world. You can't believe how good it was when you put my mother's homemade butter on the bread. When I get hungry now that's what I have a vogli *for (pronounced "woolie," it's our dialect word for yen, from the Italian* voglia*). People went wild for my mother's bread. I remember Frank Donnaruma stuffing it in his pockets.*

Sometimes, we'd dry the prosciutto and capicola in the back when the oven was going and we were baking the bread. (There's a second compartment in the oven that you open from behind the main chamber for drying and smoking.) Other times, when the bread was baking, we'd go in the woods behind the house and collect the nuts— hickory nuts, butternuts, wild walnuts, or whatever we found—and put them in the back of the oven. We'd save them to eat at night, in the winter to eat. It would give us something to do in the winter at night. We'd crack those nuts and eat them.

Of course, we roasted suckling pigs, twenty/twenty-five pounds, and chickens, when we had the large crowds in the summer. We ate under the grapevine in the backyard, with the wine and the cheese and the bread. [Told by my mother, Rose Becce Clapps]

The Well

We had to carry all our water up from the well. For cooking, for washing, for everything. We would say to each other, "Do you want to get the water, or do you want to get the wood?" We all worked hard—all of us, don't worry. It was a pain in the neck.

Then we had to heat the water. We'd have two tubs, one that had hot water and soap, and one where you had the water to rinse. We had a scrubbing board and we'd scrub the clothes. Then we'd put them in the other tub to rinse them out.

The linens, the sheets and pillowcases, white clothes got special attention. In the meantime, we had more pans on the stove heating the water for when you drained the rinse water out. For the white clothes, you'd take the Star Water bleach, and you poured the bleach onto the white clothes you already had lined in the pan, one layer and another layer, the sheets of the week. Then you poured more Star Water, then you poured the hot, hot water on top; it was almost boiling, really hot. Then you would take and bleach all these white clothes sparkling white.

When you took them out, you hung them up and sometimes we'd hang them over the bushes because that made them whiter. [Told by my mother, Rose Becce Clapps]

Washing the Floor on Saturday Morning

On Saturday morning we'd wash the floor. It was wood. Mama would splash the water on one part of the floor. Each girl would do one part of the floor. One of us would scrub that part. In the meantime, my mother would pour out some water in another place where another sister was. We'd scrub and then rinse and wring out the mop. My mother would throw more water and we'd rinse our section and then go to the next section.

We had to throw the water out in the backyard. If it had bleach in it, we had to be careful that we didn't throw it where there was something planted. We threw it on the poison ivy plants hoping to kill them.

It was such a godsend when my father installed a pump in the kitchen with a handle, and we didn't have to go down to the well to carry it all up to the kitchen from downstairs. Buckets and buckets, all day long.

It made us tough. We accepted everything, especially when the Depression came. We made do, and we were glad for what we had, happy that we had what we had. We thought we had more than other people. We were never hungry. You could go out and pull a carrot from the garden and eat it. I did that many a time.

My mother would say, "Be a niza gal. I give you something nice when I got 'em." [Told by my mother, Rose Becce Clapps]

Sunday on the Farm

SUNDAYS WE ALL GO *UP THE FARM*: ALL OF THE AUNTS, ALL OF THE UNCLES and all of the cousins.

We eat a big Sunday dinner all together as more and more children are born and we grow too large; each of our families arrives after their big Sunday dinner at home. The grownups gather around the table and the kids run wild outside.

The house overlooks a sloping field down to two lakes with a small road between them. Bedsprings tied together make fences to keep the cows in the field. The lake on this side of the road belongs to the farm. In a red brick oven down near the road, bread used to be baked very week. We don't play near the oven even though it's like a little house. It's too close to the road.

Up the back at the end of the big kitchen garden, there's a stone slaughter-house and a stone barn. There's also a small brick house, where the hired help lives. But we don't go near there either. There's a big black dog chained there. These are all up a small road on the way to the pigs. Up the pigs it stinks from the manure. We don't go up there either.

There are fields we're not supposed to run through when the hay is growing. We get into big trouble if we forget and do that. There could be beatings.

The woods out back are just beyond the stonewall at the edge of the hay-fields. The woods are filled with big rocks between the trees. Good for climbing and all kinds of games. The girls especially love one enormous rock out in one of the fields, on Mr. Turrell's land. The rock has a hole a few inches wide and we convinced each other it had been used to grind corn. So that's where we often settle in for our game of house, mothers and babies. Our husbands all have names, but they are at work. We all want to be the mother. No one wants to be the baby.

The boys go off to their games. Cops and robbers or cowboys and Indians in the woods. We go up in the woods too, to collect stuff for our house. Large leaves for our plates, small leaves and seeds pulled from the ends of grasses are our food, small sticks are our forks and spoons. We spend hours setting up our home, running back and forth in the fields and woods. But once our house is all set up we make only a small pretense of playing mommy and baby. Making the house was the fun part.

We do tricks. Who can hold the best handstand? That's Bede, who lives on the farm. She's the youngest. We do cartwheels and somersaults. We hang down from swing set bars; we try to outdo each other. We climb high up in the pear trees where we know we're not supposed to go. But no one's around to tell. We might run inside to get some lemonade.

The men are just getting up from their naps. The women have cleared the table, washed and dried the dishes, and brought out cakes and other desserts and fruit and nuts. Coffee cups are on the table. If we're eating watermelon we assure our mothers eating the seeds isn't going to hurt us. They are not good for you, they insist. We eat the white part of the rind too. Not good for you.

Then we run back outside again. We might go to the rabbit hutch or go to see the calf that was just born. We climb up in the hayloft and jump in the old hay. The boys have joined us so there's no one to tell on us. We go down by the lake and take off our shoes and socks and get our feet wet up to our knees. Sometimes there are ducks in the lake. We remind each other that we're not supposed to go here because this is where grandma's little boy, Pasquale, drowned. He was with his uncles, in a cart pulled by a skittish horse, when they were run off the road into the lake by a bus honking his horn. The horse jumped the fence into the lake.

But we know we're not going to drown. That was a long time ago that Pasquale died.

When it starts to get dark we go inside to the living room where there's a piano. No one ever sits in the living room. We are the only ones ever in there and we only use it for rehearsals. We make up different words to go to with one of the few songs one of us knows how to play, "Long, long Ago." We make up a play or dance to go with it. The grownups have to watch us later, after we've rehearsed it over and over. They always come in from the kitchen slow. By now grandma's mozzarella and prosciutto are on the table. Other cold cuts.

Fresh sliced tomatoes, arugula salad, tasting like earth. Good bread. Some sausages in oil. More coffee.

All afternoon the grownups have been arguing and talking about bringing over my grandmother's brother Gerardo from Italy. Grandma's worried about taking him away from Tolve and his family. Grandpa's sure it's a good idea. They can make a cheese business together. Gerardo can bring his oldest son. It's still not decided.

"Five more minutes, five more minutes," we say when our parents say it's time to go home. They let us play for another half hour. A few times. Eventually we'll drive in our black Pontiac Terraplane back to 56 Ward Street, and our father will carry my sister and I upstairs to bed.

Once when Uncle Rocco got mad at Aunt Bea about something—it was always something—he started to scream at her, "You get everything all wrong," he said. "You don't do anything the way I tell you!"

We were all in the kitchen, everyone kids, grownups, company.

Aunt Bea was by the sink. "Oh stop it, Rocky," she said. She was mad. In front of everyone.

My uncle's face was twisted in fury. He lifted his hand to threaten her. He didn't care.

"Oh, Rocky, okay, Rocky," my father said, in a soothing voice from where he was sitting at the other end of the table, "let's let it go."

Uncle Rocky glared at my father. "You shut up," he said. He was going start with my father next.

After that my father wouldn't go up the farm for about twenty years. Later he began to show up at the farm and sit down at the kitchen table, but he never looked at or talked to my Uncle Rocky again. My uncle came to my father's funeral because he had to. My father was his sister's husband. That's the way it was in our family.

My Only Irish Aunt

WHICH, ACTUALLY, SHE ISN'T. IRISH THAT IS. ACCUSED OF BEING *Irlandese, Irashe*, by my grandmother because she wasn't Italian, my Aunt Bea was Anglo, Irish, Scottish, but worst of all, a Yankee, an American. A stunner. She was a farmer's daughter from Upstate New York. She was raised in the way that farmers' daughters are, to work hard and to accept all the relentless responsibilities for a farm to thrive. Her parents looked as if they belonged in an American folk painting. Grandpa Ferguson kept apple orchards. Grandma Ferguson was as sweet as her daughter, my aunt. Our family won the grand prize of Aunt Bea by accident of fate and our good luck. Beatrice was dating someone from back home when she came to Waterbury with a girlfriend during World War II to get a job in a factory. Jobs were plentiful then, and she was young and a dazzling beauty and wanted to have an adventure with her friend, Evelyn.

Uncle Rocky's friend was dating Evelyn. That was how they met. Once my uncle met Beatrice Ferguson, he courted her as if his life depended on it, and really it did. She was the very best thing that ever happened to him. He couldn't have found a more beautiful, kinder, nicer, or smarter woman. It could be that his determination to court and marry her was the one and only time he was completely, 100 percent right.

He pursued her seriously, insisting on picking her up to take her home when she got off work at the factory at the end of her late shift, at eleven o'clock at night. Every night he was sitting there in his Ford Model A Roadster.

He'd pick her up and take her out to dinner. "Have a steak," he'd insist.

"I didn't even want a steak at eleven o'clock at night. Who wants a steak at that time of day? But he insisted." He wanted to show this young woman how much he valued her, would value her always. She has the distinctive look of Anglo-Irish beauties, abundant dark hair, pure pale skin, slender body, the beauty of a lady, a country lass, with the beauty of a star. Aunt Bea was nineteen years old when she met my Uncle Rocco. He was handsome, too.

She must have been convinced by my uncle's persistence, his ardor, his devotion. She broke it off with the boy back home and agreed to marry my uncle. A brilliant move on my uncle's part. I'm sure the young Beatrice had no idea she'd wind up in the middle of a large, noisy Italian family, while she was still picking apples in her father's orchards.

How I would love to know more about her, and what her life before us was like. Where did she swim? What were her girlhood days and nights like? There was a one-room schoolhouse where she was an exceptional student, skipping grades. Even now, well into her nineties, she corrects my sister and me on details. Her mind is as sharp as her beauty is long. Reticence hides her luminosity.

We know that Aunt Bea's mother, Grandma Ferguson, had the same lovely nature as her daughter—gentle streams of sweetness come from both of them. Did the two of them laugh together as they went about their work on that farm?

My aunt has one of those delightful and easily delighted natures: She laughs easily, quickly, sees the silliness in the least thing. I can picture her hands deep in a bowl of water at the sink as she washes some vegetables that have just come in from the garden full of soil. But something has struck her as funny and she throws back her head with a half a toss, her hair going back off her neck for a second, while her hands stay in the sink, or one hand comes up out of the cold water, and with the back of her wrist she wipes a bit of hair from her forehead and laughs that easy, lilting laughing of one who sees life in its full ridiculousness. She has a generous acceptance of the slip, the mistake. She has the kind of gentleness and kindness that makes us all feel safe when we are with her.

During their courting days, Uncle Rocco told her that they would live for a year on my grandparents' farm, and then they'd buy a house, or he'd build her a house of her own on the land down by the lake.

One day when they were taking a long Sunday ride in the country, my aunt pointed out a sweet house for sale. My uncle's response was swift and adamant. "I'm not buying that house or any house. I'm staying on the farm.

I'm going to inherit it. We're staying there." Was that the plan all along? "I'm going to inherit it all."

She lived on our feudal farm where she learned all the Italian ways from her impossible mother-in-law, my grandmother. She learned to make sausage, cheese, *prosciutto*, to can the tomatoes, the pears, string beans, and other vegetables from the huge kitchen garden, to fry the pumpkin flowers, to bake bread in the outdoor oven. To cook massive meals for all the farmhands and others who trouped in and out of the kitchen daily. She threw herself into all of it. Had five babies. Three *maschile*. So she fulfilled all expectations. Apparently my grandfather loved her. "Your grandfather was always good to me."

Perhaps that affection fueled my grandmother's ridiculously mean treatment of her sweet young daughter-in-law. That my grandmother was so awful to my aunt is very hard for me to reconcile—two women I love and admire, and one treating the other as if we were living as some ancient brutal tribe.

My grandmother was furious that her only son, my uncle, had married someone who wasn't Italian. Who was in fact, *Irashe*, Irish!

My grandparents continued to live on the farm throughout their lives. As Aunt Bea learned to master each detail of running the domestic side of this large enterprise, my grandmother reminded everyone this farm was "*casa mia*. My house." My grandmother called her, *puttan'*, whore.

Uncle Rocco and my grandmother fought all the time—he was still the absolute center of his mother's life. But that was a way of our family. Everyone telling everyone else what they weren't doing right.

But my uncle took belittling his wife to new heights. "You have no idea what you're doing. You never do anything right." "Why did you put that there? Don't you know I have to keep my rag there? What's wrong with you?" Everything was an opportunity for a blast of critical fury. His meanness of spirit toward his wife and children was hard to watch up-close, and we all got a good look.

Still, despite these two furies at her side all day, every day, Aunt Bea did everything with great skill, panache, and always with a kind of savvy. Maybe that's what her husband disliked so much. He was outclassed.

Meanwhile, the family tradition of *paesans* and relatives coming either to stay at or to visit the farm continued. Sometimes the young guys helped on the farm, but the elders just came to bask in the country. Some of the women helped my aunt with her endless work; some just came to enjoy the food and fresh air. They all loved Aunt Bea.

How did my Aunt Bea manage to live her life out under these circumstances and maintain her sweetness? I don't know. She did stand up to my uncle and they fought hard and long. Eventually seeing that those fights never came to any resolution, she'd just shrug her shoulders and get on with it. Too much to do to waste time on this nonsense. The best of her life was all of her children and grandchildren and great grandchildren. Many spent long hours on the farm under her care while their parents worked.

Meanwhile, we were all crowding in her kitchen, my family telling their childhood stories over and over and over. I don't think I ever heard one of them ask her what her childhood was like.

We sat in her kitchen, ate her amazing food. The table would be covered in heaps of fresh corn on the cob, roasted chicken, greens cooked with oil and garlic, loaves of fresh bread, a huge tomato and lettuce salad, a big bowl of *ciambott'*, eggplant, tomatoes, peppers, and onions. She is as good a cook as I have ever known in a family filled with brilliant cooks.

She behaved with the same sweetness to us cousins, seventeen in all, who came and went, slept over, stayed at the farm until their parents came home from work, while she raised her five children.

Aunt Bea and Uncle Rocco's firstborn, Beatrice, is my very first best friend, a friendship that continues through our lives. She has a good deal of her mother in her. Each of my aunt's children has a special quality, a kindness and a generosity gotten from their mother. She loved her babies. She loved rocking them in their carriages, carrying them around, laughing with them. She deserves their endless love. She has three sons, Rocky, Vito, and Danny, and one more daughter, Lucia. They treasure their mother. They've carried their babies to her too, and so on in turn, and now there are nine grandchildren who have created sixteen great grandchildren.

Later, when my Aunt Bea was in the hospital with pneumonia, my uncle began to write her love notes. "I miss you so much. I love you so much. You are the best thing that ever happened to me." He missed having her near him, taking care of him.

She loved being in the hospital, then in a rehab facility where it was quiet. Where she could read whenever she wanted. Then she stayed with her son Rocky and his wife, Judy. Rocky made her breakfast that she could eat at her leisure. She loves to read. She loves to write a letter. We have all gotten her lovely letters telling us about what is happening in her world, a few pages in elegant handwriting. Her pneumonia afforded her the briefest of respites—

complete freedom from the endlessly demanding life she's led. She went back home to care for my uncle during his last time.

"It's too hard on you, Mom," her children all said. "You've just had pneumonia. You can't do all of this work. You're older, too."

She always had the same answer, "I can take it." That was strength, her tenacity. Her profound stubbornness. Perhaps that spirit had always been in her, perhaps a way she learned to hold onto her own center. She was buffeted in the storm of our family all of her adult life. But she held her own.

There were many such women in the world I came from, and there are many such women whom I know today. We can take it. It's a pride in the ability to deal with anything, take on anything, a sense of inner strength.

One day after my uncle Rocky died, and she was finally living in peace and quiet, Vito, her middle child and second son, found her on the floor. She had fallen and couldn't get up. She hadn't called anyone from her cell phone. "I was just there for a few minutes," she insisted. "They make such a big deal out of everything."

In the few years after Uncle Rocky died and before Aunt Bea went to live in a lovely place for older people, the farm she had worked, cared for, cleaned, lived in, grew her family in, helped raise her grandchildren in, welcomed everyone to, became *casa sua*, her house. As it should always have been.

FOUR MOVEMENTS ON
THE THEME OF *MINESTRA*

"I want Grandma's *'nast*," is how my sister's granddaughter, Rosie said it over and over as soon she was old enough to eat real food.

In our modern secular lives, cooking seems to be what we have left of alchemy. Maybe that's why we prize it so, why our young people have taken up cooking as an art, a sport, a vision. Transforming the raw and the fresh into something we'll eat is alchemy. It's a connection to our earliest human origins, when we learned to use fire in order to make things we eat. But this particular food, *minestra*, this soup that is more than soup: it's truly full of preternatural powers.

Even though one of the things I love about cooking is its playful aspect, for me this one recipe is sacrosanct. I make it one way. Even within family and friends there are variations. Annie Carballo puts in string beans or whatever vegetables are in her fridge. Lucia convinced me to put potatoes in for our vegetarian children to give the *minestra*, Rosie's *'nast*, more substance. I make an exception for them. But only for them.

My sister, Lucia, has the opposite approach. She sees it all as improvisation. "Cooking is like jazz, you can't write down every note. Not only does everyone cook it differently—just take our own family—but everyone makes it differently every time they make it. I know it's true for me. I'm always asking myself, is it better? Is it better to cook the greens in the broth, or separately? Those questions are always alive for me. They are never settled. Do you chop the greens while they are still raw, or after they're limp and wet? This is one of the pleasures of cooking. To be open to suggestions by the ingredients and the day on which you are cooking it. I'm different every time I make it, and therefore the outcome is different."

This soup will straighten out your life, soothe your soul, and heal a broken heart.

THE RECIPE: MY VERSION

First, make a big chicken soup.

I use lots of wings and some backs to make the big broth. I will add some chicken breasts for say the last 45 minutes. My stepdaughter, Donna, buys a beautifully roasted chicken to break up in her chicken soup.

The vegetables: onions, carrots, parsley, tomatoes, and only sometimes celery. In my 14-quart stockpot I'll add to the chicken 4 to 5 onions, 5 or 6 large carrots, at least one full head of Italian parsley, 1 or 2 large cans of peeled tomatoes. Salt and pepper. It all simmers slowly, sometimes overnight. In the morning, heaven. And maybe a cup for breakfast. It's been known to happen.

Strain the broth, keeping aside any vegetables or chicken you choose. I like to keep all the carrots and some of the celery, some of the onions, tomato, and whatever chicken I can save from the pieces. De-fat the broth by skimming or chilling.

Next: the pepperoni and meatballs.

Buy 2 or 3 sticks of a good-quality pepperoni, and cut them into thick slices, skinned or not. Boil the pieces for a few minutes to tenderize and remove excess fat. This is a kind of sad substitute for all of the home-made pork products my grandmother put into her *minestra*, ends of prosciutto, dried sausage in oil, a pork rib, or some salt pork.

The meatballs.

Mix together:
3 lbs. equal parts ground pork and veal
1 bunch of fresh basil, finely chopped
6–7 cloves of crushed garlic
Lots of grated Parmigiano cheese
Salt and pepper
4 large eggs, beaten
1 cup of dried bread crumbs
Enough milk or cream to moisten the mixture.
Make very small meatballs (about ¾-inch in diameter). Boil them in water, set aside.

The greens.

At least 2 heads each of *cicoria* and *scarole* (chicory and escarole) carefully washed and rinsed to remove all of the sand and dirt off these wonderful greens. Break off all browned edges, or any parts that aren't fresh. The centers are so tender you might want to put them aside for salad. Fill huge bowls with cold water and gently swish your greens around, 1 head at a time, then drain them in a (*scolamacaron*) colander. Rinse and repeat until there's not a bit of sand or dirt at the bottom of the bowl. As each head is cleaned, steam it in a large pan with some water. Cut these large leaves into pieces and set aside. Steam the next head. You get into a rhythm. The greens are a major reason why this soup is so delicious, and makes us feel so good when we eat it. You can cheat and use frozen greens but the cooking gods will know, and you just won't be as good or as healthy a person ever again.

The assembly.

Add the greens to the meatballs, pepperoni, vegetables, and chicken pieces in the broth. Cook until the elements are married. Taste for salt and pepper.

Minestra Means Soup

MINESTRA MEANS SOUP IN ITALIAN. THAT'S ALL. BUT FOR MY FAMILY THAT vowel-driven word—notice all of the vowels are in there except the *u*—meant transcendent possibilities.

When Pretzel, my son's very young dog, was run over by a speeding car and died on the way to the vet in my son's arms—my response was to make a vat of *minestra*. I was certain that the best I had to offer was this soup with its rich layers of broths, meats, and greens. It might help a bit. It would carry with it ingestible comfort.

The word *minestra* comes from the word *minster* or serve, which suggests that it takes care of those it's given to eat, and that the *minestra* maker is a caretaker.

It's a big, layered dish, which needs a goodly amount of time to make, and which my family all cherish and love on a cold winter's day. There are times when we feel it's the only thing that can possibly make things better. It can help with grief, healing, exhaustion, sheer misery. We make it when someone comes home from a long journey, physical or psychic. It's a meal fit for death, divorce, breakups, or other terrible losses. It helps to right the earth's axis.

All cultures and families have such foods. These foods gather family stories, memories of old customs; eating this food often marks certain dramas and occasions. There's nothing new there. But if each family doesn't believe that it can have this kind of profound impact, then the dish is not worthy of its reputation.

Since this soup is ours, I have complete faith in its unique powers to heal and set things right again.

Soup is soothing liquid, meant to slide down with fluidity and ease. There isn't so much chewing as there is ingesting over deep breaths. Our *minestra* has a heartiness that partly contradicts its identity as soup, while also being the essence of it. There are the pieces of carrots, celery, onions, and chicken in it. There are the small meatballs and the pieces of pepperoni. All of it embedded in large amounts of *cicoria* and *scarole.*

The warm mist, which rises up from a just served bowl of this combination gives one a sense of eating healthily, substantially, and delicately all at the same time. There is the soft cloud of a good chicken soup, the delicious meaty vapors of the meatballs and pepperoni, and the flood of scents from the greens, which sooths, repairs, and makes one whole again.

The etymology of the word *restaurant* has, at its root, the word connected to soup. Wikipedia tells us that in sixteenth-century France there was an inexpensive concentrated soup sold by street vendors that was specifically known to help to restore a person against exhaustion, hence, the word restaurant. This in turn led in the eighteenth century to a shop called a restaurant being opened that specialized in those kinds of soups.

Perhaps if I describe the way we make it, what I'm talking about will become clearer. There are five distinct parts to this. The soup, the preparations of the two additional meats, and the preparations of the greens. Then the assembly.

All of the food that I learned to cook in my mother's kitchen, my grandmother's kitchen, my aunts' kitchens seemed immutable, forever exactly the same. But one of the most important recipes in my family tells another story.

MINESTRA, MONDAY MIDDAY
DINNER UP THE FARM

My cousin, Bede Becce Avcollie, the firstborn of my Aunt Bea and Uncle Rocco, grew up on the farm, where the oldest ways of cooking in all of our families went on the longest, because it was a pig farm and they had a huge kitchen garden. They made their own *prosciutto*, sausage, *capicola.* They canned tomatoes, pears, lots of other things too, and made their own cheese. My grandmother was the originator of all of this cooking; even while she reviled her daughter-in-law, my Aunt Bea, mercilessly because she wasn't Italian and married her only surviving son, Grandma still taught Aunt Bea, her daughter-in-law, all of her cooking ways. She learned every detail, and carried all of these traditions on for all of us. My cousin Bede knows the original recipe.

Bede recalls how they made the *minestra* every Monday for dinner.

"First my mother started with a large soup pan on the stove. Then she added salt pork or a few ribs. Sometimes she used the end of the prosciutto or some dried sausage. Sometimes some salt pork or ribs. Whatever we had in the house. Mostly she made a chicken stock, with pieces of chicken, like the backs and necks, but she sometimes made a beef stock, using soup bones. After that simmered a while, she added whole onions, carrots, celery, and a few sprigs of parsley. We always added greens from the garden, *scarole, cicoria*. But dandelions were the essential green that had to be in the soup. We picked those from the fields around the house where they grew wild. The greens were cooked separately and added to the broth at the end. When freezers came in, my mother would freeze some too. She put some chicken in at the end so it wouldn't be overcooked. We never put meatballs in our *minestra*.

"She removed all of the parsley. She took the vegetables out whole and served those in one serving dish. She put all of the meat in another serving dish. We had the *minestra* first as our soup. Then we grated our own cheese on top of it: mozzarella and parmesan. We'd have that with fresh Italian bread, and dip the bread in the soup. Then we each had some vegetables and whatever pieces of meat we wanted after the soup."

ANOTHER IMPORTANT STORY ABOUT SOUP

The Benediction
By Lucia Clapps Mudd, about our
Aunt Dora LaGuardia Claps[4]

Aunt Dora was a dumpling of an aunt. She spoke in hems and haws. With hands overlapping on her belly, she sputtered in fits and starts. "Ummh, huh, ehhe." Reticent and unsure with words, she was right as rain in the kitchen; silky homemade pasta, sugary eggy *tarall'*s, *minestra*—and what a *minestra*!

Uncle Paul was Dad's beloved uncle, a superb storyteller, and Aunt Dora was Uncle Paul's beloved wife.

Yet it came to pass that one of the favorite stories to come out of the two-family house on Oak Street was Aunt Dora's to tell.

It seems that Uncle Paul's sister, Aunt Sadie, was not well and Aunt Dora went to New York, to Maspeth, to take care of her. Aunt Sadie was sweet and mild with a large rosy dot on each cheek and soft curly hair. Her husband, Uncle John, was a fine tailor but a mean man. From his Fifth Avenue shop he dressed New York's finest—celebrities and movie stars, Cary Grant and Adolph Menjou. But he couldn't stitch together a kind word.

Aunt Dora ministered to Sadie with true devotion. She hurried about the fine house in Maspeth, cooking and cleaning and tending to Sadie. When Uncle John came home from Fifth Avenue he'd start criticizing. He liked everything done the way his mother had done it: His mother was from Vetri. He belittled and berated Sadie, even in her sick bed, finding fault, and finding it with pleasure. This really steamed the loyal and devoted sister-in-law.

This particular day, Aunt Dora set about to make her *minestra*, a complex task. She peeled and chopped, and simmered and stammered, "Humm, ehhh, uhhh," *runzeling* along with the low boil of the pots.

When Uncle John came home he started right in with his taunting. "My mother used *l'oss 'd' maial'*. Where's *l'oss 'd' maial'*?"

"Ahhh, huh, oh, you want the pork bone! Okay, then I'll give you the bone." So she reaches in and pulls the precious prosciutto bone out of the soup; brass knob coming out of the holy water. Then nice and wet and dripping she delivers it directly to Uncle John's head! *Botta bang!* "*Oiyy!*," She covers her mouth with her hands as she recalls the contact.

"Ummh, ehhe," she continues, "and then the lump came."

We laugh out loud. We applaud her. "Well done, Aunt Dora, well done!"

A benediction, a long time coming. "Huuh, umu, huuh," the priestess incants, remembering. And we praise and honor her.

SPEAKING OF *MINESTRA*, OR
THE LAST SOUP SONG
By Bill Herman

When I was a little kid—under eight years of age—my family lived on the top floor of a two-story house, whose bottom apartment was occupied by the Campanellas. We Jews referred to them fondly as the *'talieners*. The neighborhood was mixed: Jews, Italians, Irish, without exception working-class people. I was crazy about the Campanella girls, Josephine and Anna, they seemed so abundant, so pretty.

So once in a while I was in their apartment, and there, every time, I noticed an alien smell—I knew it as "Italian." I had experienced any number of Jewish homesteads and they smelled—like each other. Like mine—more or less garlicky, more or less of boiled chicken or of a recent scouring with Ajax ("the foaming cleanser"). But the Campanellas' house: sharply different, in another class altogether. Finally, one day, I began to associate it with dark, dark greens, cooking and cooked greens, though I never actually saw any. I said to myself, well, they eat different stuff. I decided I wouldn't really like home-cooked Italian food. Too much of that dark green stuff that smelled.

A few years later—I was then forty-seven—I was courting this great beauty of an Italian American woman from a big clan in Waterbury, Connecticut (notice I've switched from just plain Italian). The courtship was dessert for me, a very rich, very surprising encounter with varieties of thrilling sweetness—and yet I was wary. Things were going too well. Like all DNA-fortified males, I was blood-bound to resist commitment. I did. I faltered.

Among the things Jo did to overcome this powerful force was to ask her adviser, Lenny Kriegel, and his wife, along with members of an entire seminar that she attended, to an Italian dinner, together with me, her boyfriend, in her apartment. This enterprise struck me as daring to the point of recklessness: her apartment was a postage stamp—a one-room studio, no "L," and so small that she slept on a trundle bed that doubled as a couch. There was one armchair, a couple of small tables, and a kitchen that was a begrudging indentation in one wall. Of course, no dishwasher and a pint-sized fridge.

I ventured a little skepticism, which she waved aside with all the jaunty daredevil-confidence of the guy who walked across a rope from one world trade tower to the other. Since in her seminar there had been considerable serious talk about ethnicity and Jo being Italian, Lenny had told Jo— not asked—that he wanted an Italian dinner. At this charge, too, she smiled adorably with super-confidence and calm as a bed sheet, and said "Sure."

To me, she just said: "Make sure everybody shows up."

On the appointed night, then, I rounded up the other suspects and appeared at the door of, essentially, what most restaurants would have designated as a cloak room, and as we entered, across the spidery strands of time and memory, there wafted into my nostrils that alien smell, a faint version, of what I had used to smell in the Campanellas' apartment when I was a kid.

The crowd of us jostled around, miraculously found seats—most on the floor—had a lot of laughs greeting Jo. I asked her what we were gonna eat.

"*Minastr*," she said. "Look in the pot." There, floating in an enormous quantity of soup (I supposed) were, in addition to things I'd never dreamed could be accommodated in soup, limp waves of green stuff—the source of the aroma, as I now named it, and boy was I even more in love. I was still a little culinary Jewish kid, for whom soup was chicken or split pea. The former, guzzled straight when you were sick, with matzo balls on Passover, or with rice or noodles at Friday night dinner. Split pea was a lunch special—for variety.

I was even more in love because I knew I was gonna eat all that stuff in the soup: little meatballs! boiled pepperoni! and things I usually consumed in a salad or on a pizza. Could I do it?

Folks, that enormous bowl of *minastr'*—covered with a snowy layer of freshly grated Parmigiano-Reggiano, my first ever—gave me a momentary shiver of deracination, but I knew I couldn't hesitate and I didn't. Sublime and glorious don't begin to do it justice. A velvet rush to the taste buds, a strengthening of the sinews, a delayed message to the genitals, and in the end, my entry into the life I would soon commit to. All done in this tiny, but blissful bower of Jo's. Like being inside the heart of a rose.

That wasn't all: the second course was lasagna. The forces of male denial were thus overcome, and I can actually make this dish myself now.

MOVE TO AMERICA

Chiesta ca, or This One Here

"WHY SHOULD WE SPEND ALL THAT MONEY ON HER EDUCATION IF SHE'S not a good in school? The other one, okay, she's serious. But *chiesta ca*, this one here, com'on Rose, it's ridiculous," my father and mother's voices were rising in summer's late light on the back porch.

I'd just come out of my bedroom into the kitchen to hear what this fight was about. I could tell it was bad.

"Peter," my mother said fiercely. "You can't do that. You can't do for one and not the other." She walked up to him and said it loud into his face.

"But Rose, she's always in trouble. She's not a good student. Why are you insisting on this? You know I'm right." The voices kept rising. They didn't care that they were screaming out on the back porch where everyone could hear them. Each of them was dead set in their positions.

"Let her go to the local branch of UConn, if you want. That's good enough."

My father, who was usually my ally, wasn't that night. He wasn't wrong. But my mother, who really had a very hard time with me as her daughter, was my fierce protector that night. She wouldn't give in. Her voice was getting higher and more intense.

"Both of my girls are going to college. We sent Lucia to Simmons and we're sending Jo to Boston, too. You can't do it. I won't let you!"

She would not back down. Both of her daughters were going away to college. My sister was attending Simmons College. I was going to attend Boston University.

The fight went on for a long time. As the sun slipped down my mother became more and more insistent.

Each of their voices rising higher than I had ever heard them I was frozen in place and sick with confusion.

When my mother came in from the porch, her eyes were flashing furiously. She looked at me in a rage. "You're going to Boston University," she said. "You're going!"

I didn't thank her or hug her. She didn't hug me. Or say anything else. She went into the bedroom and slammed the door.

In the fall of 1962, I left Waterbury to go to Boston University. I had never been good in school. I probably had what is now understood to be attention deficient disorder, but then I was seen to be careless, lazy, and out of control. I was in trouble often at home and in school. I talked back at teachers. Once when a receptionist at a doctor's office kept me waiting for hours while other patients who had arrived after me were taken, I slammed the door so hard as I left in disgust that I broke the lock.

After taking an IQ test in eighth grade, my teachers looked at me in surprise. "You should be doing much better than you are in school. You're smart." As always, the question was what was wrong with me?

Still, I left Waterbury to go to Boston University as an Italian girl who went to church and didn't smoke or drink. I wouldn't even consider having sex with the boyfriend I had been madly in love with. As rebellious as I was that was out of the question.

The first Sunday after I arrived at Boston University, I went to mass in a cool, unadorned, modern, nondenominational chapel; it was austere, empty, not our small, wooden St. Lucy's back home. The next Sunday I rolled over in my bed while my three roommates continued to sleep. I rolled over and joined them. Going to mass seemed to slip off my back like an old husk.

"Pray for faith. You must continue to pray and believe," I had been told repeatedly by the priests I had turned to for help with my questions and doubts. But here in this large secular university it was easy not to go to mass. I woke up, thought about it for a very brief moment and rolled over to go back to sleep.

Boston University was too large for an ethnic kid like me. At home, decisions sprung naturally from within the tight boundaries of my world. I'd go swimming when the housework was done. I could buy that dress if I had saved enough money from babysitting or if my mother thought it was a good idea. It never occurred to anyone that we should be in charge of our own lives. Our lives belonged to the family.

My father once said quizzically, "You know, Jo, there are people in factories who spend all day reading documents. Maybe you could get a job like that. You love to read." It never occurred to him, even though he was a passionate reader himself, to suggest that I should be a high school English teacher or a librarian. It never occurred to me either.

I arrived lost at Boston University and remained that way.

But in 1962 the world was about to shift on its axis. We just didn't know it. The summer after my first year in college, a friend offered me marijuana for the first time at a drive-in movie. A gentle summer shower came down on the windshield of my friend's car as he taught me how to inhale the smoke and hold it in my lungs.

"I don't feel anything," I said, exactly as the raindrops falling on the windows began to mesmerize me. I smoked as much as other kids did then. I had sex for the first time the following summer—partly because the guy I was seeing nicknamed me Paris. The next year the civil rights movement took over another layer of our lives. By the time I dropped out after my junior year, so much had happened to move the ground beneath my feet that it would take decades of therapy to understand what it meant to leave Waterbury and travel into the larger world. Those first three years at Boston University were just the beginning of a long turbulent migration. I had to learn how to live and belong in America.

After Eden

IN THE BEGINNING I THOUGHT THE RUSSELLS WOULD BE MY PATH TO America, but when David Russell died we were all left in the country of his death. Mourning and disarray made up our days while we tried to go on, even though his small body was no longer with us.

It made no sense that our arms and legs still worked where his no longer did. How air still continued to go in and out of our lungs, how we walked from one side of a room to the other is still mysterious.

For Glady, his mother, and Jack, his father, it was a catastrophe that knocked them back so hard they weren't in their own lives for decades. Their seedling, their tadpole, their youngest male issue left a void in their firmaments. They were unmade.

The word *catastrophe* is from the Latin *catastropha*, which in turn comes from the Greek *katastrophé*, or "an overturning; a sudden end," derived from *katastrephein*, "to overturn, turn down, trample on; to come to an end." From *kata*, "down" ... to "sudden disaster": the reversal of what was expected. David's death was precisely that.

When I left my family in Waterbury to go to college in Boston, I had no idea that it was the beginning of a very long journey away from them. I just thought I was going on to continue my education. My love of this first idyllic and then tragic family influenced and changed forever the way I thought about the world, family, and myself in both.

I saw in them the wide world of sophistication, what being an American grownup meant. I thought I would live with them and by osmosis learn about this larger world that included the arts, the university, but also children, family, a mother who painted and had a cocktail before dinner.

I had been babysitting for the Russells for a couple of years by then. At the end of my sophomore year at Boston University, Glady (Gladyse) had asked me to be her next au pair the following year in exchange for room and board.

I moved in with the Russell family in September of 1964. David died that November.

At Boston University, I was lost and bewildered in immense auditoriums filled with at least hundreds but more typically thousands of students. I had none of the necessary skills: how to take useful notes, how to outline the reading materials, how to recognize the important points in a lecture. I'd sit in those auditoriums daydreaming, listening to the traffic hum out on Commonwealth Avenue, watching students whisper to one another and trying to guess what they were writing in their notebooks. I imagined I'd figure it out sometime in the future when lightning struck. I was a truant from my own life.

Living in Boston was another story. The wide horizon of the city beckoned to me in a celebratory way. I took long walks, which had no destination but still might lead now to a museum, now to a part of town that I didn't know, maybe to an interesting shop, a café, or an art film. When another student invited me to go to see *Madame Butterfly*, I went only because I was curious about what it would be like to sit in a theater attending an opera. I was filling up with an inarticulate passion for the city. It was all instinct toward the world, which lay beyond my family.

When the flower sellers arrived in spring on the street corners, the sudden displays of color would flood my body with an excitement and a hope I couldn't explain. Fields of color on gray sidewalks. People walking past them. At twilight I'd often walk to the nearest shopping street and watch people hurrying off trolleys, into shops and then home in a bath of light that made everything and everyone exceptional. Something opened up in me in response to the crowds, those colors; all this changing my ideas of how life might be lived—a sense that the unexpected might come toward you as you walked down the street. These experiences awakened immense, powerful, confusing aspirations.

At that time, young people all over America were involved in civil rights issues. I joined the Northern Student Movement, the NSM, and we marched, organized, protested and got arrested. Boston, filled with colleges and universities and students, was a perfect place for this movement to take root. We went to meetings and joined each other in actions large and small. Once we had been sitting in all night outside some government building when at dawn the flag was raised. We looked at each other in our exhaustion, stood up, and recited the Pledge of Allegiance, impressed by our virtue.

Aside from endless marching and singing, going to endless planning meetings, where the women still made the coffee, and attending too many conferences, tutoring two preteen African American girls was the most meaningful part of my involvement with the civil rights movement. They'd come over to our apartment to visit my roommate Kathy and I. We had a poster of Michelangelo's David on the wall. "Naked City," they cried in unison whenever they came over. "You two are bad. Very bad." They laughed, bending over, screamed, stamping their feet, "Ahhhhh ... *Naked City!*" We'd laugh and laugh with them. The girls always reminded me what a screeching joy it was to be a child and say what you thought the moment you thought it. We all cracked up. These kids were so great.

I decided to talk to Tiffany's mother about her homework—I was hoping I could help her see that Tiffany was special and that as a mother she should encourage her. Tiffany kept trying to talk me out of meeting her mother, saying, "She's not home," but I knew that wasn't true—and eventually I had insisted. I got into the elevator with the wounded, corrugated walls, filled with the sour smell of piss and dirt, and entered the first poor, dirty home I had ever been in. The TV in the living room was tuned to a soap opera that no one was watching. A three-year-old jumped up and down on one side of the shabby couch, while Tiffany's mother, whose hair stuck up in all directions, sat with her eyes half shut and her head nodding. A baby in a swollen smelly diaper sat on the other side of her. I hadn't known that there were tiny kids, only the older brothers. On the kitchen windows were unhemmed curtains that had once been white but now were streaked gray with dirt, and on which someone had appliquéd apples with leaves and stems with crude, uneven stitches. When had there been hope enough to stitch those apples?

That was in my sophomore year. It was the same year the Boston Strangler prowled the Boston nights. But that didn't stop me from taking walks at three or four in the morning if I were feeling restless. There was no one to stop me. One night two cops pulled up next to me. "Is anything wrong? What are you doing out here in the middle of the night?" they asked. They didn't lecture me, or give me a hard time. They quietly drove me back to my apartment and suggested it wasn't safe to be out in the middle of the night.

Glady's proposal that I become the family's au pair called to me like a lighted window on a dark street. It gave the possibility of shape to amorphous waters. If I thought Glady and Jack would show me the way to America, my Italianness gave them back a bit of the romance of their early, married life in Naples.

On the first day of their honeymoon they got a call to go down immediately to New York City for a job interview with the Italian Mission Service in Naples. Three days later they were on a ship to Naples. She always laughed when she told the story about weeping on the ship, wondering what she had gotten herself into. The ship took a month from New York to Naples. This was in 1950. Naples was still in a state of utter disarray from World War II. He was twenty-five. She was eighteen years old.

Glady worked with people who were living in the caves where they had gone to escape the bombing of their city. Jack worked to help people get the essential personal documents that were often lost or destroyed during the war. Jack learned to trade cigarettes and soap for documents. Glady spoke the Neapolitan street dialect. Jack learned *real* Italian. What I brought with me of my southern Italian family spoke to Glady.

The Russell family was one big lively organism, throbbing with vitality, bursting at its skin, burgeoning and overflowing. The children were young and flourishing, running up and down the stairs, knocking things over, bumping into each other, making good chaos before retreating to their own rooms. Enamored by the whole boisterous bunch, I became a part of their noise and activity.

There were five children in the family. Their firstborn and oldest daughter is Darshan, who was called Shan. She had sandy blond hair down to her waist when she was twelve years old. She was lanky, smart, and at ease in herself and the world. She could say what she thought with a simple assertive clarity, something that was new for me to hear from a child. She spent hours in her bedroom reading and had the aura of a young woman in an eighteenth- or nineteenth-century novel. She grew up to be a successful painter. Biff, their oldest son was bursting out of himself, full of jazz, energy, and impulse, and often in a little trouble, especially with Glady. He always had my heart because I identified with being that kid in the family. He became a professional ski instructor. Erik looked most like Glady and is deeply artistic, with a quiet but mischievous sense of humor. Even the way he played with his Legos reflected the playfulness and the concentration of an artist. He became an extraordinary designer of jewelry. David and Natalie, the little ones, were the two sweet beanbags of the family, still only really defined by their charm and the softness of their limbs. Natalie, called Talie, had a mass of strawberry curls cascading around her face with a lazy eye that gave her an especially pixilated look. Talie is now a wife, mother of four, and business partner with her husband. And there was David.

Glady and Jack were involved in the civil rights movement as well. Jack had worked with the Reverend William Sloane Coffin at Yale, and was committed to many political causes. He was part of the Boston contingent that went down to the Selma march with a group of ministers from Harvard, MIT, and Yale. Later, he joined the Boston Redevelopment Authority, leading teams of young people to rehab substandard houses. Lots of young people were welcomed into the Russells' home and family. Some of them were from Yale; others were from Jack's political work or students from MIT and Harvard. The house teemed with youthful energies.

Glady had a different way of dealing with family life. Before I moved in, she sat me down to talk about my responsibilities. She explained that none of them were set in stone, that we could always talk about and change things as we went along. "But," she pointed out with wisdom, "these things should not be left informal. Between friends it might seem as though they should be, but it's better and clearer if it's all laid out at the beginning so that there are no misunderstandings." I'd cook for them once a week, making whatever I chose. Do the dishes after dinner at night. If I wished, I'd babysit when she and Jack went out. I wasn't to have boys stay in my room. There were specific rules and responsibilities. It was a revelation to me that people living in an intimate situation might make detailed plans for one another and not assume everyone just knew how things were supposed to go. I was startled and impressed.

The Russell family lived on Beacon Street in a five floor brownstone house provided by MIT, where Jack was the Methodist chaplain. The first floor was elegantly furnished with antiques, each of which Glady had carefully chosen and which she or Jack may have restored, and about which she knew a great deal. She had a sophisticated sensibility and an artist's taste. She also painted when her home and family didn't consume her. Above the ground floor, out of public view, each of the kids were free to do what they wanted in their rooms: they could paint on the walls, keep huge tables filled with tools and projects in messy disorder, leave books piled on their beds, toys around the floor. Those rooms were their domains. This was a radical departure from what I knew. I began to think that the confines of where I came from might be loosened here.

Before the children got home from school, Glady and I would sometimes sit and have a cup of tea or coffee in the afternoon at the long pine table by windows near the kitchen. We might be planning dinner: "Do you have any ideas? I can't think of a thing to cook today."

That casualness was far from my practical family, and it seemed romantic, especially since she could admit these flaws of hers out loud. "Sometimes I'm just totally incapable of making a decision. I just get paralyzed." It seemed this might be better than knowing what to cook for dinner every night, like my family always did.

It must have been on a day like that, with the tea cooling in our cups as the sun sank off to the left of the bridge just outside the windows. We stirred our tea slowly when she asked, "Have you been up there? We have much space in this house."

At the top of the main stairway was a set of narrow, steep stairs. It was only once you reached the top step that you saw it opened into a very large room. Likely meant as an attic or servants' quarters, it was filled with the dusty, cracked, and discarded: an antique Victorian S-shaped settee with the stuffing coming out, cardboard boxes, old toys, broken furniture meant for mending someday in another future.

That room was like one of those rooms in our dreams that we'd forgotten had been there all along, waiting for us. It opened in front of me that day as if it had been waiting for me. There was a window overlooking the Charles, a small toilet closet. I stood with Glady gazing at the streams of dust slanting in the light from the window, the stale smell of disuse enveloping us.

"I could clean it up, if you wanted me to, bring it back to life," I said on a whim. I walked to the window, looked out at the traffic moving across the bridge. I imagined being with the Russell children, playing games and making things on the wide floor.

"Would you want to use it as your bedroom? You could move up here. But it is another set of stairs," Glady said, half joking, half suggesting.

I was stunned. One second later we were collaborators. The smell of old dust was dissolving at the thought that this remarkable space would become mine.

"Could I reupholster the settee?" I could make use of whatever was up there. We'd bring my bed up. For a week I scrubbed, cleaned, painted, and reupholstered, making this astonishing room my own. It could easily have been the garret in *La Bohème*.

Glady's delight in and for me gave a new sense of what could happen for me. She insisted that every visitor go up and see the transformation I had created. It was exhilarating to be a part of a household brimming with such modern attitudes, on the one hand, and an old world love of family, on the other. They made much of me. Told me that they loved the way I laughed. I was beginning to awaken to a new idea about myself.

Some evenings I'd climb through my window onto the slanting roof overlooking the Charles River, and sit there as the light changed. Once I was sitting with my sister and a friend as the glint of dusk assembled. The light from upriver sent us iridescence down the water. All of the pervasive yearning I had ever felt about wanting someone in my life with whom I could share this kind of moment was collected then. My skin and lungs were packed with aching and uncertain longing. Sitting on the roof with my knees drawn up to my chest, looking at the glow of the buildings across a shimmering river, my eyes were opening in wonder at this new way of being a family, in this place called Boston, in this place called America.

I wanted Glady's life sitting on that roof. A husband, many children, a beautiful home: she could only be that romantic figure for me. She knew about the world in a way no one I had known intimately had—her flare, her joy. The tragedies that followed only deepened the shadows around the glowing lights around Glady for me.

Jack Russell was a tall handsome young veteran when he and Glady met while attending neighboring colleges. They'd party at his fraternity on the weekends, drinking liberally. When Jack got drunk enough he'd climb up on a table say, "I'm going to go to divinity school and become a minister." It was a big joke—wasn't Jack hilarious? It always took a fair amount of alcohol for him to declare his deepest truth.

Glady's low smoky chortle emerged when she told me that story. "Not one of us took him seriously. We thought he was so funny." It dazzled me when she shared these stories about how much they drank and played. They would marry as soon as Jack graduated. Jack would go to divinity school in Scotland, but first they'd take a year for themselves.

If her family was a living organism, Glady was its pulsing heart. She was blessed with an incandescent appeal: sparkling blue eyes framed by dark lashes and eyebrows under a mass of dark curls. Her beauty seemed to emanate more from who she was rather than as result of great good fortune. In her mid-thirties, after giving birth to five children, she was still ravishing. She had a cheerful nature, and a husky laugh that rolled out of her often. More than anything she wanted a large, happy family. Her face was often lit with mischief, and she usually laughed at the endless chaos, the complications of raising a large family.

Young people were a specialty of hers, perhaps because she was really still so young herself, even though she seemed the ultimate grownup. Jack's students would often get more involved with Glady once they became a part of the welcoming household. She opened her heart to young people like me with grace and generosity. And we all adored her for it. We were grateful that she was willing to listen to us, to give us counsel, to be in her glow.

I viewed Glady through an idealized lens, and Jack, too, because they were attractive, vital, and savvy. They were worldly while still grounded in family and love. Jack was committed to religion, politics, and to building community. Glady especially seemed to embody everything I didn't dare to hope to learn about and find in the larger world: she was artistic, a wife and mother. She was sophisticated and unfussy. She was honest about who she was and wasn't.

Glady loved that I was Italian, that I called a dishtowel a *mappin'* and a colander a *scula macarun'*. She loved that I cooked all my family's Italian dishes at the drop of a hat. She loved that I loved children, her children especially. That I liked to play with them and make things with them. I reminded her of the people she worked with and adored in Naples. She loved that I was young and loved her. She gave me a new idea about myself, which included that being Italian was something to be glad about.

She was the first person who didn't think there was something wrong with me. She was the first person who thought, instead, that there was a lot right with me. This was completely new to me. It marks me still. So, of course, I still can barely see her foibles.

Glady employed a short African American man to clean her house once a week. He began to flirt with me. It made me miserable and uncomfortable because I had no idea how to deal with this. I decided that I should deal with this myself without saying anything to Glady or Jack. The next time he was there he made a more brazen proposition as I walked by him on the stairs. "Please don't talk to me like that," I said, holding his gaze, "it makes me uncomfortable," and I continued up the stairs to my room. I knew at that moment that living with a family who thought well of me had given me the presence to refuse this man without making either of us feel awful.

She shared herself too, which brought me into her warmth. She talked often about the deepest pleasures of her life. I remember her explaining that blackberry picking and skiing were two of her favorite things to do. "I could do both of those things forever and never stop," she said. There was exuberance about her when she talked about things like this. I can imagine her flying down the slopes on her very strong legs, and bending in timeless concentration to plunk berry after berry into a bucket. I think she meant that she was in a transcendent state doing both things—one a kind of flight through the cold and the other a meditative crawl in the hot sun.

Sometime during that fall they decided to give one of their old-time parties. Glady and I were standing in the living room in front of the bay windows, and Glady turned to me with delight. "We haven't done this is a very long time, but we decided to give a real party for our friends. Don't be shocked by the way our friends might behave once they start drinking," she warned me. "We want you to come to the party." My body opened itself to this surprise. I'd be here in this room at a real adult party. I was suspended with delight.

Glady was always generous with herself, but as the family faced further crises, she came to understand that she had given too much of herself away, to others, to lots of people, people precisely like me.

David had the soft, agile limbs of a six-year-old boy who seemed to always have a question about what went on around him. He had a gentle inquisitiveness, lively and earnest.

One of my jobs was to give David a bath every night in the large, old-fashioned bathtub on the second floor, where he could jostle his small body up and down, splashing water onto the tiled floor. His knees, shoulders, feet, and elbows were all caught in the corners of his wet skin. Drying him under the big towel, his skin moved easily with the soft elasticity of the very young. David was all sweet curiosity under his sandy blond hair, with his high-pitched chirp commenting on life as it gave itself to him.

He liked to walk Waldo, the neighbor's dog, on a leash. One day he said in his little boy voice, "I'm not sure if I'm weading Waldo or Waldo's weading me."

Then there was his death. And all that came after, enfolding his family in grief and confusion.

One afternoon when I arrived home from Boston University, Jack was there as I came up the steep front steps. He was standing just inside the double front door near the bottom of the stairs as if he had been waiting for me. His basso voice descended from his full height with even more solemnity than usual. "I have something to tell you," he said. "Something has happened." He told me that David had been hit by a car and had died. On impact.

I remember only saying, "No!"

A "No!" that sounded through me, resonating down into my bones and out into the cosmos. This could not be. Must not be. Can't be. Isn't. No!

That was the first time I experienced that *no*. The one that comes when we are face to face with the death of someone we love. It comes with the arrival of any death, but even more incomprehensibly when it's the death of a child. For a beautiful small boy to be *not*, brings me still to the same frozen, stunned, *No! This can't be so.*

David had been walking home from school and was crossing with the traffic signal correctly as he had been so carefully taught. He was not a reckless child. The driver of a car idling in the main lane seemed to be daydreaming as he waited for the red light to change. David stepped into the crosswalk with the light in his favor. Another car, which had been parked next to the idling one, pulled out of its space and moved next to the idling car. That first driver took the movement of the second car as a signal that the light had changed and that it was safe to go through the intersection. He stepped on the gas before he realized his mistake. He hit David, as our small boy crossed in front of his car. David died in a ghastly, horrible mistake. Jack had meant to try to get to David's school to walk him home but got caught up in a meeting at MIT. It took Jack many decades to forgive himself.

While Jack spoke to me, Glady was sitting by the window in the living room. I could feel her breathing body there. I stood in front of her in shock with her while she told me that she had gotten a phone call from her friend Myrna, the mother of David's best friend Valerie, that a child had been hit by a car. Myrna thought it might have been David. "I knew it was him. I just knew it the minute Myrna said it," Glady said as she stared into space, inhaling her cigarette.

Jack and Glady were smoking cigarette after cigarette, phone calls were being made. Phone calls to their parents. Friends. Did the other children all know at that moment? At one point Jack offered some kind piety in an attempt to bring comfort.

"Oh, Jack, just stop it," Glady said sharply, standing up, "shut up," and walked out of the living room toward the back of the house. No pieties. Not in the face of this. She had to walk away from these useless words. Her clarity rang though the cloud of emotions. I felt such a surge of respect for her that she wouldn't allow a false note, not even from Jack at this hour. I had only confused sensations after that.

A few months later, our friend Karen came to visit us on Beacon Street bringing her firstborn son for Glady to meet. I can see Glady sitting in her elegant upholstered chair saying, "I'm just so glad that I loved David so much."

I don't know how Glady and Jack survived the death of David. They did, but they did not. They went on, their four still-young children to care for. Jack's faith wasn't with him for a long time after that. He left his job at the Boston

Rehabilitation Authority. Later, after they moved to Philadelphia, Glady started a chair-caning business and an antique store. Jack became vice provost of the University of Pennsylvania. But their grief unfastened them from the best of themselves. Various crises began to hit sequentially and then simultaneously. There were breakdowns, alcoholism, drug addiction, mental illness. To me, it seemed as if those crises were born in David's death. The week they had planned to have their raucous party, the one to which I had been so delighted to have been invited, was the week David died. That happiness with which Glady had planned the party was borne of a time and place of sweet abundance. That was where they lived before David died.

If I had unconsciously assumed that Glady and Jack would be my road to America, I'm not sure I can understand, even now, how that first tragedy and all of the dysfunction that followed affected me. They were romantic figures and then they were tragic figures. Life out in America was much larger, filled with possibilities but also unsafe. The looser boundaries gave freedom but also disorder. It has taken me decades to even begin to sort this out if I have at all. This was a single episode, but the Russells were a powerful part of my beginnings. I know what their love gave me.

In time, the Russells overcame the crises that followed David's death, and healed, Jack and Glady had many rich years together. The four grown children have substantial and good lives, grounded in work, art, partnerships, marriages, families, and love.

Losing David in a split second of random urban confusion caused a dark chaos, before which there was Eden and after which they were left without form and void, and they were left looking upon the face of the deep. To overcome what had befallen them, Glady and Jack had to create their lives again out of the swirling of loss. Out of the formless dust, morning slowly came again.

My First New York Story, 1965

THE DAY I CAME TO LIVE IN NEW YORK, I WAS TRAVELING WITH JUDY, THE slightly older sister of a friend of mine. She knew how to look for an apartment for four girls, of which we were just two, who were going to live together. Judy had been living here for a year, going to graduate school. This made her a sophisticated veteran of the city. We got off the train at the 125th Street station: we'd come in on the New York, New Haven and Hartford Line in June 1965. It was just before the riots in Harlem. Joints had only recently begun to be passed from friend to friend. Free speech was the sound of campuses. Young men and women were pouring into New York, as they dropped out of places like Reed, Michigan, or Brandeis.

I would discover that fall that the French, *French people*, people who lived in *Paris*, thought New York was *terrible*. "Isn't that cool? What those French people want is a pair of jeans!" I remember someone saying to me at a party soon after I arrived. I stood there thinking, *They* look to *us*? "For our art," this guy said, "our music, our jeans. You can ask almost any price you want. For a pair of tight black jeans especially." That story got passed around. This was more exciting than the fact that I might sleep with this guy in a couple of weeks, which I did.

I rode across 125th Street with all of its dirt and sordid neighborliness so close to us in the cab. *Take a cab?* If I had known anything about politics, urban blight, economics, I might have predicted that riots would be taking place near here. And I should have known. I had been tutoring in Roxbury and the South End of Boston during my college years. I had been on picket lines and protests for at least two years already. But I was still a Waterbury Italian girl who was riding on the rails of her twenties knowing little but what was being said around me. Since I was trying to leap centuries between the world in which I had been raised and the one I just entered, I mostly didn't even know what I didn't understand.

Almost everyone I knew had been an English major—we knew a little about Hemingway, D. H. Lawrence, some knew about Chaucer, maybe Dickens, but not much else. I knew less than most because I was barely present as a student. Even though we had all been involved in the civil rights movement, had all been volunteering in ghettoes wherever we went to school, I knew little about politics. We went into poor neighborhoods, inept but feeling virtuous.

When I arrived in New York, I brought with me the moment that I heard the news that JFK had been shot—how it felt when something happens that's so terrible it can't be true. That was the first time. There were to be so many of those events to follow that the feeling wore away from overuse.

On November 22, 1963, I had just stepped off a curb to walk across a wide street on my way to the South End in Boston. I was a student at Boston University. In Waterbury we called it "going to college," but somewhere along the way I learned to call it "at school"—why did that sound more sophisticated?

Back then I was tutoring Tiffany and Jackie, then both around nine or ten, with skin as soft as pudding—in a settlement house. I was walking along thinking about something my roommate Kathy had just told me about our friend Mary, whom she had met in Art History. Kathy said that Mary had told her that the year before she had gotten pregnant and had gone away to a home for unwed girls. No one gave a shit about being called a girl then—we were just starting to say *shit* and *fuck* out loud, there was a feeling of real liberation to these words then—and that Mary had given her baby up for adoption.

This story was filled with so many strange parts: the idea that someone would get pregnant, which meant she had sex with someone—still a daring thing to do. Anyone who did and who got pregnant married immediately. It meant that Mary had slept with someone who cared for her so little, or was married, or something weird, that she had had to go away by herself to a home with other unfortunates and then to give up her baby. Have a baby! Give up a baby!

In the next year I'd start taking "the pill."

But right at that moment when I was thinking about Mary's baby, some guys driving past me kind of swerved close, the one riding shotgun—sitting in the window seat was called "riding shotgun"—one arm draped over the car door, head halfway out the window shouted something at me. I was annoyed by the interruption, until I realized he was saying, "The president's been shot in Dallas." The guy leaned out as they started to drive past me. "Yeah. He was riding in a car in a parade—down in Dallas," full of the excitement of spreading the news, they sped off. I walked across the street, away from the wood-frame houses with the screened-in porches on the back. When I walked over to the South End to tutor Tiffany on Tuesdays, I always daydreamed that I might live in one of those houses someday. Whenever I think of JFK's death, I think about the curve of that street, the promise in the shine of those windows, and of Mary—and what had happened to that baby? When I got to the settlement house, everyone was crazy with it. The president hadn't been declared dead yet. Everyone was talking. Some were crying.

I stopped in the middle of the room, more chaotic than usual, full of folding chairs and tables scattered with paper and pencils. Were there magic markers? When did magic markers come in? Tiffany came out of the disheveled crowd at the settlement house. I had no idea what I should say.

When Tiffany came out of the crowd at the settlement house the day JFK died, the usual gleam in her eyes was turned down. She said to me, "They saying the president's shot. Why'd they shoot him?" Relieved to have Tiffany come over to me, I was embarrassed that I knew so little. I felt as if I should have something important to say. "A lot of people don't like what he's doing, for poor people," I said as we sat down, the only ones sitting at the tables.

"That's why they killed him? So he won't help us?"

I realized how ridiculous I sounded by reaching for something to explain what couldn't be explained.

So what I saw when I arrived in New York with my old friend Judy wasn't unfamiliar. But Judy knew the ropes, had lived here for a year, and I only knew New York from coming into Grand Central Terminal and going to Broadway plays. I had been dreaming of living in the city without really understanding that was what had been on my mind from the moment Marjorie Weiss had said one day in sophomore year of high school: "My sister Ronnie lived in New York for a year. That's where she met her husband."

I had felt the power of that idea hit me; someone I knew or at least the sister of someone I knew—Marjorie was my closest friend—had lived in New York. That sister had her own apartment, a job. Was that something a girl could do?

Now here I was in a cab. This is what you did, you "grabbed a cab," and told him 96th and West End. The cab raced across 125th Street, honking and stopping with a jerk at the lights while Judy started explaining. "This is Harlem, it's the ghetto in New York. This is the Apollo, the famous theater where a lot of black singers got their start. Billie Holiday sang there." I had only the vaguest idea who Billie Holiday was. I had grown up on Nat King Cole and *The King and I*, Perry Como. Then rock 'n' roll. So I didn't say anything as the cab took the corner under the El at Broadway, taking with that one swerve half of that short block between 125th and Tiemann Place, where I would later live with my boyfriend who became my first husband, Danny Pisello.

It was in that apartment that Danny and I had a terrible fight because I had just started to take birth control pills and Danny had just ripped up his draft card and neither felt the other was listening. We had almost broken up that night, but we fumbled our way back to one another, not out of deep loyalty or love, but for something to hold together while everything around us fell apart. Danny was going to write his dissertation on quarks or quantum theory—there was so much confidence in physics in those days. I was going to work at the Countee Cullen Library at 135th and Lenox Avenue. We were going to affect things—until we could have a lot of kids. That was the plan before the '68 riots on the Columbia campus, the barricades in Paris, before the Red Guard in China. It was in that apartment in Harlem that I heard Martin Luther King Jr., then Bobby Kennedy had been assassinated.

But at that moment, as the cab came around the corner, a car in front of us came to a screeching halt because some boys leapt, legs flying, into the traffic, in their black high-tops, wearing clothes that were too big for them. Their clothes belonged to their older brothers—in those days kids were ashamed of too big, raggedy clothes—but just then the boys running in front of the cab were too occupied to think about shame, running across the street against the light, slapping at one another and laughing, immune from danger. The driver of the cab in slammed on the brakes and we went lurching forward hard against the soft, worn leather and then slumped back into our seats. I looked out at the corner that later would be my neighborhood, the grounds of my misery, where my husband didn't write his thesis, didn't come home at night, didn't want to be married to me.

And Judy explained, laughing, "This is the way it is whenever you come into New York, something like this always happens. You see a car accident, or you're in a car accident, or you see someone being arrested. Something dramatic happens as if to announce, 'You're here, in New York City!'"

"The last time, when I was in a cab coming back from the airport . . ." Judy started to tell me.

This was a long time before I lived in Paris with my second husband, Bill, where I learned the word *rentré* that Parisians use to describe the rush and fervor with which they return to Paris at the end of August holidays. I never forgot Judy's words from that cab, even though I had no idea that I was about to hear my first New York Story.

200 Square Feet in the Village,
or, My Soluble Fortunes

A PLACE APART

WHEN I WAS A YOUNG WOMAN LIVING IN THE WEST VILLAGE, WANDERING along crooked streets in and out of bookstores, into small shops filled with small intriguing objects from very far away, working, waiting for my life to begin, uncertain how that would happen, uncertain whether it would *ever* happen—would I ever find someone to love, have children with, have a professional life, or live in more than 200 square feet—I lived in an apartment at 26 Grove Street.

Grove Street begins at the western edge of Sheridan Square, then goes along for a few short sweet blocks, then bends to the right as it runs out to Hudson Street. I lived just before that last block. It is the heart of the old West Village. There are townhouses, brownstones, an eighteenth-century wood house, a couple of restaurants, a few small apartment buildings, and a grammar school. Walking in from Sheridan Square you come to a place apart.

My studio on the sixth floor had the feeling of a tree house or a tiny houseboat. Each possession had its own place and function: a single red wing chair, a trundle bed, an old baker's hutch, a rough bookshelf made of weathered planks and two by fours, a small television, and after a while, an antique French table with four bentwood chairs. The red wing chair was for visitors. On that table I prepared food, ate my meals, entertained my friends, sewed, made paper, and wrote in my journal. There were books, lamps, and baskets. There wasn't room for an extra spoon or spool of thread.

Two good-sized windows held flowering begonia plants that overlooked the trees and blossoming backyards of the townhouses. My plant laden glass shelves were my own miniature garden. I peered past to the urban haven below, filled with trees, flowers, hammocks, rattan chairs, dinner parties, children playing among cascading gardens. Everything I was certain I'd never have.

In moments of despair I'd stare out of the windows wondering why I had no way forward into adult life. On better days and nights, I'd throw myself on my narrow bed, reading in solitary pleasure.

Since I dropped out of college in 1965, I had worked in a day care center, in a library, until I went to work at a school where, although I was still without my undergraduate degree, each year I was given an increasingly more responsible job and very slowly I began to grow up.

I worked then as a teacher at The Walden School, a private, progressive school on Central Park West, filled with liberal, intellectual, and artistic families where many of my young friends worked too. We were on the front lines of new ideas about teaching and learning that were coming out of Britain, a movement for informal education that came to be called the open classroom. We felt enthusiastic about trying the freedoms it gave us, creating a space where children worked to their own strengths. The teachers were wild shoots growing right alongside our tender tendril students.

The open-classroom idea was seen as a challenge, and an alternative, to the problems of American life. In that moment of our youth, the '60s, society was shedding an old skin. A brilliantly excessive era, we were creating so much stuff just as it occurred to us, along the nerve endings of our brand new selves.

Teaching at Walden allowed me to make use of all of the skills I had learned from my southern Italian family of farmers, housewives, factory workers, construction workers, seamstresses, cooks: people who worked hard making and building things. We knew how to care for it, build it, sew it, decorate it, undo it, and do it right again. The physical world belonged to us. Belongs to us still. We take for granted that it will do what we want it to. At Walden I used everything that I had learned in Waterbury.

In my "resource classroom," my students and I created elaborate spaces that we'd build and live in for weeks at a time. Once my large classroom became an extensive Calder circus, with lions, lion trainers, high-wire walkers, the panoply of a vast imaginary world we got lost in as we made it. All across the room there were beings and creatures high and low—wire horses and dogs and lions jumping through "flaming" hoops.

I'd taken up papermaking recently and brought this process to the classroom. We made our own pulp from rags, old paper, and fiber from clothes dryers. We built our own deckles, making paper with different textures and embedded lace and leaves. We made these sheets into pages, and these pages into books, as a book-making studio gradually emerged. My students wrote and illustrated their stories. In another project I taught them to build small wooden handlooms. They learned to string their looms and weave fabrics from colorful yarns. We decided to dye our own yarn using ingredients we could buy in grocery stores. Each project began as a small idea that started casually, then grew, as if by itself.

None of this was planned. None of it came from a curriculum. My work always came from intuition, from the creative impulse. Given my fairly loosely defined title of resource teacher, my students and I were able to find our way to big projects organically, in moments of work, play, and experimentation. Once a new idea emerged, we threw ourselves into these projects with the commitment and passion that come with making something together. This approach happened so naturally that it didn't seem in any way unusual or even noteworthy. Since improvising—making things, creating elaborate artistic projects—came to me as easily as breathing, clearly it meant anyone could do this.

My friends and I drank too many cups of cappuccino in cafés, and whiled away too many hours talking, smoking too many cigarettes and ingesting too many other substances, going to hear very loud music and dancing our nights away. We all slept with each other too. It was all part of that moment.

I was aloft on my youth, physical beauty, energy, and ideas of our time. But the intuitions I lived by worked precisely well sometimes, but not at all at other times. When I began to live by myself for the first time on Grove Street, I didn't even know enough to make dates with my friends for the weekends, I stayed home and read, crocheted, sewed, and watched *The Twilight Zone*, *Mary Tyler Moore*, and old movies. I believed everything was supposed to happen spontaneously. The '60s supported such delusions. By now my earlier rebellious instincts seemed to be supported by the times. I didn't even own a clock, because we were supposed to be tuned into our own inner clocks. Oddly enough, I always awoke on time, got to work on time.

If someone happened to say, "Jason's brother is playing tonight. We're all going," there was my plan. When something didn't happen spontaneously, there wasn't a plan. In Waterbury, if you had nothing to do, you could walk down the street to one of our cousin's houses and hang out, and decide what to do then and there. In college, and in my apartments filled with roommates, and later with a husband, you did the same thing. I thought this was how life would always be. But not here, living alone in the Village.

Too often on Grove Street I spent weekends not talking to anyone from Friday afternoon when I left work, until Monday morning when I went back. I'd spend the weekend between reading and ruminating about how messed up my life was. Wondering why I was so lonely and isolated, I looked out my windows confused; I had no idea of how I'd get from here to there.

Just behind me then was a brief, miserable marriage, which happened not long after I had dropped out of college. My rebellious nature was still very much with me. Whenever a lovely guy showed an interest in me I dismissed him quickly. I had plenty of terrible boyfriends, men over whom I pined because they were so exciting in their utter indifference to me. Failure seemed to becoming a lifelong habit.

I had no idea why all of that had gone wrong, just as I didn't notice what went superbly right. Nor did I know what my direction should be, or how to figure it out.

Gazing out of the window from my apartment on Grove Street, I imagined a life somewhere else—Paris, St. Petersburg, a hill town in Italy—somewhere romantic. I missed living in the eighteenth or nineteenth century. There and then I could live like one of the heroines in my books, dressed in long flowing garments and boots with tiny heels. But I was *just* living alone in the West Village in the '60s, where I apparently didn't notice that we often wore long dresses and sweeping skirts and shawls that we had made ourselves, drinking our coffee and tea in brown earthenware cups.

When I took the train home to see my family in Waterbury, I'd read Tolstoy when I wasn't meditating out of the window. Perhaps that was as close as I got to living in one of my novels. If it was winter, I made sure I wore high boots tied up the front, my long dark-green coat, and my Russian fur hat. I'd pile my waist-long hair under my hat, just so that I could enjoy the theater of pulling off the hat to let my hair cascade down my back. I read Tolstoy as I traveled, so that I could look up from the book out the window, watching the trees pass by. I'd imagine the snowstorm I step down into when I got off the train.

On other days in this theater of the everyday, my friends and I wore the tiniest miniskirts, patent leather neon-yellow ankle boots, or see-through florid lace blouses, above skintight jeans with red suede sling-back high heels. The guys wore shirts with flowing collars, rich saturated colors, wide bell-bottom pants, and cool leather boots. We created our identities, depending on how we saw ourselves on any given day.

Two rushing waters moved through me, side by side: a rich, lively organic day-to-day, and a profound sense of personal failure. The good in my life was so easy and natural it was like walking down the street. The misery, on the other hand, roiled in me, insisting, what a mess, what a mess.

A WORLD APART

In one very particular way though, none of this mattered.

Reading was where I actually lived. Always had been.

As soon as I learned to read books with chapters, I was lost to them. I read books in my lap at school while the teacher screeched or murmured at the front of the classroom. I had a book in my lap on the bus to school. My working-class family was filled with readers. My parents both loved to read. My father was a more serious reader. But I lived in my books even more than the others. Reading was my boat on the waters rough and calm.

Our books came from the small storefront branch library on a scruffy patch of North Main Street. My sister, cousins, and I trooped down there after school, scouring the shelves, grab as many books as we were allowed, and afterward, walked to our bus stop to go home, our arms full of books. We went back and forth to the library like it was the grocery store, a few times a week.

There was a series of biographies, all bound in the same orange cloth covers, about historical figures that I read from one end of the shelf to the other. I have no memory of who the subjects of the books were, except for the two Roosevelt presidents. There was *Black Beauty, Black Stallion, National Velvet, Anne of Green Gables, Pollyanna, Johnny Tremaine*. There was an endless flow of books where I hid from my mother's relentless list of chores and errands, which awaited my sister and me when we got home from school.

I had escaped the rigidity of the '50s, the confines of traditional life, not being able to live up to the punishing standards of what it was to be a good girl in my family, in my neighborhood. I'd slip down to the basement with my book, hoping my mother wouldn't find me. If I was by myself, I often walked down the street holding a book up in front of me, not wanting to be parted from the pages I loved.

I was an extreme kid: loud, physical, not interested in being still or obedient, unless I was reading. I was often in the bad row at school, for talking, for answering the teacher back, always in trouble, for not doing something, for doing it too slowly, for doing it badly. Once I threw a yellow pencil across the room at a friend's head when something she said annoyed me. I was taken aback that even the other kids were upset that I did this. But I knew how to live the lives that took place in my books. In fact, I was living them. The characters were like me, not at one with the worlds into which they had been born and made to live.

One of my favorite reading hideaways was at the very top of the maple tree at the front of our lawn. Climbing trees held the same kind of transcendence for me that reading had. Making sure my mother didn't see me, I'd reach up to grab the lowest branch, bracing my feet against the trunk to pull myself up through the smaller lower branches, their leaves brushing past my face as I climbed higher. Each stretch of my arms made me feel stronger, each pull up to the next branch going higher brought me closer to myself. Sturdy branches came toward me until they reversed in strength again and I reached the branches that began to bend my under weight, but which I knew were still secure enough for me to perch there. In a reverie of being hidden in the middle of things, I watched everyone and everything coming and going. I'd gaze around from the one place where my station was high. Then I'd take out my book and settle in. The branches gently swayed under me when breezes came, rustling the leaves around me.

In my aerie I'd disappear into words and stories where I was my most complete self. In those upper branches I was in my own leafy Eden.

On Grove Street, too, I flung myself onto my trundle bed and lay back on my beautiful antique quilt, against a mound of pillows, turning the pages of novels by Woolf, Forster, Hemingway, Fitzgerald, James, Tolstoy, Turgenev. My reading was a random, unplanned, unstudied course.

Back then, reading was close to what swimming has always been for me. I enter the water; I am in the water, with the water. I am the water. I entered into a watery dream, of words flowing into one another, my body suspended in these words that were not language, but a fluid other. I swam into the pages, into streams of words, unmoored from the quotidian, wiping page after page from the right to the left, swish, flip, swipe, as regular as inhaling and exhaling. It swept me beyond the gravitational pull, out of my life, exchanging it at the border for this flow. As my mind flowed into the words and pages "I" dissolved.

The words strung together didn't lead to thoughts but to a strange fluid trance. In my transfixion between the words and images I joined the characters and lived this essentially unembodied, utterly vivid existence. It was this oddly unembodied state that made it most real to me. I was alive to it *there*.

Although the characters in my beloved novels might be as confused as I was, though they might be in despair about love, just as overwhelmed as I was, on the page, if troubled, they were *meant* to be confused, they were written to be exactly that. They were made inevitable by their authors, and lived in novels where they didn't face the annoying ambiguity or confusion of reality.

In everyday time the threads of most thoughts dart around our brain, pulling us along: a fragment of a dream flashes, and then disappears too quickly. We search for it again, but instead come upon another stray bit of memory, a phone rings, we notice a blouse we meant to mend, a bill shows itself. Something comes on the radio that reminds us to download a piece of music, or a movie we'd meant to watch. It's the nature of consciousness that lots of what comes to our attention isn't voluntary. Some would say none of it is.

But once we embark on the path of contemplation that reading is, we inhabit the world the author has made out of letters and words. It's exactly the writer's job to mark the path, to make the words and sentences move us from here to there. This sentence, then this one, go along here now onto this tangent of character, that detour for history, follow this idea—it's the reader's job to follow quietly along. All of which pulls at us and distracts us all day long has been pruned away by the author.

In a great novel, or even in a good one, we're brought straight into deep REM sleep, and we awake refreshed. It makes a meditation, a state of reverie. The life of a reader is the life of a dreamer.

In one way, I am describing a reverie, but in another way, what is deeply incised in me is a physical state. I have entrenched muscle memories of my life as a reader. I can feel the pillows under my head in my childhood bed—the one I shared with my sister, Lucia. I can feel the small table next to my bed, where I might have placed a *capicola* and pickled eggplant sandwich. Or it might be a melted cheese sandwich, of browned and bubbled provolone on a thick slice of good buttered Italian bread, hot, and waiting.

Reading was all of these contradictions to me—an unthinking state, an altered state of consciousness, and a deeply physical place. It was where I was learning about how lives are lived, but it was also just a place in which to live my life. I loved the very terrain of reading, the land itself where only reading existed, in all the places where I read, up in my tree, down in the cool, dark basement of our ranch house at 2279 North Main Street, and in my studio at 26 Grove Street. With the days and nights blowing and burning just past the begonias that filled my windows, in my tiny *barco*, I'd sink down and away from my delicious world, in which I knew myself to be a failure.

I'd read, for example, *Portrait of a Lady*, thinking I'd find my way by following Isabel Archer. I don't think I even understood the disastrous choice she makes. *To the Lighthouse* seemed a study on how a woman should be. Tolstoy was forever a comfort, that immense canvas where I could imagine riding in carriages and trains wearing fur, being madly in love with the wrong man, then the right man. If I ran out of something to read I'd return to my girlhood favorites—Hemingway, Fitzgerald, the Brontë sisters—dreaming along their streets of weather.

The Brontë sisters enhanced my ideas of being a sister, about having a close life with other girls, about having been an au pair in college and being now a schoolteacher. I was proud to be in their long shadows. *Wuthering Heights* and the moors didn't seem isolated or distant to me. It has always been my ironworker father's favorite novel; he read pieces of it at night after dinner, intermittently and often. Our southern Italian background was at one with Heathcliff's gypsy passions. Heathcliff made sense to us: dark spirit, romantic, ferocious, demanding.

In the '60s novels had a presence that's hard to imagine now. All other forms of prose seemed simply second rate. Poetry wasn't even on my horizon. The memoir was a book written by generals and potentates after they retired. Belles lettres was a charming, minor genre. Other art forms were never as interesting.

Novels aren't about learning about "otherness" but about the "sameness" of the human condition. These were our intimates. Being involved in literature was a way of life then. The eighteenth- and the nineteenth-century novel was the high literature of our time, the second half of the twentieth century. Those books were as much a part of our daily lives as our Formica-topped tables and knotty pine paneled rooms. The novel was ours. We inhabited the novel.

It was a higher calling to study literature seriously. English departments were huge, influential forces in both small liberal arts colleges and large universities. They had vast teaching staffs. English faculties often ran college governing bodies because they claimed the largest enrollments. We read everything, but the novel was the form of our time, just as epic poetry and drama had reigned during other times. It rivered through our lives, as powerful as a force of nature.

In some sense I was on the margins of this magnificent world because when I was at Boston University I had no idea how to study literature, or anything else. I was floating through the books, living in their streams but not thinking about them, writing about them, understanding what they were doing. That was why I dropped out. On the other hand, it gave my reading a more central place because it was my private world, undiluted by analysis and commentary.

My life from childhood on through my twenties and thirties was a magnificent life of the book. I suspect I thought it was a failure of imagination that I hadn't yet moved from the page to where my actual life waited for me. I was always working on how to become more like those heroines: the more I submerged myself in those novels, the more my life seemed real to me. I wanted to be those protagonists: difficult, extraordinary. That's all it would take, I was convinced, while I lay curled up on my solitary bed, for my real life to finally begin.

Those novels made me want to read about the writers of those books. Reading biographies of writers was a guilty pleasure, which I dove into with abandon. Those biographies gave the girl I used to be pictures of the way they had maneuvered their writerly waters.

You could say I read biographies as my own field guides. I understood little about myself other than that I was a reader and a teacher. I wanted to know how all those others had attained that mythical status, "being a writer."

I'd kept diaries throughout my girlhood and early twenties, but I didn't particularly attach any importance to them. They were just a place to complain. 1968: I'm a mess. Have to figure out who I am. 1969: He's left me for his wife. I am furious and sad. 1970: I can't seem to find my way. I'm so upset.

I had no idea what writing was—just rivers of words, years of books embedded in my brain, images long ago incised into the way I thought.

While the biographies didn't tell me much about how to write, they did give me a sense of those who wrote, an oar in their waters. Quite frequently these writers drank too much, betrayed their friends, ignored and hurt their families. Often, they were narcissistic beyond anything I would ever wish to be. They put their own desires and needs before anyone else's. There was no greater sin where I came from.

Still, I was gripped by these often appalling stories. These writers also lived in windowed rooms, sat at wooden tables, got distracted from the hard work of writing by the footsteps at their doors. They often had a lust for fine paper, pens, kid gloves. It's the human details that compelled me then and compel me still. Did you know that Tolstoy and his brothers were allowed on rotating nights to crawl into their grandmother's bed and listen to the blind storyteller who came to her room every night to lull her to sleep with his stories? Does the intimacy, the claustrophobia of that image move you as it does me?

Protest politics, illegal drugs, sex, nude beaches, theater of the self, sure: defiance of conventional social norms was ordinary. Trying to write? Forbidden seas.

The '60s included constant upheaval, celebration, rock 'n' roll, rhythm and soul, doors bursting open, new kinds of politics, but also hesitation, confusion, foolishness, and pain. Civil rights opened the world to my generation in college—making us feel we could change the world. There were boyfriends and important female friendships. There was unrequited love, and love: then a bad, brief marriage, then an almost marriage. The death of a small child I cared for in a bizarre accident. Feminism exploded into my life. I had a miscarriage in Italy when I didn't know I was pregnant. My closest friend, Elizabeth Powelson, was murdered at the hands of someone she knew. Just after that I was in a car accident where one side of my face was ripped open. All this convinced me this was just the way my life would go, lurching from upheaval, to the awful, to the tragic. A helpless feeling about my inability to create a life that moved forward sent me spiraling around and down.

Books were still my lucid water, but despair seemed to be more and more my other constant companion. Fate's frequent visits of tragedy and hardship pushed me into deeper, darker waters, and, eventually into another way of descending into the world of other, under, the dreamscape: therapy. Therapy, like reading, like dreaming, is its own terrain. You live in it to exclusion of all that disappears to distant and dim perimeters. Like writing.

MY OTHER SOLUBLE FORTUNE

The conversion from reading into writing was so meandering that it took not years but decades. So many stops and starts, so many parts and pieces that it's hard to write about. But it is exactly the transubstantiation of reading into writing, of turning words pouring into me to words pouring out of me that is the crux.

For passionate readers, this fervent love often creates a savage longing to create writing, which means so much to us. But that doesn't mean we know anything about how to write. We're just stuck with this longing. So, some plunge in with blind faith, start with scraps and intuitions, and hope we're led to the evanescent.

I was still living on Grove Street, working at The Walden School during all of this transformation. I entered therapy after I had been in the car accident and had a miscarriage and Elizabeth had been murdered. Therapy began for me and has been the most substantial piece of my education.

Therapy enabled me to transcend the unconscious in a new way, to understand how my life had become the shape it had, and how to try to create a life more like the one I wanted. It also allowed me to very slowly take myself into my own hands. All of this meant swimming deep where it was hard to breathe or see, or even move.

It also sent me into finishing my undergraduate degree in the early '70s. I stumbled my way through finishing that degree. I began to date slightly more appropriate men a little more frequently. I began a master's degree in American studies at the City College of New York in the early '70s. I still had no idea how to study consistently, or write an academic paper. I fumbled my way through the beginning of that program until I met my future husband, Bill Herman, who, while he was in the department, wasn't my professor (neither of us would cross that line—part of why we were right for each other). He began to teach me the fundamentals of being a graduate student: how to concentrate, how to read for the academy, how to construct an academic paper. And now I had love in my life.

The very last course I took when I was finishing up my master's was a writing course with Francine du Plessix Gray. In my utter naivete I thought taking a course by a leading practitioner of the New Journalism would help me write my academic dissertation. What it did was begin my long journey to becoming a serious writer.

Francine was a heart-stopping teacher. Her well-shaped assignments, her articulation in class, set up a stream of writing for me. My instincts were good from all those years of reading. Under her guidance, work poured out of me. It began to seem as if this dream previously refused might move into the light.

Francine liked what I was writing in her course well enough to bring it to the *New Yorker*. After she showed him my work, an editor, William Maxwell, asked to meet me. I remember a quiet seriousness in his office: large windows, a desk, a room in browns and tans, a man with a kind and sober manner. Beyond that I remember only a single moment of that meeting, when he said, "You are a writer. And you will write. You have a voice." The certainty of his gentle words rang in my head as I left his office in a daze. I found myself outside in a dark bathroom stall in a state of momentary amnesia. I didn't black out, but had lost my way: all I could think was: Where am I? What am I doing here? How could he know this about my writing? I didn't.

I was so disoriented by Maxwell's validation that I stopped writing for months. I had no ability to deal with being thought well of. No idea how to walk across the bridge from where I had come from. I had never been a high achiever in any realm that I understood. I wasn't used to approval from anyone, certainly not from someone who guarded the door of what I considered a sanctuary of the high holy altar. My writing barely managed to survive that meeting.

But a door was opened. I wrote on and off. I had a few pieces published in tiny literary magazines. Some poems, some lyrical meditations. I was writing by inspiration only, which essentially isn't much about writing. But some were more fully formed narratives about my life back in Waterbury. I was trying to write fiction, but I really had no idea how stories were made. My writing came directly out of my unconscious, mirroring the way I had always read. I'd start to write from an image or a scrap of an idea of language, let them lead me into the rest of the work. For days, I'd carry around whatever fragments had slipped into consciousness, and seemingly out of nowhere, when I walked down the street apparently thinking about something else, a first sentence would form. I was grateful to the First Sentence gods and the Ur sounds they gave me.

When a story or poem or emerged in that way—from an idea that had been flitting in and out of my awareness for years, I knew how to work. But when something wasn't right and didn't work, I had no idea what to do next, other than to put more hours into it. Or put it aside and begin something else. Then I'd pick it up later and see if I had any new energy for it. Not bad ideas about writing, as far as they go. I'd ask myself—what is going wrong? What is stopping me from moving forward?

It seemed I'd never be able to write, as I wanted, with sustained deep immersion. I'd told myself, for example, that I wasn't interested in plot. This was an idea, a stance, which filled the air in those days. It was some vague notion that we in the avant-garde were above such trivial matters. One day I mentioned to an old friend that my writing didn't have much plot. "Why not?," he asked, perplexed.

I didn't have an answer. I had gone as far as I could with what I knew. My own writing slid into the background. I wrote intermittently, feverishly, or not at all.

I finished my master's degree. But all of it was still painfully difficult for me. My course with Francine du Plessix Gray had changed the course of my life. All I wanted to do was write. Even though she had opened a door wide for me, I was still unable to walk through it.

Bill and I had fallen deeply in love and married. I even left my tiny studio on Grove Street. I was teaching as an adjunct at City College, and teaching those courses was another essential element of my education.

During those years I was in the stir of a new family. I was devoted to Bill, to raising our son James. I was also committed to my job at City College, where I taught basic writing courses. The challenge of helping my students never failed to grip me: always pressing myself further, to figure out how to help them break down the stages of writing into doable small bits. How to go from brainstorming, to ideas, to words, to research: shaping, rewriting, revising; this seemed to me to be the key to giving my students control of their work. I didn't want academic writing to be the mystery for them that it had been for me. As I taught them, I taught myself more and more about writing.

Eventually my course load began to include literature: reading it, analyzing it, and teaching my students how to write papers about it.

Once in a literature class I assigned one of my favorite stories, "The Swimmer" by John Cheever. The glimmering image of a man swimming across a neighborhood at the height of summer through a string of jewel-like pools compelled me—I loved this story for its set of structured images. When I began preparing for my class, I discovered how unconscious my reading had been. Until then, I had no idea that Cheever's story was about a tragic life, a whole life, the cycle of the year, and so many other rich and complex ideas and images. I saw how the deep riches of the story enhanced that stunning central image—how carefully sustained the arc of the story moved, slowly and soberly through each very different swimming pool.

It was an awakening, a transporting moment that would set my reading onto a new course: now I was taking stories apart in all my reading, seeing what the underpinnings were, the understructure, the net of language and image.

My habit of *dissolving* into the text, becoming the words, so the blurring of words and "the me" was gone. Instead, my reading became an alert poring over. I hunched over the text, more of an artisan than an artist, noting, thinking consciously: What had they made? How had they made it?

My own writing was usually on hiatus during the time we raised James. I only returned to it intermittently. During those years we lived on the Upper West Side, and he was very much like me, very ADHD, and he took up an immense amount of our time and attention. We were determined that he wasn't going to be seen, as I had been, as careless or lazy. We traveled a lot. We lived in Paris for one semester, Torino, for another. I had various full-time jobs, but mostly I always went back to teaching as an adjunct, because it kept me in connection to my love of books and writing. Writing was still my lost dream.

James was a teenager by then, taking his first steps toward leaving us. All the centrifugal force of my love could only impede him if I kept my focus on him. It was a return to my other savage passion: writing.

A good deal of my early writing had been done on foolscap, a cheap yellow paper that we used for drafts back in typewriter days. I scanned all my material. I found I liked a lot of what I had written. I was especially intrigued by the last story I had worked on years before. The story had been such a defeat that I put my writing away because I had no idea how to make it work. I liked the characters, who were pretty well developed. But although I could see what a mess it was overall, I could also see where the story worked. All that was needed, really, was a big edit, more pages gone than kept, a structure.

My friend's old question about why I didn't believe in plot returned to me. I couldn't avoid a legitimate answer any longer: it was because I didn't know how to work with plot. His question stood for all the questions I had never dared to ask. Because then I might have to answer them.

I'm smart, I'm a teacher, I thought. This is what I do. I teach things. I can teach myself how to do this. What is it that I don't know how to do? How do stories work? What is structure? What is plot? That began one of the most fertile times in my writing life. I worked at my kitchen table, usually leaving my laptop there overnight, and flipped the screen up in the morning before I took my first sip of tea, starting the day by looking over what I had written the day before.

There were often four or five teenagers staying over in our rather small apartment on 109th Street and Riverside Drive on the weekends. It didn't matter that much to me. I'd push my machine aside, make them breakfast, then go back to work. Some days I worked twelve hours, some even more. I worked pretty much any time that was free. I carried my laptop into bed with me and wrote till I dropped into sleep. I stopped exercising. I stopped cooking dinner. I taught and I wrote. I worked through drafts of stories over and over, endless rewrites.

What was the idea behind the story? How would the events of the story unfold along an intentional structure? What was the pattern of language and image I needed as a substructure? How would the action of the characters support that idea? I began to feel as if I had more control over what I was writing. I began to understand there was so much about writing I hadn't known.

The anxiety that I experienced as a novice writer was based on the idea that writing always involves secrets that I would never understand. But writing, like all learning, is a matter of discovering how to break down a dizzyingly complex whole into small tasks that are worked on in a systematic and repetitive manner.

Gradually, I learned enough so that the whole process became less volatile, less fraught. Although writing can still excite me, and cause me frustration and fury, I understand more about how to get control of the wild currents racing through me. It's work. Just work.

When we write we touch the live wire of life. Daring to create out of nothingness, something. Isn't that what the gods do? Isn't that what the Greeks so clearly laid out for us, and the lodestar by which we take bearings here in the West? This work rises from Eros, the life force; instinct. It has a direct link to the erotic impulse, the impulse to give birth, to make life, to make. That's why for so many of us writing has a forbidden quality. Who do we think we are to dare? Which is why the work has to be tempered with Thanatos, the death instinct. That piece of us recognizes—even while we can't comprehend it, even while we push it aside to get on with living—that we *will* certainly decay and die. In the face of this fearsome Thanatos, what we can do is to work, take control of that which *can* be controlled. Some serious whistling in the dark is our best hope to defy, even deny, this inevitability, by acting like the gods who give us life and take it away. So we imitate them. Feeling the creative rush, we surrender. We allow our hand to reach out and touch the live wire. But then we must also give Thanatos its due, by force, by will, we keep our hand on the live wire, absorb the shocks and burns that Eros's fiery impulse creates, so that we can master the current. If Eros is hot steel, Thanatos is the hammer tempering it.

When William Maxwell at the *New Yorker* said, "You are a writer. You will write. You have a voice," I briefly filled with amnesia because he was talking to someone who didn't exist yet: a writer.

Now when my work stalls and stops I try to act as my own teacher. I sit myself down and ask questions. Now what isn't working with this piece? What is it that is missing? What needs doing to make it work? Then I struggle to make myself do the smallest task that is in my control. Look up the definition of a word I want to use precisely. Rewrite one sentence over and over until it's right. If I'm able to stick to these small jobs, bits and pieces gather into writing again, pile into sentences.

Writing is always about leaving the shores of the ordinary world and plunging into the waters of the imagination, the unconscious, the preternaturally conscious: it *is* the altered state. Writing starts in our everyday, in us—in our ideas, our knowledge, in the way images and language come to us. Eventually it must also come back to the ordinary because it must be readable, comprehensible, and even possibly publishable. But the ordinary is what we must leave behind in order to make something out of nothing. We have to be willing to venture out into uninhabited landscapes, unruly waters, the dreamscape: there we face wilderness, beasts, and wise women to transport ourselves and our readers into the other. Reading was where I first learned to transcend those boundaries. Now that converted into writing.

If reading had been my soluble fortune, always, now writing is where I submerge in the primordial sea. My best work happens when I am so completely in the flow that I work exactly at the point where language emerges from my unconsciousness. Usually I'm writing away when I sense that something ineffable, something akin to thought, crawling up from my swampy unconscious, trying to coalesce. Fragments begin to push into the ether, trembling toward language. If I stay with this, the barely real, with these corners of images and traces of sounds, then threads of words can form, and they will pool and collide on this unholy shoreline. Words, ideas, sentences, crawl and rush, aggregate, as if on their own. If the day has grace, if this primal slurry heats, if it combines into tissue, that tissue can be called writing.

Much later in life, I dream again and again about coming upon a small neighborhood that I know intimately, but it's one I had forgotten my way to. I'm relieved to have stumbled upon it again. In every dream variation, the neighborhood has small streets that twist and turn, beckoning me to follow. I wend my way, each bend leading me further into the heart of this neighborhood. I enter a small shop or a small café, each so evanescent that it could too easily return to the forgotten. Sometimes I'm called to climb up a set of stairs—wide, sober, concrete, or rickety, steep, wooden. Inside the building, at the top of my climb, I find a tiny compartment of a home. Once I enter, I am both embraced and set free—I am where I belong. In those dreams I have found my way back to an ancient personal omphalos. It took me years of those dreams before I recognized that the dreams were about living at 26 Grove Street, home to the origins of myself.

My Friend Elizabeth

My sister, Liz, was a wonderful, joyous person. Everyone was experimenting then and Liz was no exception. There were some men who came into her life that we wish hadn't, but still that shouldn't have led to her death. I live with her loss every day.
—Elizabeth's brother, Roger Powelson

THE IMAGES I HAVE LEFT OF LIZ COME TO ME AS IF ON A SCRIM THAT flickers dreamlike on a translucent tissue where I see the classically beautiful young blonde woman, with wide-set almond eyes the day I meet her. She's come with her boyfriend Steven; down to the apartment I share with three other women in New York, at 520 West 110th Street, just off Broadway, to introduce her to us. She had great bones. She seems a bit shy, maybe uncomfortable. But now, I'd say she looked like someone who was holding a lot inside. She's coiled tight, strong and taut.

Steven came to New York to attend graduate school at Columbia and lived upstairs from us with three other grad students. Liz had arrived to New York to join him after dropping out of Reed. We were all in and out of each other's apartments.

I was working at a daycare center in Bronx as an assistant teacher. Liz always had some kind of a temporary job while she took courses here and there, went back and forth between Walnut Creek and New York.

She was an unmoored as I was. We were two young women in deep confusions. We were attracted to each other as friends precisely because we were profoundly unlike the other. But we were very alike in one way. Unmoored.

Liz and I became friends very quickly, then closest friends, a natural falling together. But our early friendship flickers in shadow. This was in 1965, as the world shifted round us. We were twenty-one years old, everything in us still lifted. Up. Our feet barely held to the ground. There were drugs and a breaking away from the confining past. But mostly we overcame gravity, from the sheer joy of just being young and alive.

Friendship can be intense for everyone, but female friendship has its own particular ways. It's a kind of falling in love. Often it's so intense as to be a secondary female characteristic. There is bonding over our biology, our sexuality, our dealing with the question of babies—that has a primal hold over all of the women I have known. We are bound by being daughters, sisters, mothers, aunts, girlfriends, wives, and friends.

Does this primacy between women arise from the blood flowing out of us once a month for decades? Does it arise from the fundamental question of whether our biology will determine long stretches of our lives, whether we do or don't devote ourselves to family? During our girlhoods it had still been assumed we'd be helpmeets, dependents, less than. Our bond also arose from our struggle to know our place, to take up less room.

Girls and women have always been central to my life, and my friendship with Liz was dead center for me.

In this intimacy, there exists between women an intense need to talk, talk, talk, about everything as it swirls around our psyches: worries, fears, and when we're young especially, about love. Liz and I had that, even though there are large rips and tears in this fabric of love and friendship. Absences, confusions. Then it turned out there were secrets too.

OTHER

She was west to my east, her Walnut Creek, California, to my Waterbury, Connecticut. She was light, tight, all California, all other to me. I was dark, sudden, all industrial New England, all other to her. She was used to walking above the extreme Pacific Coast with a longing that floated her above her own life. I dove deep in cold New England lakes formed in ancient rocks, and held my breath as long as I could.

She, the daughter of a psychiatrist, lived in a professional, intellectual, upper-middle-class home in Berkeley. Her father was head of the University of California's mental health program. I, the daughter of an ironworker, lived in the midst of my sprawling Italian, working-middle-class family. Her parents had dinner parties, held parties that went on late into the night in the backyard of their beautiful home. Her family discussed things artistic, psychological, and intellectual. They went to jazz clubs. My large ethnic family sang Nat King Cole and old Neapolitan songs, saw each other every day, dropping in, sitting in each other's kitchens for one more cup of coffee. These gatherings called for food, talk, talk, talk, any excuse so we could all be herded together.

She was the oldest girl in a family of five. She had four brothers. Her parents' marriage was unraveling. I was the younger of two girls, born of parents who longed for, but couldn't have, more children. My parents were blessed with lifelong love for each other. Her family became more and more dysfunctional over the time I knew her, even though she didn't really talk about it. Liz's parents' marriage fell apart over the last years of her life. It included too much drinking, screaming fights, infidelity, arguments, beatings by her father, Harvey. Her father was probably already having an affair with the woman he'd marry next. None of this was talked about by the Powelson children until decades later, long after Liz was gone. She never talked about any of this to me.

My family yelled and screamed and hit their children when we dared to disobey, but you couldn't tear us apart with a crowbar: we were bound together, planted in each other.

I brought Liz up to visit my family in Waterbury a few times. I didn't *yet* know that I came from working-class people, or that my family was a family of immigrants. They were just my family. I wonder what she felt about the odd mix of our big working farm on the edge of a factory town, my family living in a small ranch house down the hill from the farm, surrounded by large Victorian homes, and new streets of other small white box houses right down from the Scoville house, with its dank reek of animals and manure. I still didn't understand that Liz and I were from different classes.

I can see Liz in the living room of my grandmother's house, laughing, saying, "You come from such an old-fashioned world."

I had no idea what she meant. "You use words like *valise* and *parlor, sofa, divan*," she laughed in a friendly way.

"What do you say for the parlor or divan?," I asked, a bit startled. I had never before seen myself reflected this way.

"We call it the front room or the great room. We say couch. We say suitcase." I had never before heard anyone say *front room* or *great room* for a living room, but I knew the words *couch* and *suitcase*. My best friend and I were standing in my grandmother's parlor. It was all intimacy and connection. But a crack had just opened.

America had arrived in that parlor, starting a tiny fissure in the place I called home, by making me self-conscious but also self-aware. Though it took decades to understand where I was from, what part of me wasn't fully American, I can measure everything from that minute. What Liz revealed to me that day was just a glimmer of all that must have seemed strange about my family to an upper-middle-class girl from Walnut Creek, California.

BEAUTY

Liz had the kind of beauty that arrested male attention. I watched when men met her for the first time. They'd pause as if adjusting themselves to this world that held Elizabeth, trying to figure out what to do about this creature and her intense beauty. She knew she had this impact on men and held her stillness inside while she laughed quietly with them, pleased that they were taken with her, but holding them at a slight remove.

CONJURING THE DEAD

Sometimes I feel I can conjure my departed back to me, commune with them, have long conversations with them, understand their answers to my appeals. With Liz, perhaps because it was so long ago, perhaps because I barely remember who I was back then, this isn't true. She's more of a ghost, just as my youth is to me more of a suggestion than a certainty. I have these tattered scraps, worn tissue thin, falling into dust. Liz is a part of them.

Her brothers gave me more about Liz recently. When their father was being harsh she'd say, "Let me talk to him for you. I'll bring him around." And she would. She was the only one who could get him to listen, so she protected her brothers from her father's extremes. Angus remembers a rainy day when he was bored because he had to stay inside and Liz found him restless and unhappy. "What's the matter?" she asked.

" 'I don't have anything to do. I'm bored.' It was raining that day. I was about ten. She was in college already."

"You don't know what to do because it's raining? But the rain can be so much fun." She made them both put on raincoats and boots and grab umbrellas. Angus told me recently, "We went out into the rain and splashed through puddles, we kicked the water. We played out in the rain for at least an hour. When we came back to the house, she said, "See it was fun. Don't let the rain stop you from enjoying yourself." It's such a vivid memory of her taking time to show me something really special."

But I'm riveted by how much I didn't know. That we never discussed. That I never will know.

I do remember Liz talking about the fact that during her childhood, her parents had hired Fred Dyer-Bennet, a local architect, to design their new family home. It was an elegant, modern design, with a large common room, a full glass wall looking out on a wonderful view. The boys had the smallest bedrooms, fitted with bunk beds so they wouldn't care to stay in their rooms. Instead they'd have to pour out into the large common room to play and eat. They loved it, but it didn't work for Liz. As the only girl and the eldest, she had the only large bedroom. But her doors had no locks. "I hated it," she said. "I was the only girl and I wanted some privacy, and this was supposed to be so great."

Often we were walking up New York avenues, talking, her laughing a rich chortle. I can hear her rich chortle of a laugh accompanying what she's saying during these walking conversations.

Another conversation. I can see us walking up Broadway, her footfalls clipping along Broadway. We're near 110th Street. She's furious at her mother, about whom she usually doesn't say much. Her mother has had a letter published in the *Village Voice* about how important it is for a woman to have an orgasm. She says something like, "People think that it's so great to have a mother like that—so open about sex. I don't like it. I don't want my mother publishing letters about orgasms in the *Village Voice*."

I remember her saying only one other thing about her mother, maybe on that same walk. "I have this one song that keeps going over and over in my head, 'I don't care what Mama don't allow, I'm going play my guitar anyhow.'" An important piece of information is being given to me. I just want to be free of my mother, but she's in my head all the time (she may have even used those exact words). I want her out of my head. There's no laughter accompanying that memory. There is only the hard clack of her heels against the concrete, only the evocation of her difficult mother expressed in her footsteps, only her anger.

Such strangeness: a psychiatrist father who is harsh with his children, a mother who writes letters to the press about orgasms, a gorgeous new home that doesn't afford the only girl child her privacy, and parents who couldn't understand why that should matter to her. All this is beyond my ken. She is my best friend, but it's so confusing that I don't think beyond her words for decades.

After Liz and Steven were married, they lived in a triangular apartment in a slightly odd triangular building called the Cliff Dwellers at Ninety-sixth Street and Riverside Drive. It had a wide view along Riverside Park and the Hudson River.

I was living on Tiemann Place with my first husband, who was getting his PhD in physics at Columbia. We were close enough to see each other often—with all of our other friends, or just the two of us. We took long walks in the park in every season.

Once when I was visiting Liz, I was gazing out the window. She looked at me laughing and said to me, "A friend of my mother's was here yesterday and she said, 'What a gorgeous view,' then she turned around and said, 'and what a grungy apartment.'" Liz told this story laughing, as if it were charming. Was rudeness dressed up as honesty and wit seen as charming where she came from? It sounded plain mean to me.

By 1968 we had both been married briefly and divorced; we had taken and left various jobs, and we both lived downtown. I worked at Walden. She had temp jobs and was finishing her degree at General Studies at Columbia. I hadn't returned to school yet. She lived at 225 East Twenty-eighth Street. I lived at 26 Grove Street. We saw each other often, and went out and walked and talked.

But one important conversation was by phone. I was standing next to my bed on Grove Street in my small studio apartment. She'd just gotten a new job at the American Civil Liberties Union. She was so glad about this real job with good people, interesting work. Perhaps a bit of solid earth had begun to gather under her feet, hold her up.

She was in a mischievous mood, rebellious and pleased with herself. That time she was laughing with pleasure and a maybe a bit of "look what I've gone and done."

"I wanted to tell you something," she said that day. "I've put your name down as my . . . I wanted this put in your name." I was embarrassed to say I didn't exactly understand what she was telling me. I felt disoriented and nonplussed. Was she saying she put me down as next of kin? I have no memory of what I may have said. I can still feel the discomfort in my uneasy skin, the confusion in my body, the quilt against my leg as I attempted to understand what she was saying. I want to say, I don't understand what you're talking about. But I was too embarrassed to say anything.

It was only after she died that someone called me to tell me that Liz had named me as her benefactor on her death insurance policy. It was double indemnity because she had been murdered.

MURDER

We were still best friends the night Liz was murdered in her apartment on March 13, 1970. We know she opened the door to someone she welcomed inside. That person was surely the last person to see her alive.

When Liz was murdered (was she murdered?), when Liz was killed (was it intentional?), when Liz died (who was in the room?). Many of us are pretty sure who it was. There were two silk stockings around her neck.

Someone had wrapped those stockings so tight around her beautiful arched throat that she couldn't breathe, so tight, until there was no more air going into her lungs, no oxygen flowing into her heart, her blood, not up to her brain, until the electrical impulses slowed, then skipped, then stopped.

I hadn't spoken to her for a few weeks. I had no idea there was an eviction pending. She had been away the week before with friends from work. They were upstate skiing. Her friends later told me that she mostly stayed inside, wearing sweat pants. Very relaxed, her friends said. Very happy.

How did that eviction notice come to be pasted on her door that night? She was working for the American Civil Liberties Union then, so someone there could have helped her out. I'm sure. It was the first job she really liked. It was the beginning of a new path forward. A good job. People who valued her. Saw how wonderful she was.

I'd guess that the man whose apartment she was going to move into the next day knew about the impending eviction. I don't know his name or when she started seeing him. Her brother Roger was told that she had been living a wild life, involved with a group of people who were trading sexual partners. But she had decided to put that life behind her. She was going to make a life with a good guy, with someone who cared about her. I assume now that it was the guy she was about to move in with who Liz was on the phone with that night when someone came to her door?

THE UNCREATION OF LANGUAGE

What happens to our brains when we find out someone has died? There's simultaneously a freezing of the brain and a jolt of electrical impulses flooding through us. Maybe it's at that moment when our language gets uncreated, because after that news—someone we love is no more—what is there to say, since we can no longer talk to them, watch their faces as the flow of talk goes back and forth, listen to our voices swing in shared cadences?

Instead there begins the long slow disuse of the parts of our brain we've designated for that person, for that love, for those conversations, for that image of the two of you at the ocean, the two of you talking in small downtown cafés, the two of you walking the streets of New York, talking, always talking and laughing. I don't have a single photograph of Liz and me together, but I still can't imagine why.

MR. X

I'm sure X felt the attraction to Elizabeth's beauty that most men felt. But that time I believe she felt it too—for X, that inexorable pull to the other.

The first time I heard about X, we were walking up Lexington Avenue toward her apartment in the East Twenties, and she was talking about a new guy she was seeing. This conversation too, is embedded in the sensation of walking side by side, imbued with the intense energy in her walk, as if she were always wearing Cuban heels, and her feet were clipping along the sidewalk with a distinct set of beats and taps in rhythm.

He led an encounter group she was a member of. She told me he was exciting, funny, and fascinating. Charismatic.

Laughing, she told me that he asked the group, "Why we do always take pictures of our faces? Why don't we take pictures of our asses instead of our faces?" His irreverence delighted her. She allowed him to photograph her ass. Isn't that great? She was alive in her connection to him. He had brought a piece of her into electric being. He was a revelation to her. She was sleeping with him.

X's work with the group was unusual. He was thrilling. He had singled her out from the group for special attention. He gave her pleasure. She was in his thrall as men have always been in hers.

At another time, Liz told me that X was married but that he was trying to talk her into having sex with him and his wife. She told me with her full-throated laugh, but this time there was something about the laugh that was uneasy, something that made me think she was considering it, or even that she'd already slept with them. Some who knew her believed that she had been involved in other sexual antics with a whole group of people. It could have been true.

She told me that she had never had real sexual pleasure before X. The joy of sexual pleasure, of orgasm, was her sexual awakening. That was what drew her deep into his sphere, his control. We never talked about sex at any other time.

EVICTION NOTICE

There was that eviction notice on her front door the night she was murdered. Apparently she intended to move in with someone whom she had been dating. Her friends at her job saw him as a good guy, the right kind of guy for her. This was going on while she was still seeing X and living whatever kind of life she had with him. Although she talked to me about X, oddly, she had never mentioned this other man to me. Others knew about him.

We know who was on the phone when she said, "Someone's at the door. I have to see who it is." She went to open the door and let that person into her apartment. "I have to go now," she is reported to have said, laughing.

"We'll finish this later." Then she hung up the phone.

She didn't go into work the next day. People in her office tried to reach her. When the police arrived, they found the eviction notice, the door closed and locked, and Liz on her bed with the pantyhose around her strong young neck. It was a Friday, March 13. There were two small puncture wounds to her chest, but an autopsy determined that she had died of manual strangulation.

The silky instrument that took her breath away—an insult too profane—took her young bright life. From her, from all of us.

THE FUNERAL

Liz's mother, Marian, told her brother, Roger, that X attended the funeral. She was sure it *was* X who had killed her daughter, Liz. Marian told Roger that X's hands wouldn't stop shaking at the funeral, and that he couldn't look her in the eye. Others thought so too.

At first I couldn't get myself to go into the funeral home. Someone told us there was a disagreement in Liz's family about whether the casket should be opened or closed, between Harvey and Steven, on one side, and Marian and two of Liz's brothers, on the other. I didn't want to walk into a situation like that when we were there to say goodbye. I stood outside with my sister and her husband and my boyfriend Jon, overwhelmed by how I felt. Eventually we went inside and sat. People were asked to speak about Elizabeth. Friends stood up to say what people say on those occasions. She was finally getting her life together. She had really made such good changes and was on her way. Her life had turned toward the good now.

I could feel the hardwood under my body—I was miserable with what I thought were ridiculously glossed encomiums. There was so much disconnect between the Liz who was being talked about in that room, and the Liz who talked to me about X.

There was the fact that she was dead. That she had been murdered. That she had welcomed someone into her home who put silk stockings around her neck. Who had strangled her.

I stood up. "I'm furious at Liz. How could she do this to herself? How could she do this to all of us who loved her? How could she let this happen?" I meant, how could she open the door to someone who would wrap silk stockings around her neck? How had she come to such a place that she had taken a risk that opened the door to her own murderer?

I walked out of the funeral. Jon came with me. He thought I was brave to say what was actually on my mind, to go against convention. Now I can see that I was overwhelmed by so much sadness that it burst into a rush of fury. I was so angry at the universe that I had lost her.

I didn't introduce myself to her family. I don't remember even seeing them. Her brothers Bruce and David were there. Roger was at sea as a Merchant Marine when he got the news.

I saw Steven outside the funeral parlor that day, then later when he was in New York. Recently he told me how Liz's father called and asked to fly with him to New York to identify Liz's body. It was horrible for him to go down to the morgue with her father. How sickening it was to see the terrified look in her eyes. "I'll never forget that look in her eyes. I'll live with that for the rest of my life." Then he saw X at the police station, where we all had been called in to talk to detectives. When I suggested to the detectives that they look at X, they told me others had suggested the same, but that X had an airtight alibi.

Steven said that Liz was unfaithful and deceptive to him—before and while they were married. He talks about times when she acted oddly. She'd be out at night without him, and then say things that weren't too convincing about where she had been. Once, Steven came home earlier than expected. Their bed was unmade and rumpled and the handyman was just leaving the apartment in what seemed to Steven like haste. Liz had hurried off to take a shower. "I just took it. I couldn't get myself to believe it at first. I just wouldn't allow myself to believe it for so long. So I didn't confront her. But I was sure she had just had sex with him. I was sure that she was always sleeping with other men too. I had to confront that truth. I became sure of it."

Soon after that, Steven and Liz were in California when it became apparent that their marriage was in trouble. Harvey and Joan, Harvey's second wife, asked them to do marriage counseling with them as a couple. The foursome was bizarre. Joan had been Harvey's patient originally. For years Harvey had denounced psychiatrists for having affairs with their patients, then he married a former patient with whom he had been having an affair for many years. He and the woman he left Liz's mother for were going to help Steven and Liz work on their marriage.

Harvey encouraged Steven to leave Liz, because he didn't think she was expressing real love for him. Steven fell deeply under Harvey and Joan's influence. He wanted Harvey's approval more than anything else. Liz was becoming like her mother, Harvey said to Steven. Who was showing love for whom here? And who isn't? Why didn't her father insist on talking to his daughter if he thought she was going so wrong, his first born, who had always been his favorite? Where were her parents when things were going wrong for her?

Harvey essentially abandoned his children once he took up with Joan, while he was still married. When Angus lived with Harvey and Joan after his father left, Harvey beat his youngest son so badly he feared he'd kill him. Then he put Angus in a foster home "to protect him," Harvey claimed. By that point, Marian was already off the rails.

A few days after Liz's death, I went to my bank on Sheridan Square. There on the line were two men talking. "My friend Liz died a few days ago," one said. "She was found in her apartment, strangled to death." I was on the line next to theirs. He was talking about my Liz. I was sure. Yet he was talking about Liz as an intimate detail from his own life. I had never met him or seen him. I felt such turmoil and bewilderment in hearing my friend's death talked about like this in public, on a bank line, as if it were *his* news. Should I have interrupted his grief, would it have been rude to ask, "How did you know Liz?" I just stood on line by myself thinking something like, you don't know anything about Liz. I don't even know you and I'm her best friend, hugging my incomprehension and my grief close.

Much later on, when I learned about a sexual act called erotic asphyxiation (the intentional restriction of oxygen to the brain for the purposes of sexual arousal), it was a jolt, almost as strong as the one I had when I was told that Liz had been strangled.

Perhaps this was what X talked Liz into, an act of sexual enhancement that went radically wrong. If one or both were high at the time (a possibility), it might explain a loss of control during this deadly act of pleasure that in the end created her death. Even if it began consensually, only one of them was winding the stockings tight around a neck and the other's breathing stopped. I believe that's called murder.

In death our beloved ones get further and further away because our love can't be reanimated by another conversation, another letter, another note, another hug, another photograph. Just one more conversation, we ask. Just one more, as if that would satisfy.

In the end we are left with the terrified look in her eyes, and the man who put it there walking out of her apartment, leaving the door open behind him.

The youth Liz and I shared, our energy, our leaps beyond the ordinary, drained away with her death. Death, the downward end of overcoming gravity, is the greatest gravitas, the deepest dark we go into. Liz looked down into death seeking the sweetness of pleasure. When she went into the darkness, some of me went with her.

On Not Writing My Thesis

I LAY IN THE HAMMOCK OUT ON THE BACK PORCH OF MY SISTER AND brother-in-law's country house, the same way I had in previous summers. The porch overlooked the small pond, the cows, and the fields. There was a low stone wall between the fields. Nearby was an old apple orchard, the trees were bent and unpruned; we still got small oddly shaped fruit in the fall. The upper fields were dotted with black-and-white dairy cows, wild grasses, Queen Anne's lace, mallows, other wildflowers, and cow pies. The hills spread gently from side to side, and rose up to woods. There had been an old road up over that ridge through the woods, but it had all grown over to a rough dirt path. There was just the one road in or out of this small valley now, leading to a small wooden bridge over the creek. From there I could see down to the other two farms on this small, unpaved road. The fields called to be walked in. But I rarely did. I read Chekhov and Hemingway while the sun baked down on me, as I lay in the hammock, barely swaying.

This was in 1974. Bill and I were still fighting about whether we'd have children or not. That held us in permanent suspension during that era. We had no idea what to do about this absolute unbridgeable chasm.

The previous summer a butterfly with bands of black and translucent stripes settled on my elbow as I was reading. I watched it until Bill came out onto the deck. I had called to him to look at it. But he wasn't with me this summer.

I was rereading Hemingway's Nick Adams stories again. It was a book that always gave me hope. The simplicity of his language made it all seem inevitable that someday I would write too. It would happen. Not now, but eventually. Then I'd put Hemingway down and read Chekhov; he was the real focus of my reading that summer.

I'd go out to the hammock on the deck in the morning right after my coffee, before I started to work. My master's thesis was upstairs on the desk Bill had built for me last year from old barn wood. The thesis was already late. It had been due in June. It was August now, and I'd been here since July. "I'll do it over the summer," I had promised my advisor.

Each morning I went back upstairs after I had read for a while, sat at the soft gray weathered desk, and looked at the pages I hadn't worked on the day before.

The thesis was one of the things about getting this degree that had terrified me most. The thesis and the language exam. Real students knew how to tackle that kind of work. But not me. I had already failed the language exam once, having prepared for it in my familiarly inconsistent way. I had been teaching basic writing courses while I was supposed to be writing my thesis. I had fallen in love with my teaching, and my creative writing and the thesis was pushed to one side. But now all the courses were all done: my students' and mine.

And Bill and I had fallen deeply in love by then. He was giving me such a hard time.

In the middle of that winter I got sick of waiting around for him to make a decision. I had had it with the smart answers he would give as a way of getting out of the inevitable question: Was he or wasn't he willing to have children with me?

What would *he* do about someone who refused to answer his serious questions?, I asked him one day. I'd leave them, he'd said, so I took his advice and left.

Now it was summer and I had come up to my sister's country house with my friend Myra to write my thesis. I would really concentrate on it upstate, in Otsego County, New York. I was sure. But I hadn't gotten far into it upstairs. I'd write letters, some prose, try out lines of a poem. But I couldn't face the real work of slogging through ideas and coming up with a substantial outline. Then I'd go back downstairs and read more Chekhov. And those short hours each day lifted me from the misery of having no idea of how to move forward. I just couldn't see how I was going to get this thesis done. I was terrified every day.

I ate a lot that summer and gained weight. Myra said I never looked better. That made sense, that I'd look my best when I felt my worse.

One day I showed Myra something I had written while I was whiling away time, not working on my thesis on Pietro di Donato.

Bill had begun to come upstate on weekends. We were wavering back and forth. Now yes. Now never. Promises had started to be made. We'd all three take long rides on the backcountry roads around sunset. Once, in a barn where they sold old things, I found a large comfortable armchair that cost fifty dollars. When we had to drive out to pick it up, Bill was enraged. What was I doing buying an armchair? He demanded I pull over and let him get out of the car. I drove down the road for quite a way before I circled back to pick him up.

After Bill came to be with Myra and me upstate in the country, every day after lunch I'd go back upstairs to work—really I meant it this time—I was going to work all afternoon. But it just didn't happen. By the end, I only wrote five pages. It would turn out that they weren't bad. But at the time I had no idea that I had done so little that summer.

More and more, if I went upstairs after lunch, I'd come down quickly to read some more. I read the full-length plays by Chekhov, and pretty much gave up trying to work on the thesis. Even Myra and I were fighting, although I have no idea about what. It was a rotten summer. But it was almost over. We went back to the city.

In the fall I was back to reading Hemingway, instead of Chekhov. I often reread *A Moveable Feast* in the fall back then. Took me years to see how nasty he was. I was simply involved with the romance of his life, Hemingway and Hadley and Bumby. Mostly what I remember about that summer was lying in the hammock and reading Chekhov, and heat, just like on the summer estates in Chekhov's writing, only I had been in upstate New York instead of somewhere in Russia.

Eventually over the course of the fall, Bill promised he'd have kids with me. We decided to move in together. Eventually I wrote something that passed for a thesis. I don't remember how I finally did. I passed my language exam with flying colors because Bill taught me how to study. It had actually been easy, once I sat down and stayed still for even short repeated periods of time. I hadn't realized this before.

Bill and I went back to my sister's country house the next summer. We slept in the same room I hadn't been able to work in before. Now I wrote downstairs in the kitchen. Bill wrote upstairs in the room with the beautiful view of the cow pastures, the pond, and the woods. By the end of that summer I thought I might be pregnant, although it would turn out that I wasn't.

ITALIA, SEMPRE ITALIA

PART ONE: SOUTHERN ITALY

The Stones of Dialect

My house is my language. That's where my home is.
—Dacia Mariani

An ancestral village is a house in which we see ourselves, even if we have never put one foot down on its stones, never walked its streets, never gossiped in its doorways. My grandparents' two tiny *paesi*, Tolve and Avigliano, in the province of Potenza in the region of Lucania in southern Italy, are those ancestral villages for my sister, Lucia, and me. In our childhood, they housed a version of who we were, which came from the way our grandparents' skin had the whiff of food, or work, in it—oils and salts—when we kissed them, the way the food on their tables was hot, delicious, sometimes bitter, the way they hurled themselves at their labors, flew into arguments with each other, told their stories in their dialects. It's from here that our habits, our cooking, our linens, our tools, our speech, our way of being come from.

All four of our grandparents were born in those *paesi:* their families had been there at least for centuries, maybe millennia. Only a single line of heritage, the Claps, were latecomers, arriving in the fifteenth century.

Where we are born and raised gives us a fixed point. I am here. Here I am. Because our people once had another *here*, homes that they had known as mother village, which they belonged to and which belonged to them, the very names of those towns cast an ever-present veil of absence in our family. The immediacy of those *paesi* was still in them. For us, their descendants, those villages were mythical, but also visceral.

If these towns aren't where we or our parents were born or lived, they are where our families are "from." We knew then and know still that not only are we "from" Tolve and Avigliano, but that we are Tolvese and we are Aviglianese. Our connection with those two towns was so internal that we wouldn't have language to talk about this shadow life for decades. Our shadow life. There and not there. Here and not here.

Lucia and I were born and raised in Waterbury, Connecticut, our other ancestral village, so of course we are also American. If language is a home, for those of us who don't share that language of origin those homes in some ways will always just out of reach. Even when we struggled to learn our family's first language, we did so far from those *paesi* of origin. So what does it mean that we belong to a place where for all our early years we hadn't even put one foot down on the stones of those *corsi, viale, vicolini*, and where we still couldn't speak that mother tongue?

Our language, and in this case our dialects too, are from a time that precedes memory. Very early on there is the touch of skin, light and dark shapes, sounds. Slowly those sounds shape into words that give names to reality. The sounds of our dialects are embedded in us as an archaic architecture of learning that goes as far back as learning language goes for us. Even though we only knew the dialect words that filled our everyday sentences—*tu sei patz', fracomod', chiana chian'*—their cadences and rhythms created for us the imagined stones and walls of those *paesi*. Our dialects gave us the first Tolve we knew, the first Avigliano we knew.

Our family elders, like all immigrants, talked relentlessly about what had been left behind, all that glistened through the lens of memory, the lens of heartbreak. All that was better there, all that had been lost to them forever once they came to *"L'merica."*

The longing for home was most deeply felt by my maternal grandmother, Lucia Santorsa, who had never expected or intended to leave her beloved home and family. There had been an abrupt break with her family once my grandfather refused to come back to Tolve as he had promised throughout their courtship, early marriage, and even after their first child, my oldest aunt, Arcangela, was born. He sent her a letter telling her he wasn't coming back to Tolve anymore. Her only choice was either to come to America, or live in Tolve as a young mother without him, without a life as a wife, all that she had yearned for, planned for, and had been lead to expect. Longing and loss colored her life. No doubt one reason why my sister and I work so hard to keep our connections, is to repair the rip that America was for her.

My grandparents' voices were gravelly and almost hoarse, as if their words were shaped by the small pebbles and clumps of dirt in the fields of the *masserie* in Tolve, or charred by the fire and dust of the blacksmith shop in Avigliano, before their words escaped into the air that we breathed.

It's Sunday afternoon in our third-floor rent on 56 Ward Street. The family is visiting, probably on an anniversary or birthday—any excuse for a party. All of the kids have just come from playing outside. We are flooding into each other, around one or another of our kitchen tables, where there is talk of "the other side." What it's like on the other side, what is better there, what is lost, is described in the glow of loss. The air is so clean, the water tastes so delicious, the olive and lemon groves are so plentiful, the *ieri finocchio*, wild fennel, so sweet. These conversations, after many excited interruptions, often ended in sighs and trailing sentences, the talk now of the groves of lemon and olive trees that were stolen through dirty deals, the land that had to be sold because a father died, or a serious illness in the family, the sadness about hungry children.

The talk at those Sunday tables went back and forth between dialect and broken English—more of it in dialect, but there had to have been enough in broken English for me to understand, because I remember many such conversations.

Intimi, the sounds of those dialects, bring back crowded kitchens, the smell of garlic sautéing in oil, *pisciat'* diapers, family. Our Lucano dialects both drop the ending vowels of words and also slide sounds together. They both have a soft *shwa* sound and a blurring of words into one another. There may be some early Greek sounds left, the sound of the *u* as an article, or a word ending from Arabic, some Spanish influence, probably some French, and probably others lost to time. What language did the original Lucanian tribe speak? What did that sound like? Is there any of it left in our dialect? That line back disappears at the edge of history. *Chissa?*

"I was spooked the first time I heard that kind of perfect clear English come out of the mouth of an old person," my sister says about meeting an older American woman who spoke beautiful English. "The sound of English only came out of young people. There had to be another person inside this old person."

Sometime after World War II, into the '50s, about once a year a phone call to Tolve would be made from the farm kitchen. That day would stand apart. "We're going to make a call to Italy." That sentence went around the family. My mother would call a day or two ahead and ask owners of the Bar Tabac in Tolve, with its single phone on the wall, to tell our family to come to the Tabac at an appointed hour on a Sunday afternoon. We'd all gather at the farm for dinner, waiting for the appointed time to come. There was a call to an American operator, who in turn called an Italian telephone operator. My mother would speak to that operator to place the call. All of this was slow and arduous, back and forth across the ocean from America to Italy.

"Okay, okay, Mama, we've gotten through," my mother twisted back toward the kitchen to call my grandmother to the phone. "*Viene' ca Mama. È Zi'Domenica.*" We crowded close in to the long black telephone on the wall of the very small landing at the bottom of a narrow stairway.

The kids were spectators here. When she had one of one of my grandmother's sisters on the phone, my mother went through the series of opening salutations, each prescribed, and politely handed the phone to her mother. Each of my grandmother's children would talk to their aunts and uncles and cousins. Each person shouted into those receivers to carry their voices across all of that way "to the other side."

After, my mother would calculate to the penny how much each family had to pay for the call.

When she was about three years old, my cousin, Beatrice, whose family lived on the farm with my grandmother and grandfather, would regularly sit with my grandfather, Vito Becce, on the daybed in the kitchen, where he taught her to sing the old Neapolitan songs about the beautiful sun-filled land that had been left behind and were so dear to Italian immigrants, like "Osole mio." She was called on to sing them for all who visited at the farm. "I wonder what I sounded like?" she speculates now. "What can I have sounded like?" she laughs.

Beatrice heard long letters from Tolve being read by my grandfather to my grandmother at the Formica table. Pages might be spent sending us greetings from each member of the family. There was a proscribed sequence that had to be said before any news was told. Some of those letters asked us to please send for them and bring them to America since they were "*le pecore che stanno davanti al lupo,*" like sheep staring at a wolf.

Beatrice heard daily fights in dialect between our grandparents and between her father and both grandparents. She heard my grandmother call her mother, my Aunt Bea, one of the loveliest women on earth, *puttan'* (whore) just because Aunt Bea wasn't Italian, and was married to my grandmother's only surviving and beloved son, Rocco. For my cousin, the intimacy of our dialect was inflected with fury. She lived in the din of easy fury. A different kind of intimacy.

My relationship with my grandmother was very different. My mother was a favorite daughter and Lucia and I were fortunate enough to have my grandmother's tough Italian sweetness bestowed on us.

My grandmother and I had only partial language between us. With her children she spoke in dialect. With her grandchildren, she spoke broken English mixed with some dialect, but she was most comfortable in her dialect. However familiar it sounded, I only understood bits and pieces of it. When I later studied standard Italian, she almost never understood what I was trying to say. We found in our need for each other a way to make the best of the small amount of language we had in common.

This was a language of our greatest intimacy, our mother speaking to her mother about all that mattered most, my grandmother talking to our grandfather, all of their children talking to their parents and each other. Those sounds were the walls of intimacy.

The first time we went to Italy in 1963, as very young adults, Lucia remembers being completely overwhelmed by hearing everyone in Tolve speaking in our dialect. But not just speaking dialect. "To hear all these strangers, people we didn't know who all sounded exactly like Grandma. The entire town. How could that be? It was such a shock."

Our many visits over the decades have been attempts to inhabit the place that has always housed an essential piece of our psyches. It was only once we began to visit there that we came to know just how deeply it was embedded in all of us—in ways that we could never had known until we our feet touched the stones of *scorsi, vie, viali*, the tiny streets.

As we walked those *stradolini*, almost every woman emerged from her doorway saying, "Come in, come in and have a cup of coffee with us," tugging at us, wanting us to visit their homes, where there was a huge *matrimonia* bed taking up a large part of the room. Those urgent invitations sprung from the ancient roots of hospitality, which were so powerfully the same as in our family and what had seemed so excessive in the way my mother behaved, suddenly made beautiful sense.

My cousin, Diane, tells me that when she went to Tolve for the first time in 1993, there was a guy leading his donkey through the streets with sacks of grain on the donkey's back. "It's 1993! A donkey on the street carrying grain!" But what struck Diane most intensely was the way in which Tolvese women came out of their front doors, "And they'd stand there, you know, and give us that look. Standing there with their hands on the hips? I have so many pictures of my mother standing that way. Is it genetic that they stand that way?" Diane asks. This way Tolvese women stand with their hands on their hips has a strength and defiance in it, as if to say, "*Em beh*, who are you, what are you doing here?" I've been asked that more than a few times when I've wandered in the streets on my own. "Why are you here? Who are your people?" the chin goes out and up. Once I give a last name and chat a bit, I'm free to go, but first I must answer to them. Under everything is also the question, why do you want to come back here?

After we began to visit and sit in our families' homes, drink cups of coffee, eat plates of handmade *strascinati*, we made a fixed connection to these villages. We have maps in our heads; we know how to drive in the back way, past *la ripe* (the ravine into whose sides all of the *cantine* are dug). We began to have a geography of streets, churches, caffès, markets, and fields.

Now when we visit our cousins, we stumble through in "proper" Italian, which we've worked very hard on. When we hear our cousins speaking in dialect as our elders did, a window opens to Waterbury, back to their Tolve, back to our very first visit to our homes of origin. The talk flows differently into our ears and down into old crevices in our brains.

In recent visits we walk the stone patterned streets in Tolve or Avigliano, arm in arm with our cousins, chatting on our way back from a many-coursed lunch. We stroll and look at the elegant buildings they have renovated in Tolve, or at the doors they or their fathers carved in Avigliano, or we pray in front of the ex-votos to San Rocco in Tolve; we are in Italy of the twenty-first century. But when we turn from the tiny streets into the tiny courtyards, and climb the *scaline* where my grandparents were once little ones, where I'm sure they suffered spankings, *palliade* on their *culi*, for not coming when their mothers called, I feel a rending in the membrane of time, where decades and centuries fall away. Our people lived in these towns the way people lived for centuries, as farmers and herders, as cheese makers, gathering olives, lemons, from their trees, pressing the olives into oil, pressing grapes into wine. Their homes were built the way homes were built for millennia, stone upon stone, house against house. We are in another time and place *e ai questi momentini siamo Lucane*. In these brief moments we are women from Lucania.

As the years go by, this identification becomes something I pursue, work at, and carefully construct on travel, reading, and study. I have put one building block after another in place so I can know more and more about where I come from. Why I am the way I am.

But all of this is only in order to be able to write about my Italy. About the very first night that we arrived in Tolve at midnight on San Rocco, on Ferragosto, which starts at the mid-August holiday, the highest of high holidays in the south of Italy.

My mother, Rose Becce, daring to sit in the driver's seat. She's about thirteen years old. Her sister Vicki is to the far left and her sister Toni is to the far left.

The farm was the last working farm in Waterbury. It's still there intact, although no one lives there. It remains our omphalos.

My grandfather with his daughters, his son, nieces, and a nephew, and his first two grandchildren, Gene and Bob.

Antoinette Becce Padula, Aunt Toni, as a young woman sewing.

Aunt Toni at one of the factories where she did a forewoman's job without the pay or title. The bosses came to her for advice.

Aunt Toni gardened well into her nineties, here with her tomatoes. "I'm fine as long as I stay busy. Otherwise I get depressed."

Beatrice Ferguson Becce, Aunt Bea (my only Irish aunt—that is to say, not Italian) as a very young woman just after she came to Waterbury from her family's farm in upstate New York.

Aunt Bea with a table full of food in the farm kitchen as it was every day. Everyone was always welcome to that table.

(right) Aunt Dora, Addolorato La Guardia Clapps. Aunt Dora, who hit Uncle John with the bone from the *minestra*, sitting for once.

My father, Peter Clapps, about nineteen years old as a young ironworker.

My father, who loved to read and spent hours in his reading chair.

My sister, Lucia, and I praying as we did every night; Christmas, 1947.

My cousins on Halloween, left to right: Bede, me, Jo, Diane, Lucia, Carol, and Linda.

As my father was building our house on North Main Street.

Lucia Anne Becce's first birthday. Main people: my cousin Rocky behind his
father, Uncle Rocky, Lucia Anne on his lap; Aunt Bea, Uncle Joe, and Vicki Jean
on his lap; other cousins at the edges.

Two photographs of Elizabeth shortly before she died.

One of Gladys's passport pictures.

Here I am as a young teacher at The Walden School.

My sister, Lucia Clapps Mudd.

Leaning into my father at Idlewild Airport just before I left for Europe in 1966. My parents always drove in from Connecticut to New York to drive us to the airport in New York whenever we traveled abroad.

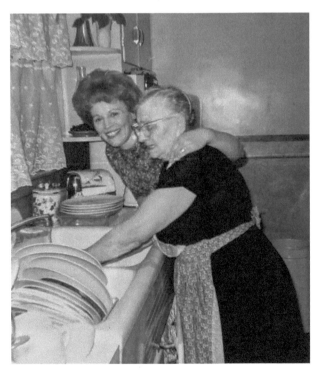

Two Italian women, my mother Rose Becce Clapps and her mother, my grandmother, Lucia Santorsa Becce, in my mother's kitchen.

My maternal grandmother's *quartiere di Tolve, Provincia di Potenza, Basilicata.*

The same medieval *quartiere.*

My mother with *le zie*, Zia Domenica and Zi' Annarosa. This was the first time my mother met her aunts on her mother's side of the family.

My mother and father on the same visit in front of the stairs that led to the hay loft where Zi' Rocco and Zi' Annarosa hid a Jewish family during the war. My great uncle found them hiding in the woods and brought them home. This story was told to us casually when I asked a question about the stairs on a visit in 2011. It had never been mentioned before.

Lucia and John's farm upstate in Davenport, New York, where our family all spent a great deal of time together.

Peter Mudd, Will Mudd, and my son, James Paul Herman, with me on the bed in the kitchen upstate.

My mother with Anna Mudd on the back deck of the farm upstate.

James and me under the same tree.

Bill and James

Donna Ann Herman with her brother James Paul Herman.

Bill and me together in Riverside Park.

My beloved husband, Bill Herman.

Siamo Arrivati

WE DESCEND THE STEPS OF THE TRAIN AT POTENZA, ONTO A PLATFORM where the dim lighting makes it hard to see. We search for faces that search for us. But there are none.

The other passengers quickly hurry toward porters or waiting buses. Some wave to families who are there to meet them. They rush into each other's quick kisses, one for each cheek. "*Carmelina, vien'ca'*," a husband waves his wife to him, even as he rushes toward her. A family gestures toward their arriving people to come then grabs their *valige* and stuffs them into their tiny Fiats.

This is not like the humming stations we've seen coming down from Naples, where platform peddlers of *panini* and *zucca* chanted calls for their wares. Looking around for someone who might help us figure out what to do, we see mostly the backs of families hurrying away. It's almost midnight. It's pretty clear that the telegram that we sent from London wasn't delivered.

The platform is emptying quickly. The train station is at the bottom of the hill. While Potenza begins about a quarter of a mile up and keeps going up and up and up. The buildings are piled up there. It's not at all clear how to get up there. It's too far to walk.

What sounds like old truck engines starting turns out to be the rumble of dusty buses passengers are hurrying to board. Soon the buses begin to pull out; each one bucks forward to begin a long hesitant journey to the hilltowns away from here.

"Maybe one is going to Tolve," Lucia says. When she returns to me with our pile of luggage, she tells me that the last bus for Tolve left an hour ago. "There won't be another until nine in the morning. But I'm not completely sure I understood them or if they understood me. What do you think we should do?"

We've been traveling for fifteen hours, flying out of New York yesterday: New York to London, London to Rome, Rome to Naples. It's our first trip to Europe.

When we came down the steps of the huge plane in Rome, we emerged into the Italian sun. The sky is wider; it has a gentle clarity. The blue is transparent, soft, and lucid. The baggage carriers were singing and shouting to each other in Italian, and quickly the sun began to bake off the stale air we carried with us from the long plane rides. The shouts in Italian, the smell of diesel fuel, and the sensations of Italian sun and sky tell us we have arrived in a field of light. This is the light that has been missing in the shadow of absence that is a part of our family.

Walking across the Roman tarmac, I turn back to catch my sister's eye. She has the same smile that is on my face. "We're here," she says in hushed tones, "really here." We share the same disbelief and wonder.

The sky is wider; the blue is pure and lucid. The light is more transparent. Only Italian comes on waves to our ears. We are in Italy.

It will never again happen that we land in Europe for the first time sharing that moment of sheer ecstasy: complete newness. Later we will learn to say *siamo arrivati, siamo arrivati*. Now we are merely stunned with pleasure.

The moment passed too quickly as we climbed into the cool buzz of the next plane waiting right on the tarmac to fly to Naples.

In Naples we take the train for Potenza. We are almost in Tolve. We're almost all the way there to the *paese* we've known about always, Grandma Becce's Tolve. Our Tolve.

Grandma had been so delighted that the way our plans unfolded we'd arrive in Tolve on the very first night of San Rocco. She had covered her mouth to hide her missing teeth and laughed and laughed with delight, "San Rocco."

The Potenza train station is just kilometers away from Grandma's Tolve. The buses are gone by now and there are few people left on the platform. The porters are dressed in red caps and black uniforms. The caps are squashed from years of wear, the jackets are rumpled; the pants baggy and dirty. They park their beaten-up, heavy wood and metal luggage carts against the wall of the station.

Lucia says, "I'm going to ask if there's a hotel nearby." Once more she approaches the few people left on the platform. We are trying to contain our panic.

When she returns she says, "I asked some people who said we should stay in Potenza tonight, and go by bus to Tolve in the morning. That's the only way."

"But how will we get up to one of the hotels? Are there any nearby?" I peer up to where the buildings start. "Are buses going up there now?"

"No, no one had any suggestions about how to get to a hotel. Just that's what we should do." She pauses, helpless,

"But," she continues "there are two men, they're mailmen. They say that they were just setting out for Tolve now. But I don't know whether to believe them."

"Why not?" I ask. I can see them looking at us.

"These other people, they looked funny when the men—the mailmen—said they would take us. But I don't know. Maybe I was just imagining it. The mail truck is like a little station wagon. They said they have plenty of room.

"Do you want to stay here? Or should we go?"

I look back up at the hill to Potenza. It's so dark and distant. "Let's see this truck."

But it's not a truck. It's a tiny, dirty red Fiat. It doesn't look like a mail truck—no official lettering—but that feels more reassuring. It's an ordinary tiny Italian car. These men assume we've come over to get in it. We hesitate and ask again if there's a hotel nearby.

They smile pleasantly. They're not men. They're young Italian guys. Slight and handsome.

"You are going up to Tolve? Tonight? Why are you going up tonight?"

They smile very pleasantly and gesture to the doors of the Fiat, "To deliver the mail," they answer innocently.

"At night?" I ask incredulously. But when they answer I have no idea what they've just said.

It's at least 11:00 p.m. by now. The two young men are conferring with each other in quiet tones. They shrug and turn back to us.

The station is almost empty now. One or two others left. We're on our own.

Lucia and I look at each other, eyes wide, our shoulders forward. We get in the backseats of the two-door car. Our *valigie* have been put in the trunk.

Now we are the ones riding in a vehicle that jerks and strains up the hill out of the station. Lucia and I hold hands tight. The road winds away from Potenza and very quickly we are out on a country road with empty fields on either side. Ahead the lights thin into darkness. We slow down for a fork in the road where the signs point to places in many different directions. None of them says, Tolve. We proceed down one of the turnoffs.

"Is this the right way?" I ask. What can I expect them to answer?

"*Oh, sì, sì, certo.*" The road keeps getting darker. On a distant hill we can see a few tiny clustered lights.

"*Questo è Tolve?*" I ask.

"*No, non è.*" Soon this cluster of lights disappears.

Both Lucia and I have been peering, craning our necks to see through the darkness. I look at her now. We're searching for any sign of Tolve. "We can't panic," she whispers.

I take out a hatpin and show it to her. I'm holding it so tight my hand hurts with the effort. I scrounge around in my pocketbook (*borsa*, I remind myself), for another weapon. I find an overly large bobby-pin and I slip it to her. "Maybe we're just being silly," I whisper.

As I say this to Lucia, the guy who isn't driving begins to sing to the driver. There's something about his sing-song that doesn't sound right. I try to concentrate and see if I can make out what he's saying. I hear this much, "*Queste ragazze sono . . .* These girls are . . ." But I can't figure out the rest. He's singing in code. I'm sure of that. But what is he saying?

Lucia and I look at each other. I interrupt his singing, "*Che distante è Tolve?*"

"*Trenta chilometri.*" I try to remember what a kilometer is, compared to a mile. Eighteen or so miles.

We wind around one hairpin turn after another. At times a few lights on the top of a distant hill appear only to disappear. None of them, it seems, is Tolve. When those lights are gone, the blackness gets deeper. Another town. Again not Tolve. "How long will it take to get to Tolve?"

"*Circa un'ora.*" About an hour.

"*Ma è già un'mezz'ora.*" But it's already a half an hour, I say to test what he's saying. He answers something that I can't understand.

Suddenly, the guy who isn't driving says something to the driver that I can't understand to the driver and we pull over.

This is it. I look at Lucia, where I see my panic reflected. "What do you think?" her eyes widen and she shrugs.

"*Ma che fai?*" What are you doing? I demand when he gets out of the car.

I think he has said, "*Ho bisogno,*" I've got a need. Need for what? My memory recalls two meanings. Which need?

I don't want his private parts coming out of his pants for any reason. Struggles in these black fields where no one could hear us flash through my brain. No one would even know to look for us for days and days. No one has any clue where we are right now.

My grandmother's high-pitched dialect begins to flood up from me, all jumbled up: "You have to get back in the car right now. Right now. No you can't take a piss. No. Take us to Tolve, right now, right now. I'm afraid. Our people are waiting for us up there right now. *Subito, subito.* Right away."

He leans into the car window and looks at the driver who is sitting there. I begin to rant like all of the older women in my family when they are really furious. He hesitates, "*Ma . . . ,*" but then he meekly gets back into the car.

We begin to drive again. "Do you think maybe he really had to pee?" Lucia asks me. I shrug. I have no idea.

They start asking who lives up in Tolve. Our Uncle we say. Then we say, another uncle has just come from America. We both begin to pile family members onto the list. Our parents are there now waiting for us too, right now. We keep adding names until it seems our whole clan is awaiting our arrival. They expected us hours ago.

Soon, one of the young men interrupts and points. "See those lights, that's Tolve."

There's a vision of lights—more than in any other hill town we've seen. "Why is it so bright?" Lucia asks.

"La Festa, San Rocco," they answer laughing.

"*Sì, sì, d'accordo. Ma certo,*" we answer. Yes, of course.

It seems to be about five miles ahead of us. We weave through the last hills and it disappears and reappears and disappears each time a bit larger, a bit brighter. First it's a crown of lights, then it's a carousel of lights, soon it's a huge wedding cake strung with tiers of lights.

When we finally begin climbing up the last hill into the town, I see low white stucco buildings. This then is not a memory, not an imagined place, but one both real and strange, with small houses, bare bulbs of lights strung in an endless series between the buildings on every street. It's midnight. And now we see that each and every street is packed with people. There's no opening to drive through this massed crowd of celebrants. Despite the glow of electric light bulbs, it's clear we have arrived at a medieval festival, San Rocco.

The car is engulfed by people talking, laughing, eating. They are speaking our dialect. They are eating our food. They don't really even notice that the car is there. They continue what they're doing. There are men in dark corduroy suits, somber and serious. The older women wear long black skirts, woolen scarves covering their heads. Like the older men, they are short and round, like our people. The young are slight, lithe. Young boys squirm at will through the barely moving crowd. These boys come up to the windows and peer in, make faces at us, laugh at us, and leave quickly. We are part of the spectacle. Everyone is.

Our driver becomes impatient and begins to honk the horn in short, quick blasts. People look at him in surprise and annoyance. One young father jerks his chin up to say, *Em beh,* where do you think you're going?

The driver leans out of the window, *"Macchina,* let us through." The towns people turn away shrugging their shoulders. We know we belong with them, not in this metallic encumbrance. He tries a new approach, "Where is Via Roma?" he asks politely. "This is Via Roma."

"Well where is number ten, the home of Vito Santorsa?" Vito Santorsa, my grandmother's oldest brother. *"Vito è un paesano,"* elicits directions: "Up the street, past the piazza, right across from the Chiesa San Rocco." This time they smile and point.

We crawl forward and finally reach the piazza with its *fontana* in the middle. There's a raised stage and an opera is being sung. We watch it as we inch ahead. One of the young men joins in a poignant aria being sung on the raised platform. Bodies surround us on every side, as they inch forward, we inch forward. He doesn't use his horn anymore. We just crawl along with the mass of people we are a part of now. Many of our people here wear wooden shoes. We are merging into another time.

"This is an important feast," one of the young men turns to us to explain," People come from everywhere. They walk for three days to get here. They sleep in the streets to come to San Rocco. He makes real miracles."

The lights above the stage slowly move behind us. We are the only car we see as we make our way. People are buying street food, moving slowly. There are small mountains of watermelons piled at the edges of the piazza.

No one seems to be listening to the opera too closely, although many are facing the platform. They are talking and calling to each other with their hands to come closer.

Past the wall to wall crowd in the piazza we move faster. We ask our way to Vito Santorsa's house. Across from the church. We stop in front of a row of small stucco buildings. And someone points to one in the middle, *numero diecc'.* Number 10.

There's a young girl holding a baby high in her arms in the doorway. Is she our cousin? There are women sitting in front of the doorway next door: 10. Our young driver gets out to ask if this is Vito Santorsa's house. We have two girls here from America, *Americane*. As if to say can you believe that?

Yes, yes, this is the house. But he might not be home.

A short, sturdy, older man is called from inside. He steps from the doorway hurriedly, putting on an old fedora with one hand, and slipping his arm into his jacket. He wears a vest and a shirt without a collar. He pauses in his black corduroy suit, looking at the *macchina* in confusion. His hair is almost white, and he has a generous white mustache to go with it. The rest of his face is covered in gray stubble. His skin is familiar, one of our faces, with its sun darkened folds. He's at once familiar and strange.

"*Ecco sono le ragazze Americane.*" The young man points proudly to us in the car. Here are the American girls.

We get out and come toward him hesitantly. He stands awaiting an explanation. Who are we, and what are we doing at his door, coming in a car?

We can speak enough to say, "*Siamo le figlie della figlia della tua sorella Lucia.*"

We are the daughters of the daughter of your sister, Lucia. He looks at us, his eyes squinting in confusion, then widening in surprise. He is stunned. We stand staring at each other. Seconds of silence follow as he gazes at us without a word, trying to cross years of absence. His eyes cloud, then water, then his arms stretch to gather us to him, his voice is grainy when he says as he hugs us, "*Le figlie della figlia della mia sorella Lucia?*"

He is our Zi'Vit, rumpled, fedora on his head, his neck collarless, the folds of his face covered in gray stubble, his eyes the same color as Grandma's, and we know we are not in America. We are in Italy, we are in Tolve at the Festa di San Rocco, at 10 Via Roma, and we are the daughters of the daughter of his sister, Lucia. We have arrived. *Siamo arrivati.*

"That Winter Evening"

ANTONIO COSTABILE

ANTONIO COSTABILE WAS BORN IN TOLVE, POTENZA, BASILICATA (LUCANIA). His mother and our grandfather's mother were sisters. He was a lawyer, and finding a lawyer among our Tolvese relatives was very surprising, coming, as we do, from deeply rural people. Our grandfather left Tolve for America because of debt owed to the church when the wheat crop failed.

When we met Antonio on our first visit, in 1964, he was living in Potenza and was a practicing lawyer and a historian by avocation. He was a spellbinding storyteller with some remarkable tales about a time when the town voted to seize private land still held under feudal control (100 to 20 in favor!) by casting *ceci* and *fave* beans. And he told us of rhymes chanted as couples circled the oldest tree in the village to marry themselves! These events, he explained, were the result of the influence of the French Revolution.

The last time we saw Antonio he went to his desk drawer and took out the story that follows, saying, "You girls seem to be interested in these things." And thus passed into our hands this tale so wonderfully told which, in its extraordinary turn of events, gives us a treasured picture of life in the old country of our ancestors.

Antonio's story, carried on the swing of his prose, somehow simultaneously nineteenth century and modern, has about it the air of a folk story, from a folk culture, told in a savvy novelist's style. This was where my grandparents were born and raised. Where they fell in love and courted and married. Antonio gave us another missing piece of our past.

That Winter Evening
Antonio Costabile

PROLOGUE

This story, presented as a framed engraving of its time, is in truth, a pretext for remembering and describing the life of our old village and its people—real or imagined—in that small corner of the world where we spend the most beautiful years of our lives.

In that remote, never forsaken corner of the world, where pigs wandered blissfully and hens flapped in the dust and sang the praises of a newly laid egg, where asses brayed with hunger, thirst, or love, and dogs coupled freely in our streets, which were littered with piles of manure and innumerable flies, unknowingly, we acquired the necessary antibodies that would protect us from every contagion—political, moral, or environmental. There, with the war and its subsequent upheavals, we were tempered to confront the grave adversities that the future reserved for our generation.

Nevertheless, like most studious young people then, we, too, were idealistic, romantic, and a little poetic.

On the marvelous nights of the full moon, next to the little church, "Purgatorio," we faced each other across balconies and, with our favorite poet, Leopardi, interrogated the moon that shone in the sky above Pazzano.

And, even if a sudden creak of a rusty shutter broke the silence of the evening, and then, the night soil flung onto the cobblestones fouled the air and forced us to shut ourselves behind the balcony windows, even then, the shining moon, silent and full of mystery, continued to light our fantasies and illuminate our dreams from beyond the glass.

And now, after man has stepped onto that heavenly body, and scientific progress has swept away romance, dreams, religious beliefs, secular errors and all the wretchedness of the past, now one dares to believe that there is no longer anyone who might look toward heaven and, with the poet, pose our naive questions of yesterday.

Prometheus, the Titan who stole the spark from Jove, and will ever represent the enduring progress of mankind, has prevailed and carried the spark of modern life even to that remote corner of the world—our home town.

Yes, it is beautiful, believe me, to think about the moral and material miseries of the past in this marvelous present.

Mecca, short for Domenica, lived in the neighborhood of the old castle, near the little church, "*Purgatorio*," in a narrow, dirty street that some patriots of the past had proudly dedicated to a victorious battle of the second war for Italian independence, Via Palestra.

She occupied a room on the ground floor, which was at one time the stable of an old noble's palace.

There weren't any windows, and the air and light filtered in through the upper half of the so-called *mezzaporta*, the half door, which was, out of necessity, always left open. The cat and the hens went in and out freely through a special, circular opening.

Inside the house on the left was a hearth, black and shiny from old smoke. The walls of the hearth were marked with mysterious Egyptian-like hieroglyphics from macaroni, which had been thrown there as part of the traditional Christmas Eve vigil, the same night that rings of dough were fried in new oil to make the famous *scurpedde*, as they're called in the local dialect.

That night, a large pot hung from a chain in the fireplace. Boiling water was readied to receive the *manate*, a local homemade pasta, white with semolina flour, which was spread on plastic sheets everywhere—across the bed, on the big chest, all over the table—indicative of the appetites of those about to sit together at the table.

Vito di Ciullo, the temporary sacristan (who, along with Vito Zucarieddo, was the only one who still wore *cotori*, the traditional, calf-length, leather boots), had just rung the bells for the Ave Maria at the small neighborhood church, and everyone had already returned to their homes.

Damp air forecast the coming snow. Thick smoke from olivewood burning in fireplaces rose above the low rooftops, and mixed with fog and the odor of garlic and oil being fried for the peasants' suppers.

In Mecca's house there weren't any electric lights. They cost too much. And just that night by sheer coincidence, the oil lantern wasn't working because the wick was all used up. Mecca had gone around to all the little shops in the neighborhood, from Luigi Milinari's to Vito Lafica's, but no one had wicks to sell because they were by now obsolete. Even "Pizzitacchio," normally the best supplied of shopkeepers, didn't have any, although he had solemnly promised, with that eunuch's cackle of his, that he would get them even if he had to bring them from Naples.

Mecca, who was used to doing without, did not lose heart and was resigned to thinking that that night, like so many others in the past, she would have to content herself with the light from the fireplace, which, after all, created greater intimacy. Because in Mecca's house that evening, notwithstanding the small setbacks, there was an unusual feeling in the air, gay and full of promise.

And the flame from the fireplace, which bore sole responsibility for providing light, performed its task better than one could have hoped.

With cheerful cracking sounds, and a fantastic mixture of blue, yellow, red, green, and turquoise fireworks, so beautiful to behold (these last were attributed to the malicious tongues of the neighbors and were, in truth, not welcome, and were immediately extinguished with a quick jet of water), the fire lit up the house magnificently, and projected onto the walls the enlarged profiles of the three people seated around the hearth, as in Plato's famous "myth of the cave."

She, Mecca.

Her daughter, Maddalena.

He, Rocco, Maddelena's fiancée.

Maddalena was a big girl with a freckled face, red hair rubbed with oil, and shining black eyes. Well built and round as a jar, she had the large and low hips of a peasant girl.

Rocco, who was called "Il Casalese" because he lived below in the "Casale" neighborhood, the most populated part of town just above the "Barricani" (the ancient gates that barred the dogs: i.e., non-Christians), Rocco was a tall, athletic young man with the legs of a horseman, the gray eyes of a falcon, an aquiline nose, the olive coloring of an Arab, and a mustache like Charlie Chaplin's.

He was a shepherd.

And you could tell at a distance that he was a shepherd, because of that certain scent of the woods, almost animalistic, a synthesis of wild flowers, the pigpen, smoke, the den, the fox, the asphodella (a species of the lily family), and sour milk, that characteristic odor, in short, that was referred to in the dialect by the word *cacchime*, which cannot be translated into Italian without denigration.

It goes without saying that to the fine nose of Maddalena, his scent was a perfume more inebriating than the incense of the solemn ceremonies of the church, and more exciting than any drug.

Mecca, like most people, had a *soprannome*, Mecca Ponente, meaning Westward Mecca. No one knew why. Ponente couldn't have meant west as in the setting sun, because she was neither declining nor waning.

Mecca attributed it to that far-off place west of town by the river, below Rossano, where she went on foot with a basket on her head, her hands at her side, toward the rise, the so-called *scirscitora*, a place for washing clothes, and then, while these were drying in the sun on the thorn bushes, she would undress, stretch, rinse and refresh herself in the fresh water without inhibition.

She was exactly like Diana of mythology, indifferent to any shepherd who might spy on her, and thus, be condemned to be an involuntary Acteon.

Mecca was no longer young, but she was bursting with health.

She was well built, radiant, and sensuous. In her traditional dress with the flowered bodice, wrapped sash, and long skirt, she diligently kept the best of herself hidden.

She was said to be "almost" a widow, and talking to the neighbors she would compare herself, melancholically, to the fields lying fallow, waiting in vain for the blessed rains.

For Mecca, those dry days continued, a drought without end.

In short, she felt the weight of solitude, and bore the passing of everyday events with resignation, repressing the natural instincts.

With every new event, however, she hoped for the unforeseen and the unforeseeable.

She lived alone with Maddalena, because her husband, Caniuccio, had been in prison for a long time and would remain there for many more years; she didn't know how many—ten, fifteen, a lifetime. During the festival of San Rocco, the patron saint of the town, he had been involved in a swindle that ended in murder.

Maddalena and Rocco had met each other at the Sanctuario di Fondi, where they had both gone on a procession for penitence in the month of May.

They had lost no time in becoming engaged.

Together they made the ritual three turns around the church holding each others' hands. Then, together they had gone into the woods and flung themselves on the swing that Rocco had hung from an oak tree and, finally, tired and happy, had stretched themselves out blissfully in a green field like young heifers out in the world, and ate a simple breakfast.

Together, yes, but always under the watchful eye of Mecca.

That winter evening, Rocco "had come to fifteen," as they used to say, that is, he had returned from the fields for his fortnightly time off and went to call on Maddalena, who waited for him feverishly.

Side by side, the two young people looked at each other meaningfully in the light of the fire. Sitting close, they inflamed each other with desire, while Mecca, pretending indifference, prepared dinner. The *minestra* was seasoned that night without sparing the rich tomato *conserva*, or the pecorino cheese brought by Rocco, or the hot pepper, that aphrodisiac which makes one restless. Mecca dished up the steaming *minestra* and invited the young people to come to the table for the evening supper.

Now, with the cauldron removed, the light from the fire was clearer and illuminated the faces and the table, which was set out with the steaming pot of soup and a towering double-handled jug of good wine for the occasion; the wine came from *comare* Paolina Giordano, the proprietress of the wine cellar below the Arch of the Towers. She knew how to pour out the real thing, not the watered-down stuff.

The walls of the house better lit, showed themselves to be bare and poor. In one corner was a large chest that was everything for Mecca—reliquary, pantry, wardrobe, strongbox, file, and desk.

At the center of the house was a bed standing like an enormous catafalque on iron legs covered for the occasion by a red comforter, which was gaudy and still smelled of moth balls.

The uniform roughness of the walls, which hadn't been plastered for years, was interrupted only above the bed by an old colored print of the patron saint of the town, the glorious San Rocco.

That print, now blackened by smoke and rendered more valuable by the lacework of fly excrement, had been bought by Mecca many years before under the Arch of the Towers from the vendors, who for decades came from the Abruzzi to sell sacred and profane pictures, cult objects and popular books. But she had immediately regretted her acquisition, because she felt that the saint in that effigy didn't resemble the beautiful, smiling statue in the church at all.

In this picture, no offence intended, San Rocco looked more like a Calabrese brigand, or at least like an old officer of the *Carabinieri*, the kind who turned up every once in a while at the local barracks in full uniform. In Mecca's picture, San Rocco wore a three-cornered hat that was missing its colored feather; he had a drooping black mustache, a coarse and ill-mannered stare, and, with the index finger of his right hand, he pointed in a menacing gesture to the enormous, scarlet ulcer on his leg.

In the silence of the house, only the cracking of the burning coals could be heard, along with the rhythmic sounds made by those three table companions swallowing the *manate* in its hot and savory broth.

Each in turn drank deeply from the wine jug, exhaled profoundly, sounding like the inner tube of a car wheel going flat.

Meanwhile, under the narrow table, the hostilities, so to speak, had begun.

The wandering knees of Rocco and Maddalena sought each other out and, in a sensual contact full of promise pressed against each other until it hurt.

Once in a while, Rocco's knee, trespassing, would touch Mecca's, but in truth, she wouldn't withdraw, even if a sudden shiver that was certainly not from cold ran through her body from her head to her food.

Outside, it was silent. It was snowing.

Not a living soul was to be seen in the street, not even Canio d'Erario, who was always the last to return from the fields in the dark of late evening. He had passed a while ago, with his horse noisily pawing the slippery cobblestones.

All the many neighbors—Pasquale Pisciafuoco, Caniuccio, Ciccantonio, Rocco Grannino, Peppuccio Roccuzzo, Mecca Miranda, Filomena Mustazzo, Antonio Furtucone, Marietta Spaccone, and finally, Rocco La Massariola, who was always the last—had already been sleeping awhile.

The dogs, the real bosses of the night, though normally roaming free were neither barking nor running around. That night, only the cats gathered.

In the darkness of big doorways and in the streets, the female cats meowed sinisterly and carried on a dialogue with the toms without restraint.

In their own way, they were negotiating love pacts, alternating long laments with sudden lacerating cries—flights and quick returns—expression of promise, consent, and repulsion.

Until suddenly, male and female would quickly couple, rolling around in the snow now hot under the furious scuffle.

Desire was mysteriously in the air that evening in everything, in the animals, in the people, in the warm intimacy of the hovels blackened with smoke.

It snowed without interruption for hours. Gusts of wind, like invisible ghosts in flight, sped through the narrow alleys, banging shutters, raising spirals of powdery snow, and finally quieting down, leaving silence to reign in the night.

By now the snow, which had spread its white lace on the church, on the bell tower of "Purgatorio," on the houses next door, and hid the crumbling ruins of a house that had fallen a century before and never been rebuilt; by now the snow had conferred on that remote corner of the town an unusual reality, one of the fairies and of dreams.

Even the solitary lantern hanging from a brace in the corner of Palazzo Perrone, its faint light almost afraid of offending the dark, was beating out the rhythm of the wind for the dance of the snowflakes.

A little further away, the ancient stone masks (two big, chubby, sculptured faces with iron rings in their teeth, which at one time only knew the reins of finely bred horses and now only those of the whore's donkey) were also white with snow.

By now it was deep in the night.

The bell in the clock tower near the Florenzano Arch, below the Palazzo Amato, had tolled the hours with a sound softened by the snow, but no one, neither Rocco, nor Mecca, nor Maddalena had counted them.

How many hours.

Ten, eleven, twelve, twenty, who knew?

That exceptional medieval clock, at one time the official town clock, had lost all credibility because, now and then, because of indifferent maintenance, it tolled all the hours of the day at one time and then went silent.

For Mecca, Maddalena, and Rocco, who were used to going to bed with the hens at the tolling of the Ave Maria, their vigil seemed more like Christmas Eve.

And why was it important to know the time or the hour? They had eaten, drunk, and were sated. They were finally happy.

Mecca knew that only when one is sated is one happy. Only when one is sated and happy does one go, as they said in the town, in search of the "*erba vento*," the magic herb.

Because it is then, in truth, that one's suppressed desires, renounced in solitude, are awakened.

That night, for once, Mecca felt happy, while Maddalena dreamt with her eyes open.

Rocco, as if waking from a long hibernation, from a spell, suddenly stirred himself. He got up. He wanted to go home. He went to the entrance, opened the door, looked out, and immediately came back, bringing a wave of cold air in with him.

"So much snow," he exclaimed. "It's late and I have to go."

Mecca immediately reproached him. "Are you crazy? Where do you want to go at this hour? How do you expect to get to the Barricani? You can't even see the streets. Stay here. We'll get along as best we can."

There was in that voice a certain tone of persuasiveness, invitation, warmth, motherliness, and, at the same time, mysterious sensuality. Maddalena nodded in agreement, her cheeks red, her eyes hopeful.

Rocco had a moment of uncertainty and timidity. He knew that a fiancé doesn't ever sleep in the house of his betrothed before the wedding.

In the dim light, however, he turned his glance fleetingly toward the two women and then toward the big chest.

He would have to sleep up there, on top of the chest. Being used to the sacrifices of the shepherd, one night in those conditions wouldn't be the end of the world.

Mecca, who had intuited everything, immediately cut him off and speaking for her daughter too, said to him, "No, dear Rocco, we can't let you sleep on the chest like a dog. All year long you sleep in the sheepfold without being able to rest your bones in a bed. Now that you are in our house, we can't let you twist and turn up there. Ours is a small house," she added, "but the bed, as you see, is as large as the Piazza Fontana, and we can stay there comfortably, all of us, each in his own place."

"Are we, or are we not, one family?"

And then, almost to drive away any lingering doubts or confusion, she added, "After all, at this hour and with this weather, who will see us?"

"Rocco, go undress yourself, and get in on the edge of the bed," she said to him in a peremptory tone."

Rocco did not respond. He was confused, bewildered. Even if the decision of his future mother-in-law seemed absurd to him—a man in the same bed with two women—nevertheless, he felt unable to refuse. A refusal might seem like a denial of their familial connection, an offense to their hospitality, even a lack of affection toward his fiancé, and also, in keeping with the morals of the times, cowardice.

"And then, at this hour, with this weather, who will see us?" These last words of Mecca resounded in his head like an invitation, a precautionary absolution.

All three of them undressed in silence in the room, which was by now almost dark.

Maddalena jumped like a colt into the left side of the bed, trying not to crunch the dry corn husks that filled the large mattress in place of wool.

Rocco, instead, sank in noisily, like an avalanche at the extreme opposite side, rigorously respecting the command he had received.

Both Rocco and Maddalena disappeared under the red comforter at far sides of the bed, turning their shoulders away in modesty.

Only Mecca remained at the foot of the bed, undecided about what to do.

Should she lie down in the middle, to make a barrier between her daughter and son-in-law, or stretch out across the foot of the bed? Or, should she sacrifice herself and spend the night by the fireplace?

None of these ideas was possible. There were no other covers. The fire was spent. There wasn't any light and, truth be told, she didn't want to spend a cold and endless night like that away from her own bed.

And what if there were an accident; leaving those two alone in the same bed was impossible.

Mecca knew from experience that if a man and a woman were alone, unseen by anyone, a coupling was inevitable; it was almost a law of nature.

Imagine then, these favorable conditions, in the dark, in the same bed, with the fire that smoldered in the bodies of those two.

A shiver of cold forced the only decision possible—the bed.

She got up on the chair on Rocco's side, lifted the comforter, and energetically pushed him over with her body. Without making any noise, she made herself comfortable, as they say, like a bird in a nest.

That contact, skin to skin, with the hairy body of a man, the heat of the bed, and the glow she still felt from their indulgent consumption of wine and *minestra*, along with the long forced abstinence, suddenly stunned her.

A hundred bells began to sound a warning in her head.

Her heart beat now with a frenetic rhythm, as if wanting to escape from her skin.

She had the impression that someone wanted to suffocate her, while a strange tingling sensation ran through her body from her head to her foot.

And what heat she felt! Sant'Antonio, what heat!

The coals that were dying on the hearth were suddenly on her cheeks, on her lips, inside her body, igniting a desire that she could not remember having known before.

She wanted to cry out and call for help, but she was out of breath, and her head was filled with incredible confusion.

She needed to resist; resist at all cost.

But how?

Thinking of her husband so far away, of the neighbors in their houses, of the world, and all the saints. She felt unable to reason anymore; she no longer understood a thing.

To the devil with everyone. Even if a biblical flood were to come, she would willingly be shipwrecked in the deluge. Death. Yes, even death she would accept willingly. She would not even refuse death.

In fact, there was no longer anything she refused. Not even the foot, nor the hand, nor the knee of Rocco, and then . . . then . . . everything.

To the depths.

Destiny wanted it this way.

The snow continued to fall for the rest of the night and for the rest of the night poor Rocco, under the red comforter, was compelled to lavish himself on the left and the right without respite, in equal measure, without slighting anyone—now Mecca, now Maddalena.

Eliphas Levi recounted in *The Book of Splendours*, that King David, in his time, did the same thing as Rocco, not under a red comforter and not in the dark, but in the town square while the people of Israel applauded every embrace, like a goal scored at a soccer match.

The snow and the winter passed.

Spring came.

The rain married the sun; flowers, plants, and seeds in the fallow ground began to germinate. Mecca and Maddalena germinated as well. Both were pregnant.

As the months passed, this new situation did not escape the vigilant eyes of their neighbors, of the local women, but even more of the local men who, because of Caniuccio's imprisonment, watched over the two women with great care.

Word went from mouth to mouth.

The priest, scandalized, talked in church without naming names, of mortal sins, of lust, of divine sanctions, of Sodom and Gomorrah. Some of the faithful laughed knowing that, in accordance with a peculiar moral code, they had to do what the priest said and not what he did.

The ballads they knew were now enriched with a new song composed by Larizza and his cronies, the local town poets.

This verse was sung with gusto by the peasant women in the fields, from the weeding and threshing of the wheat under the lion sun of summer, to the gathering of the olives in winter, just as the stories of Orlando or Guerino had been sung in countless town squares in the past.

Years later, someone remembered the refrain that praised the labors of Rocco, like that of Hercules.

> Leave the one and do the other. *Lascia e piglia.*
> Leave the one and do the other. *Lascia e piglia.*
> First the daughter *Prima la figlia,*
> Then the mother *e poi la mama.*

In order to avoid morbid curiosity, the two women no longer left the house. Undaunted, Rocco continued to meet his obligations, and to assist the two women lovingly. When the women of the town, friends and neighbors, saw him pass by, they called to each other in turn to admire him as if he were superman.

The only dark point of the story was the thought of Caniuccio, Mecca's imprisoned husband.

But, escape from prison wasn't possible, and Mecca could have peace for many years before her husband would be able to return home.

Although she couldn't know this with certainty.

At that time, the letter carrier was a cobbler of some intelligence who went around in the inaccessible alleys and passageways of the town with the agility of a cheetah; with all due respect to the discretion of the postal service, he knew unfailingly the contents of all the correspondence before making deliveries to the legitimate addresses.

In addition, he was as talkative as a jackdaw.

Then one day, wishing to do his part in the story, and knowing that all the neighbors would be listening, he called out in a loud voice in front of Mecca's house, "Mecca Ponente, come outside. There is a letter for you from Porto Azzurro. You husband wants to hear from you immediately." And so it was.

The diligent friend assigned to watch over Mecca in Caniuccio's absence had communicated to the imprisoned husband that his family would be enriched by two additions.

He had not specified, however, whose work this was.

It was the time when Il Duce was conferring rewards on those patriotic mothers who brought forth newborn "Children of the Wolf," in homage to Romulus and Remus. Caniuccio, on learning the news in prison, was distraught. For some weeks he did not sleep day or night.

He was tormented, not so much by the deed, as by the thought that there was someone in the town capable of not fearing him.

This someone had to be either crazy or suicidal.

He repeated to himself that to become the cuckold to wife and daughter at the same time had never been heard of in the whole history of the town.

He was crazed.

His mind whirled with proposals of vendettas.

He would plunge the switchblade into the chest of his wife, his daughter, and that infamous one.

But the infamous one. Who was he? His *compare* had prudently not told him. Only Mecca could reveal this to him directly.

So, taking courage, Caniuccio decided to write a letter in code to his wife, in order to get around the prison censors without giving away the news of his disgrace, which would surely give the other prisoners the chance to mock him.

He wrote his wife a very short letter, like that famous one of Caesar, adopting San Paolo the apostle as a phallic symbol. "Dear wife, let me know who made San Paolo walk in my house?"

When the God Neptune discovered that Aeolus had unleashed the stormy winds without his permission, he flew into a rage, threatening his deadly anger, but then instead, he calmed the turbulent water with his trident.

And everything ended there.

Here, however, at this tempestuous news, a vendetta, blood must follow. Offended honor had to be washed with blood. There was no alternative. The death sentence was inevitable.

Punctually at the due date, Mecca and Maddalena brought into the world two beautiful baby boys whom Donna Ida, the midwife, never stopped praising from house to house.

When the births were reported to the civic officer of the commune, Don Attilio Pastore, he couldn't touch food for two days. Thoughtful, rational, and stubborn as he was, he could not establish the proper familial relationship of Mecca's child to the rest of the family. Was the boy son and grandson, brother and uncle, or . . . what else?

Fortunately, Rocco had run for cover, marrying Maddalena before the happy event, thus resolving one of Don Attilio's difficult dilemmas.

But this baby, the son of Maddalena, what relationship did he have to the child of Mecca, the grandmother?

"*Gesù, Gesù,*" Don Attilio concluded without resolving the riddle. Better not to think about it. Better not to think about it.

Rocco continued as a shepherd. Mecca washed clothes, and Maddalena looked after the children. Not a cloud disturbed the family menagerie of wife, son-in-law, and mother-in-law. Until one day, according to Mecca, the envy of the neighbors prevailed.

A general amnesty was declared following an auspicious event in the royal household, granting Caniuccio his freedom.

A telegram to the mayor warned that Caniuccio would arrive in town any day. It was like a thunderbolt in a calm sky. The word of Caniuccio's liberation quickly got around, and the news shook the town from its habitual torpor. Finally something new.

At Mecca's house and in her little street, there was great agitation, a continuous coming and going of *Carabinieri*, civil authorities, and curious bystanders.

The mayor came, the political secretary, the parish priest, the womenfolk, and the neighbors. Swarms of boys, seeing all the commotion, went wild, like at the Festa di Santa Lucia at the nearby Purgatorio church.

Everyone was certain, however, that the two stone faces of the Palazzo Perrone, involuntary guardians of that fine night, would, with the arrival of Caniuccio, become witnesses to a tragedy without precedent.

Blood would run—so much blood it would dye the cobblestones red; all the puddles and mud mingling, as happened on New Year's Eve, when the pigs were slaughtered.

The mayor, for his part, took stock of the Carabinieri without delay.

He mobilized Filippo Cilenti and Matteo Frisara, the two municipal guards, to patrol Mecca Ponente's house night and day, with orders to dig a trench, if necessary, to preserve the safety of the family and the "Children of the Wolf."

Filippo Cilenti, whose pronounced stutter gave him an authoritative tone, reassured the major of his diligence, showing him the bulky revolver he always carried in his belt, which had been loaded since the end of the First World War, but which, in truth, he had never taken from its holster.

Matteo Frisara, notwithstanding his age, assured the mayor of his diligence and vigilance.

All the neighbors, as if anticipating an impending storm or procession of goose-stepping fascists, gathered-in hens and offspring and withdrew courageously into their houses to observe these developments without being seen.

They knew that Caniuccio was a stupid and dangerous scoundrel; that he knew how to handle a knife with the ability of a D'Artagnan; that he had no scruples at all, something that had been demonstrated on many occasions in the past, just imagine now, after so many years of perfecting the skill in the school of prison.

Thanks to Caniuccio, Don Ciccio Papapietro, the old carpenter, would finally have a good opportunity to sell those dusty caskets he had in his shop on the side of the Arch of the Towers, which he had never been able to sell because of superstition since the time of the Spanish flu epidemic.

Thus, curiosity in the town was raised to an agonizing pitch.

"Has he arrived?" the neighbors asked anxiously of those passing by.

No one knew anything. Only Vito the Red, also called "Sing Sing" (a man who bore a remarkable resemblance to Ho Chi Minh), ran by, oblivious to everything, as he had an urgent need to run to the town dump.

Michele il Lupinaro, who, lacking eyebrows and hair and with that yellow face resembled the famous Chinese general, Chang Kai-shek, cried out that he had learned with certainty in his town, Potenza, that Caniuccio would come that night.

Caterina di Poppa, the wife of Ciccantonio, continued to knit her socks in the entrance of her house undaunted. "In my life," she said, "I've seen everything—the cooked and the raw."

Everyone, even if their houses were far away, came to Via Palestra out of curiosity.

Even Vito Vavalone, Rosario Capitanessa, Rocco Giuricicchio, Peppe Ruspone, Pietro Pipinaccio, Saverio Sciavardella, Velaso Annateresa, Luca Camplacasa, Rocco Cazzottola, Rocco Vito Recchiolungo, usually immune to everything, feigning indifference, passed through Via Palestra casting sideways glances.

Don Nicola Biscotti (who always knew everything, being from Potenza and the brother of a teacher) stopped in Mecca's neighborhood and announced with authority, "Don't pay any attention. They are all telling you tall tales. I know that Caniuccio will not come in the surrey of Nicola Vecchiarella or in Giolanno's, but in the new car of Antonio Maria LaCapra tomorrow.

Everyone was curious and everyone had something to say.

Seated inside the house behind the open door, while the babies slept so innocently on the famous double bed, Rocco, Mecca, and Maddalena, waited, resigned and in silence, like those condemned to death, the fulfillment of their destiny.

The bells of the Ave Maria that at one time were so festive, now seemed like a death knell. The clock tower announced the hours one after another in the heads of those poor souls, hours, which never seemed to pass.

Caniuccio did not arrive that day.

It was summer. The humid heat, mixed with the stench of garbage and manure in the streets, made the air, heavy, almost solid.

Clouds of flies swarmed in the street and inside the house, making the wait even more dreadful.

Caniuccio arrived during the heat of the day, when everyone was inside behind closed doors—with rag shoes, the blue handkerchief of a rascal around his neck, graying mustache, his hat tilted forward, his eyes lowered, his face with the characteristic color of an ex-convict.

Old cronies, acquaintances, boys, and all the curious went to wait for him at the Trave Della Corda, the place at the edge of town where games were played and people assembled to carry San Antonio Abate in procession on his Saint's day.

Caniuccio crossed the piazza, the main street, the Arch of the Towers.

Arriving at the entrance of the house, he thanked everyone, shook hands with them all, and begged them to go away.

Quickly, he pushed the half door open, and, as if he were trying to escape an invisible follower, entered suddenly. He slammed the door behind him with a great bang and pushed the rusty bolt closed with a piercing screech.

The silence of a tomb followed.

The wait became agonizing for the neighbors.

Filippo Cilenti and Matteo Frisara, the Mayor's armed guards, who were already at the place and ready (so to speak) to fire, having seen Caniuccio in such good shape, thought it best to withdraw from the front line and crouch even further away in the large doorway of Donna Lucrezia Fiore across from Luisa Capocaccia's house.

They had families too and under such circumstances, it was better to be prudent. Not enough was known.

Nicola Damone derived his authority from being the town crier and the messenger for the office of the municipal tax collector.

Extremely courageously, like all the others, he went to report the first name, last name, nickname, and ages of all the protagonists to the authorities.

The hours passed by slowly. Everyone was certain that a horrible tragedy was being committed in that house.

"But why doesn't anyone intervene?" the neighbors anxiously asked themselves from their secure positions.

The guards, state police, carabinieri, the mayor, the political secretary, the parish priest, where were they?

Too much time had passed, or it seemed that too much time had passed. "By now, it is done. The crime has been committed," they thought. Now that assassin, thirsty for vengeance and for blood, was arranging their corpses.

But no one moved. They were all paralyzed, like those stone faces near the Palazzo. A sinister creaking, the shrill and prolonged sound of the rusty bold, made everyone turn their eyes toward Mecca's door.

There couldn't be any doubt. That scoundrel had killed all of them and now was going to throw the victims onto the street.

To obey the code of honor.

After the sinister creaking, Caniuccio appeared in the frame of the door. He stepped out onto the threshold.

In his arms, on one side, he held the son of his . . . wife, and on the other side, the son of his daughter, like two victory trophies. The innocent babies were beautiful, lively, and smiling.

Courageously, everybody came out from their houses and their respective places of refuge. Neighbors far and near ran from everywhere to enjoy the unusual spectacle.

Caniuccio had revoked the code of honor.

The nightmare was finished.

Rocco came out too.

He elbowed his way into the crowd with the usual slow, rhythmic step of the shepherd, absorbed in thought. He set off again toward the cantina of *Comare* Paolina Giordano under the Arch of the Towers to fill the jug with the miraculous wine of that great occasion.

In the hours ahead, however, each would eat, drink, and sleep in their rightful places.

That winter evening, and the snow, were left behind forever.

My Neapolitan Wedding

I GOT MARRIED IN ITALY ONCE. IN NAPOLI IN THE *MUNICIPIO* IN THE summer of 1967, for the wrong reasons to the wrong guy. It was a marriage that barely lasted a year.

Danny and I were American kids and we weren't. We were American kids with Italian backgrounds. His people come from Sicily. Mine from Lucania. We'd grown up in the same kind of families.

I met him at a Columbia party. He was working on his PhD in physics and he was funny as hell, and he could dance. I've always loved smart and he was from the world I knew and loved. He was in a band, of course, on drums. What more could an Italian girl from Waterbury, Connecticut, ask for?

We both lived on the Upper West Side of Manhattan. But we were still going back and forth from the Upper West Side to our traditional Italian families, and we hoped they wouldn't be swept up in all this revolution.

We were poised over a chasm between the ancient world of our relatives and the untidy new one that was sweeping into America. I had no idea where I truly belonged. We just rode on the waves of the music into this new land. Both worlds owned Danny and me. I thought we'd be able to leap easily across that chasm with lightness in our strong, young legs. Back and forth we went for a while.

This was when it began to be clear to American kids that we were the center of everything—not our parents, not our government, not dream capitals like Paris or Rome at whose altars we knelt once we left our parents' ranch homes, the homes they had worked so hard to a build and own. We didn't know how we had accomplished this huge change. And in truth we really hadn't. Fate blew us into the center of a vortex and there we found ourselves, dancing and protesting and chanting and having our minds blown. All of this happened so quickly my body didn't really absorb what happened until decades later.

Danny and I had been dating and going between my apartment and his, when he left one summer to go to Bologna for a physics conference. He was to deliver a paper there. Before he left, the last thing on his mind was me traveling with him. The friends he was traveling with were a married couple, and the wife was definitely a part of this trip. "I'm traveling light," he'd said, laughing sheepishly before he left.

After the conference, Danny was left to himself. That was when I got a call suggesting I come over and meet him in Paris.

He missed me. Terribly. "Come over we'll have a great time." I was both flattered and furious. He had clearly not wanted me with him before he left, but now that he was lonely . . . what Italian girl doesn't want to be longed for by her Italian guy?

But what would I tell my parents? In those days I'd never fly off to Italy on a trip to meet up with Danny without talking to them. They still always drove in from Waterbury to New York to take Lucia and me to the airport. We were still that kind of Italian family.

Several phone calls later, Danny's language had changed. "I need you to come over. I want to be with someone who loves me. You're the only person who loves me like that. Tell your parents we're going to get married."

Married? Where? Why? No, this doesn't make any sense; my parents said immediately when I talked to them about Danny's idea. I was happy to be longed for. I loved the idea of an adventure. I didn't want to be married without my family. Just to clear my head, I took a walk up the hill to visit my grandmother and sit at the marble-patterned Formica table in the middle of the kitchen while the televisions played an old Joan Crawford movie.

"Grandma, Danny wants me to come to Italy to marry him. I don't know what to do." This is idle conversation. My grandmother and my Aunt Bea drank coffee together at the table and picked off the tiny points around the pumpkin flowers, *shishel*, that my Aunt Bea was preparing to dip in egg and flour and fry. By the time the first ones came out of the frying pan and we were eating, my grandmother was explaining to me why I'd better go to marry him.

"When I marry you granfader, in Italia—we have two *matrimonie, civico e alla chiesa*. Un on one day, *un, l'altra*, the nexta day. *Ma* you grandfader, he wanta me sleep with him *dopo la ceremonia civico*. I no do that. He so mad a me. He hadda the church. I was his wiva. I so sorry I do that to him. Always I think about that. It make him too mad at me. Alla my liva I'm a so sorry about this ting. Go, go to Italia. You haffa too."

I walked down the hill and told my parents that Grandma said I should go. I could see the expression on my mother's face change. She was going to have to take this idea seriously. Her mother's face sank to her own mother's authority. If her mother said I should go, she had to give in. It was the same for my father. My grandmother said I should go.

It was many years before I'd realized that I had unknowingly shifted the ground beneath all of our feet by calling on my grandmother. I had changed my fate unwittingly. My grandmother had pulled me across another abyss, with a force that went back to her life in the early 1900s.

Later, I thought that I might have gone to my grandmother, unconsciously thinking she had all the power, and that if she endorsed it the decision would be made. Now I'm more inclined to think it was an unplanned first lesson about how power worked. Accepting my grandmother's decision was dumb. But I saw that she was really trying to undo an old regret of her own, and that her advice had nothing to do with me or with the time we were living in.

Danny was just lonely. He wanted me to come and hold his hand, because I was a good Italian girlfriend who cooked for him and did all the caring things good girl Italians did while still being a hip young thing. What a *strambol'* of values were mixed in that pot.

Before I left to see Danny in Italy, Lucia and I went down to the West Village to Fred Leighton's boutique, where his Mexican peasant clothes were festooned with embroidered flowers and lace. I chose a dress made from wide bands of white lace, very simple and sweet, whose hem ended inches above the knees. I packed it, and a white lace *mantilla* to wear to my wedding in Italy.

For the first few days, Danny was thrilled that I had come. We stayed in a lavish hotel on Via Veneto with the money our parents gave us because we were getting married. There was a luxurious red marble bathroom with a huge bathtub.

We traveled to Naples to meet up with his friends from the Bologna conference and where we thought we could get married without too much trouble. Our visit with Danny's friends was lovely, but we had to find our own way through the maze of Neapolitan bureaucracy. I still wonder if we had even considered the possibility that this would not be easy. Did we make a phone call to the American Embassy before I traveled? *Niente.* I don't think it even occurred to us.

We spent all of our days searching Naples for a clerk with the proper official stamp to thud out our right to be married. We waited on long lines in offices where clerks discussed bicycle races with each other, swatting flies away for ten minutes. When Danny and I finally got to the head of the line, they slammed the gates down in front of us, one minute before noon. When we went back later in the afternoon, the office was closed. The next day was a Catholic holiday, one I had never heard of. "My people, my people," I thought. Finally, a young secretary at the Embassy gave us the name of an American sergeant who'd arrange it all, unofficially. We paid the sergeant in cash, and went back a couple of days later to pick up our license.

The drudgery of making these arrangements was wearing away the romance of this adventure. But while the tension between Danny and me rose, my passion for Naples took hold. I love its sprawling excitement, shabby and elegant, its old-world cosmopolitan nature. It's a place that has been everything for thousands of years, under the strong arm of a ridiculous number of regimes and kingdoms and nations. Nothing will surprise it, but it will always surprise us. Yet it's not a city of cynicism, it's the reverse, more alive, more human: people walking always with each other, arm in arm, sometimes four across. People greeting each other with quick joy, kisses, jokes. But this was in hard contrast to what was going on between Danny and me.

By the time we had a marriage license to bring to the *Municipio* on August 17, 1967, we were getting married because that was what we had said we were going to do. There really was no way back.

At the *Municipio* there were flocks of tiny old men dressed in shabby, patched suits scrambling to offer their witness services, "*Testimone, seicento lire*," their raspy voices called out to us.

"No, no," Danny waved them off. "We don't need them." It had cost fifty dollars for the sergeant to issue the license. Danny didn't want to pay anymore. "*Basta*," he said. The witnesses had wanted a few lira for their testimony.

We climbed the grand wide marble stairs in the crumbling Municipio to *l'ufficio matrimonio*. There were swallows flying overhead in the high vaults above the stairs.

After, we waited for an hour in the antechamber, standing in the clot of couples waiting at the door of the wedding office, until it was our turn and the clerk wanted to know where our witnesses were. We needed two of them. Bewildered, I looked around the large empty room and I saw that it was empty except for a row of tall red velvet carved chairs, deep red. One huge desk almost floated in the middle of the huge chamber.

Fretta, fretta. Hurry. A small man wearing a dirty tie tapped my arm. Listen, there's a line outside. There were a lot of other people waiting. *Subito.* Quickly. The clerk pressed us, we could put any names we wanted to on the *documenti*, but we had to get witnesses immediately. The couple behind us from the outer chamber was hurried inside to be my sister and Danny's friend. The large hand of the man behind the large desk gestured in downward sweeps that it was time for them to come forward to the battered table.

Later that day we went for a long walk. We must have wandered up the hill in the *Quartieri Spagnoli*. It was a sunny day, and when I saw a group of small children playing in the street I was immediately intrigued by them. Little Neapolitan kids whose tight, strong, small bodies and smudged faces reminded me of my cousins when we played in the woods. As we walked toward these *scugnizzi*, one blond-haired little girl, half urchin, came over to me. I was bringing some simple Italian to my lips when she unleashed furious dialect at me and, looking me dead in the eye, spat right on one of my shoes. I assume it was the length of my dress that gave this tiny Neapolitan her authority to be so *scustumad'*, so rude toward me.

The night we got married, we took the train to Sorrento and checked into a small, unassuming hotel. When we entered the dreary room I saw that there were narrow twin beds covered in dark, sober bedspreads. It seemed like a bad omen to me—sleeping apart on our wedding night.

"Would you go down and ask them to change our room?" I asked Danny. He wanted no part of this idea. We were both tired.

"I don't want to do that. It doesn't matter to me." He stood turned away from me.

"But it does to me," I said. "It's our wedding night."

"I know, and I'm saying I don't care."

We traveled up and down and in and out of all the towns on the Amalfi Coast—Maiore, Minore, Positano, Amalfi. Those hotels were elegant. We must have had a lovely time. When we went to see my relatives in Tolve, he yelled at me in front of my aunts and cousins. He thought that they would appreciate that he was a real Italian man. Then it was time to come home. On the plane home he finished his meal a little earlier than I did and reached over to take my dessert and began to eat it before I had the chance to say, "Hey, that's mine."

"I know, but you'd give it to me if I asked."

"But you didn't ask."

Although we stayed together most of a year, toward the end he came and went as he wanted to, sleeping with a beautiful red-haired woman who pretended to be my friend whenever she came to our house. She told me how much Danny loved me, how much she loved me. That was when I knew they were sleeping with each other.

One day we went to Central Park and drank a bottle of champagne lying on the grass alongside Poet's Walk. On the way home Danny descended into one of his dark, withdrawn moods. When we got home I said, "I know why you withdraw when we fight. I know you hate that. But we had a lovely day today." I was standing in our tiny hallway on Tiemann Place where we could hear the IRT rumble overhead day and night.

"I don't want to be married to you." Unadorned truth.

When I left a few days later I knew that there was never anything I could have done about any of this.

There was a lot of crying and regret—his—but I had finally come to my senses.

Naples is still one of my favorite places, and I don't mind even a little bit that I fell in love with that grand old *città* while I was making promises to cherish and obey the wrong husband.

PART TWO:
THE OPPOSITE OF SOUTHERN ITALY

After the Manner of Women

MY ITALIAN MOTHER

MY MOTHER OFTEN TOLD THE FOLLOWING STORY. "MY DAUGHTER, LUCIA, was engaged to be married to this young man. His name was Jory Squibb." My mother always lowered her chin at this point, and looked out from under the hint of an overhang of her very pale eyebrows, then she went on in her small solemn voice. "They were from Michigan." She meant they were American. They were different from us. They had money.

"Naturally, I had to meet his family." At this point she adjusted herself in her chair so that her listener would have time to consider the obvious weight of her dilemma. "So I called his mother up and I said to her, 'Mrs. Squibb, I'm Rose Clapps, Lucia's mother. Our children are going to be married, and I would like to have you and your husband to come to dinner at our house.'

"Now, I had to do this, because it was only right. I was the mother of the girl. The mother of the girl has to have the parents of the young man to her house. But I was very, very nervous. I mean she was Mrs. Squibb."

If she were at home telling this story, my mother would flutter her right hand toward the blue café curtains she had sewn, washed, and starched herself. She'd give a backhand wave to the candy dish on the counter next to ripped *mappin'* to explain the difference between her way of life, and the life of Mrs. Squibb. If she were not sitting at the kitchen table, she would say hesitantly, at a loss to explain it, "Well, we are who we are."

"I was so nervous that I was actually sick"—she would clear her throat—"I mean I couldn't . . . just . . . we weren't in her league. I didn't know what to do. How could I have her to my house? I had to, but . . . I mean, I couldn't . . . just . . . not. Then I decided." My mother always took a deep breath at this point, to have the pleasure of resolving it again to her satisfaction. "She would be Mrs. Squibb, and I'd be Rose."

My sister Lucia decided she wasn't going to marry Jory in the hours just before the bridal shower Auntie Ag, her godmother, gave her at Mecca's, our favorite restaurant to have *abizz'* (pizza) when we didn't make it ourselves. But it was too late to cancel the shower. Lucia had to live through it. So that night we ate upstairs in Mecca's new private room, a classy southern Italian feast. It was the early sixties, so it was the first shower I'd ever been to that didn't take place in a living room filled with chairs borrowed from our families. The Mrs. Squibb and Rose dinner never took place.

It's my mother's "I'd be Rose" that gets to you. She knew her place. She'd be herself, but not presumptuously so. Not a Mrs., just a Rose. I've had my conflicts with my mother, but you have to love her for that story. Isn't that what all of us are struggling for most of our lives? To be Rose. Only who we are.

I thought of that story after the first time I met Simone. Simone, you could say, was Mrs. Squibb to me. Bill and I had been invited to teach at the University of Turin for one semester. Simone had been assigned as our host. An elegant, educated, poised, Northern Italian woman—*una Torinese pura*—she was Torinese and Torino was Simone.

TORINO: AT FIRST

I knew so little about the place. It was a city in Italy, and that was all Bill and I needed. We traveled often in the Mediterranean, and almost always managed to start in Italy. I had heard vaguely of the miracle of the Shroud of Turin. As for Torino itself, in America at our most knowledgeable, we might think of it as the home of Fiat. Although Fiat has been the economic heart of Torino, its factories in nearby Lingotto are tucked away where you're not going to see it, unless you stumble upon it or seek it out. These factories drew thousands of southern Italians—Lucani, Calabresi, Siciliani—to new work in the north. But they have little to do with the Torino one walks through, and lives in, everyday.

An industrial magnet, Torino is even more a court town, sophisticated and yet oddly provincial. It's a place of high manners and big closed doors. The

Torinesi comport themselves with elegant, prescribed manners and attitudes that can flourish magnificently and perfectly in a closed society.

It has a long tradition of intellectual life. Cesare Pavese and Primo Levi were born there, as was Luigi Einaudi, whose great house, one of the city's many, published their books. It's where the very idea of the unification of Italy arose and was achieved. It was the center of the *partigiani* in World War II. I knew nothing of this before we went to live there.

I learned just how sober and restrained a city Torino was. Very early in her efforts to school me in proper Torinese manners and ways, Simone explained to me in perfect, formal English, "We are a mountain people, we Piemontese; we come from the mountains where we are surrounded, closed off. We are used to that. We keep to ourselves. We don't let anyone in. That is why no one knows about our town. We don't invite strangers in."

My husband, and my nine-year-old son, James, and I were the strangers, but we were under the impression we had been invited in, with all of the usual excessive Italian hospitality this implied. Simone's statement offered, on the one hand, a welcoming explanation of the culture on whose shores we have arrived but also told us to expect being held at a certain distance, an arm stiffened against our approach.

In the United States I had been brought up to think of myself as an Italian almost more than as an American. Italian was who we were. It defined us. But in Torino we were the Americans, for the Torinesi and eventually for ourselves.

Bill would come to say that "The nice thing about Torino is that it's easy to get to Italy from there." Torino is the capital of the region of Piemonte, but Piemonte can be the least Italian of regions. It has something of Switzerland about it, in the Alps they share. It has much of France about it, a long legacy of switching territory and borders under its ruling House of Savoy. It is the only place where I have spent an extended time that left me longing for America, and it is the only place I have wept over when I left it.

What I saw when I arrived were the beautiful old baroque squares lined with arcades, large boulevards lined with handsome apartments and shops. Behind these boulevards are small *viali* that lead into tiny *piazzette*, which open, then quickly close and lead up, like a series of anterooms, to the grand Palazzo Saluzzo Paesana, and to the living room of Torino, Piazza San Carlo. This is some of what made me weep when we left, even though I ached with loneliness and isolation for most of our time there.

Torino was clothed in the solemnity of its past, worn like an exquisite, but understated, dress, hand sewn in a couture salon of a previous century, of a fabric that simply couldn't be created again. This dress would have been detailed with beads, tiny tucks, infinitesimal stitches made for a European courtly grandmother in dazzling youth. Although she came to be known only as a staid, upright grandmother, the dress told of her early beauty, of the rooms she had entered and devastated.

Piazza San Carlo is lined with tall, capacious arcades to protect its citizens from the harsh sun or driving rain. The shops on the Piazza are filled with expensive goods made of cashmere, tweed, linen, silk, and leather.

All over Torino were fine theaters, museums, bookshops, streets lined with luxurious food stores, open *mercati*. In short, it was a lovely old *European* city that evoked centuries of power. Now it was no longer filled with as much power, or as much money, or as much tourism, or as much modernity, as Milan or Genoa or Rome. But it has wealth, and it is both more provincial and, if not more beautiful, more evocative than its rivals.

Although its companies like Fiat and Olivetti are industrial powerhouses that drive the strong regional economy, they sit far enough from this sleepy dream of the past for Torino to live on in a slightly dusty, but very endearing, way. Visitors who came to see us while we lived there said things like, "Torino looks like St. Petersburg." Or, "It's as I imagine Vienna must have looked at one time."

The sense of living in another time and place was reinforced by the fact that I only once heard English spoken by someone I didn't know. I heard how foreign her American voice sounded in the market, how her American words rang out to her friend, breaking into the strange dream I didn't know I was in.

In Torino there were as many herb shops, *erboristerie*, as bookstores. There you stepped into a pharmaceutical world still made of forest, leaves, twigs, and rocks. The smells brought to mind steeping teapots and deep mineral baths where all your ills—psychic and physical—will be washed away.

Because Torino, unlike so much else of Italy, hadn't yet proffered its hand to tourism, parked cars filled these old formal Italian *piazze* and their emissions blackened San Carlo's beautiful old buildings—originally colored the deepest of Italian umbers—with a veil of dirt.

But there were cafés, bars, and thriving bookstores, bookstalls, book tables everywhere. Theatrical posters announced productions of obscure works, a run of Pirandello, a cycle of Shakespeare, or some Sam Shepard. The colors of seventeenth- and eighteenth-century buildings drifted achingly among ocher, umber, and sienna.

On Saturday, the day of pleasure shopping, every arrestingly good-looking young person in Torino came to the center of town dressed superbly. The beautiful young women wore skirts that swayed perfectly about their knees as they strode arm in arm through the arcades of San Carlo, laughing to the music of being young and stunning. Their pocketbooks made of rich leathers, swung to the tap of high heels, the sway of their skirts, and the swing of their hips. All of this hypnotic performance was for the handsome young men. Their long arms draped just so over each other's shoulders, they wore crisp shirts with sweaters loosely around their necks. In perfectly pressed pants, they moved in time to their own laughing and teasing and the crease of shoe leather against the stones. Their physical intimacy made me jealous of their right to their *italianità*. They promenaded all day into early evening, when armed with their purchases for next week's promenade, they crowded the cafés.

All Saturday, shoppers repaired to the cafés that lined Piazza San Carlo where upright *camerieri* awaited orders for coffee, gelato, biscotti. Older men and women ordered vermouths and other local aperitivi like Punt e Mes or Antica Formula, the herbal bittersweet in perfect balance. Sitting in these cafés among the Torinesi was like actually traveling back to another world. But young love had to find its way in this place of the past.

I'd lose sight of these young people until, on some other evening, I'd glimpse that they had managed to uncouple themselves from their friends, and to recouple into pairs longing for romance. They'd walk slowly toward the paths along the Po to become *inamorati*.

I never actually saw these young *bimbi* let go of their friends' shoulders or elbows to find their way to each other. Did they smile across the café tables under the arcades of Via Roma? Did the young men suggest a walk toward the Borgo Medioevale, a reproduction of the medieval village and castle in the Parco Valentino, chatting about when they had been taken there as children by their older sisters or cousins? Did their fingertips reach out slowly toward one another as they pretended to talk about the shirt they had just purchased? Did they first hold hands when they stopped by a tree, or watched the little boys kick a ball with their fathers?

I'd see them as they wandered slowly on the paths along the banks of the Po holding hands, then kissing on benches along the path, their intertwining. Next they'd be on a blanket on the grass, in those luscious tantalizing embraces that are sex without consummation. At least back then they had no access to bedroom, couch, car, roof, barn, or woods to hide themselves, and so built a wall of privacy by simply blocking out, not what we could see, but everything beyond each other, so enwrapped were they. I only saw them as their peers did, as boys and girls and then locked as couples. Did their family ever find them there? Did they know where they were? Had their parents been subjected to this same lovely torture?

PRELUDE

I didn't know anything about Torino or Piemonte the night I met Simone Novarre and her family when they were in New York for a brief visit over Christmas. All I knew was that she was a serious James Joyce scholar and a senior professor at the University of Torino, where we were going for one semester. She was elegant, upright, accomplished, and spoke perfect English. I was thrilled and intimidated.

I had recently turned forty-five. I'd made my deals with fate. I decided it was time for me to finally loosen the ancient grip of fear and timidity that my ancient provincial roots had on me. I decided I would be up to this time in Torino. I would enjoy it.

Simone's husband, Federico, was one of those European men with a soft, kind manner that makes you feel you are in a safe, serious, gallant world. He was also the director of one of the oldest publishing houses in Torino.

I liked them both immediately, but it was Chiara, their ten-year-old daughter, with whom I fell in love. She had a pale face with large, soft brown eyes that flashed from inside her small, contained being. Until then I thought this kind of face belonged to children from the south, from places like Naples or Marseille. The kind of face you see in old photographs of children from World War II, or the children in the tiny hill towns of my Lucania.

These children peer eagerly out as if their eyes are portals in the small fortresses of their lives. Their faces are also pale, their bodies are quiet, even their clothes are somber, but their eyes are bouncing beams of light. Is it because they are raised to stay within themselves, or because they are raised inside thick, firm walls of rules that when they stare beyond the familiar to the larger world, their eyes widen with curiosity? The children I knew most intimately in America lose this glint by the time they can run with ease. Our children are out in the world early, expected to take on everything they encounter easily, so that they have to close something down inside themselves for protection.

The night that I met the Simone and her family for the first time we were having dinner at the home of one of Bill's colleagues. Simone and her family were staying with that family while they visited New York City. Chiara had on a simple navy blue woolen dress trimmed with a white collar and cuffs. I felt I could try my simple Italian on her without being judged too harshly. Soon, the way she looked eagerly from face to face as adults spoke around her, the way she tucked her napkin in around her neck and ate with relish each of the dishes set before her, led me to complete surrender. Chiara was a child from my past—eager, obedient, worried about being good. When she came to a vegetable she didn't like she turned her face up to her mother's. "Mama," her eyes wide, brows raised, her forehead furrowed, a whisper of quick Italian. Simone nodded, murmured quick words in return, then turned to our hostess. "Would you excuse Chiara from eating this? She doesn't want to hurt your feelings." Simone seemed always to know how to deal with things with great poise and delicacy. Chiara, relieved, sat there eating, looking about her, demanding almost no attention other than to ask what was this dish or this one—is it good Mama?—then darting a smile to the hostess, as we talked and talked. She reminded me of my best friend from childhood, my cousin, Beatrice, the same large dark eyes set in her simple, seemingly almost plain face which suddenly transformed as I gazed at her across the table, into pale, subtle beauty.

I remarked at how beautiful I thought she was. "Yes," Simone said lifting her chin, "she surprises even us now. Sometimes when we look at her, we see it. It was not what we had expected."

Near ten o'clock, before dessert had been served, she said to her mother she was very tired and wanted to go to bed. "Fine," said Simone, "your father will take you up."

"No, no," Chiara protested. "I want you," quietly but with a look of real loss on her face.

"Don't you like your father's kisses?" I understood Simone to ask her.

"Yes, but I want you."

"Go," Simone said firmly and quietly. "I will come up in a little while and give you a kiss." With a small pout on her simple large features, Chiara held her father's hand and left the dining room.

After Chiara left, Simone said with a small tilt to her head and with a deep pride, "I didn't think I wanted to have a child, but I am so glad that I changed my mind. It teaches you everything. People are surprised to hear me say this, because I am a professional woman. I make a point of saying it," she said with such confidence. "It's really everything. You know so little until you become a parent." A woman who has everything, I thought, and knew it.

A little later Simone went upstairs to kiss Chiara goodnight, then returned quickly. I was surprised and impressed. Everything taken care of with equal dispatch. Nothing like the way I lived my life. I would never have brought my only son, then nine, with me. He wouldn't have sat still at the table. He wouldn't have eaten the grownup food. He would have begged to be allowed to go and watch television.

It was a lovely evening. We had talked about New York, Torino, a little about books, about the centenary James Joyce conference that Simone had organized in Dublin. Bill and I had been there too. Wasn't that funny? No, Bill hadn't presented. Though I was sure my effusiveness about Chiara was too intense, I felt I had comported myself with my only recently acquired, adult self-possession. As we drove home I wondered: what about the fact that my family is from the south of Italy? What will the Torinesi think of that? I knew about all the southern Italian workers who had moved to Torino to work in the Fiat factory. Young members of my family in Italy had been among them, to the great pride of their parents, my great aunts and uncles.

Well, I thought, thinking of Simone's regal blond head, her straight carriage, her elegant English, she'll be Simone and I'll be Joanna.

My mother Rose was brought up to work extremely hard, to rush to fill all duties and obligations, and to take her pleasure with great joy where and when it presented itself. My husband says she liked to have a good time. My father said with great affection, "She's a good-time Charlie." I am one of the few people who had difficulty with her. She was fairly universally loved. But our blood must have pulsed differently, or maybe too simultaneously, because we fought the whole of our many years together. She thought me too wild, out of control. I thought of her as too prissy and concerned, always and mostly, with the rules of comportment.

When I lived in Torino my mother was seventy-three and was still the prettiest woman at the dance. She had bleached-blond hair, done in local Waterbury fashion. It was a hairdo that, with the same carefully placed and fixed sweeps and curls is not unlike the formal coiffures of the old European courts. It mattered very much to her how she looked, and she looked fabulous. She dressed carefully. She never went out without makeup, high heels, with scarf and bag to match her clothes. When I was a child she also wore gloves and a hat to match for our outings.

She had, moreover, the confidence that comes to a favorite daughter. Chosen by her father to take care of his business correspondence when she was seven years old, she inherited a mantle of work, trust, and approval. Though she would never have allowed herself to think of herself this way, she was clearly his favorite daughter, perhaps even his favorite child. She married well and was a leading light among her peers on how things should be done. She was well thought of, she thought well of herself, and she was, according to my father, the prettiest woman wherever they went. She would have fit into Torino perfectly, like she did in most places.

I am said to look like her, but my hair is dark and loose. I care about clothes and how I dress, but I want more freedom than her world permits. I wear no girdles. I wear low comfortable shoes, or very high heels. Never having been the prettiest woman at any dance, I turned early to looking sexy, dramatic, smart to mark an occasion. Eventually, though, I just wanted to look presentable and to feel comfortable. My husband said to me early in our courtship, "You look like young Anna Magnani." He was worried I would hear the whole of that remark. And I did, sexy yes, but more interesting than pretty. So that is what I looked like then. Not pretty, but other things. I had to fashion my own world, one so different from hers.

SIMONE IN NEW YORK

When Simone and her family were visiting in New York that Christmas before we left to live in Torino, we arranged an outing focused mostly on our two children. It was to be our day as hosts. James hadn't been with us the night, that I met the Novarre's for the first time. He had been staying with my mother for a few days, so we could finish packing and making the arrangements for a long sojourn abroad.

James adored my mother. She was a perfect grandmother. She was full of gifts, remembrances, and love. She marked each occasion with florid attention. She came to every play, sat by the bath for hours "playing baker man," baked cookies, sent cards, always brought small gifts of toys to mark each day she spent with her grandchildren as a special moment. Excessive for someone else, for small grandchildren and their grandmother, these fussings were exactly right. She never tired of her job as a grandmother with any of her grandchildren, there was nothing but love in every direction. The day we were hosting the Novarres, Bill went to pick them up, and James and I were to meet them in front of the restaurant where we were having lunch. After that we would set out to see the West Side of Manhattan, go to several museums, and later have dinner.

Simone insisted repeatedly on the phone, "This must be a day for the children, not for ourselves the adults." Good values, I thought. My new love, Chiara, had probably had it with all these academic dinners.

James looks a good deal like me. He has my dark eyes, the same curve to his cheeks, but he is topped with a soft haze of light-colored hair like my mother's must have been at one time. Sometimes too, he looks like my mother—never more so than when he smiles in his largest, happiest way. I never love him more than when I see her smile on his face. Such a joining.

But his spirit is not like his grandmother's. It's like mine, like my father's. It is full of intensity, energy, high highs and low lows. It's full of play, passion, spirit. Our brains are quick, high pitched, rarely cool. We are quiet only when we are exhausted or absolutely alone, which we rarely are. We crave stimulation, companionship, movement the way other people need air. But in rare quiet times, a deep peace can come over us. Walking in the woods, reading a book, very early in the morning, very late at night. I worry about what from my family I have carried forward. Being the bearer of my father's spirit has concerned me because I have not worn it easily. But it is not a spirit to be worn lightly. Perhaps, too, because I am not a man, and surely because it cost me my mother. I am not her daughter as much as I am my father's daughter.

When I knew I was pregnant, I knew two things. I wanted a boy and I wanted him to be a wild one. I wanted to prove that it was possible to mother such a child without making that intensity seem bad. I am not at all certain I raised James always right or well, that I served either his spirit or the customs of the conventional world. People still come up to me and say, "Remember that time that James . . ." and then tell me about one of his adventures. For them, James was a shock and a surprise, but I never remembered their story because that was our everyday with James. James was just as hard to raise as, apparently, I must have been.

When James and I arrived at Popovers on Amsterdam Avenue, it was, as usual, crowded. But in New York the week after Christmas, every restaurant is. So I had come armed with a small fuzzy toy, called a Koosh Ball. We played catch in front of the restaurant while we waited for them. When we saw them and went to greet them, James moved close to my body. I saw Chiara move close to Simone at the same moment. That was almost the last tranquil moment of my day. After that, a collision of cultures, personalities, values, and other confusions clanged around the six of us.

We went in knowing we could count on a table fairly soon. Ten minutes, we were reassured by the hostess. "I'm going to take the children out to play on the sidewalk," I announced, proud of my child-centered resourcefulness. On Simone's face was a small piece of tension that I didn't understand or even really absorb until much later.

The kids and I went outside and played catch on the sidewalk. Chiara and James seemed to be getting along well without any words. We played monkey in the middle. I was mostly the monkey.

Soon, Simone arrived on the sidewalk, her brows raised, one hand extended to Chiara: "We must go in now," each word more clearly pronounced than the last. She barely looked at me. The situation had been righted. Nothing can make my innards wince more than the feeling that I am out of sync with those whose good opinion I desire. Nothing more than a small gesture is needed for me to feel that obtaining someone else's good opinion is beyond me.

We went in and James sat to my right, his knees bent so that he could more readily reach the breadbasket. "I'm hungry Mom," he said. "I want a hamburger and french fries. When are they going to bring the food?" We hadn't ordered yet.

"How about if that's all you have now, Pumpkin?" I said when he had eaten two large slices of bread slathered with butter. Bill was talking to Federico about the publishing industry in Torino. Simone was sitting to my left.

"But he won't eat lunch if he has so much bread, will he?" Simone turned to remind me.

"Yes, probably that's true," I answered, doing my best to lift my chin—I got it about half way up. I was still determined to hide the struggles that were an everyday part of my life with James. My own lack of conviction surfaced constantly in those days, whenever I was feeling uncertain about which world of rules I was living in: was I in the Upper West Side, let him eat bread, what do I care world? Or the, he must listen to me, I am in his Italian mother universe? I looked over to see Chiara's dark eyes looking from her mother to James, then at me. Simone's eye darted down and away from me.

Simone shook off my words and turned to bring up a small wrapped box and handed it to me. She was protecting me from embarrassment, covering for me. "I brought you something from Italy."

No rules in my family are more precisely regulated and nuanced than the gift-giving rules: you arrive at someone's house with your hands full. Usually food, either something that you have prepared, or that you have bought for more than you can actually afford. For every occasion there are strict rules about how much to spend, what trouble you should go to, shaped by decades of what was given to you or your family on similar occasions. If you violate these protocols, at some point it will be discussed. You will be discussed. What you should have given, or done, makes the rounds of the family gossip. This is deeply Italian. We keep to rules of gift giving and hospitality that are as ancient as Homer.

When Chiara's box was placed on my plate, a package of Italian obligations and counterobligations landed next to it. I had given two Koosh Balls to Chiara. It had not occurred to me that we were already entering the gift relationship. I had assumed that would wait for our arrival in Italy.

"Oh that's so lovely of you to think of me." I smiled broadly, making sure to show ample gratitude.

"No, no," Simone smiled full of goodness, then looked off at an American family across from us whose two small boys were eating soup, "it's just a little something from Italy."

I pulled the delicate beige tissue open, and lifted a square of heavy dark-blue silk with deep red flowers in one corner. The silk was dense like satin. I held the weight of it between my fingers to show how much I loved it, running my fingers along the hand-rolled hem. Hermes, it said, then in script the word, *Paris*. My eyes traced the undulations of each letter, as I noticed that Simone's eyes were tracing mine.

"Well, all of these scarves are made in Italy anyway," she tossed her head, shaking her short blond coif.

"Oh, it's so elegant. You're just too lovely to have brought this to me." I hid my bewilderment and pulled myself into the appropriate posture.

I kissed her delicately on the cheek. "You're very kind," I said, aware that James was reaching for a fourth piece of bread.

"Mom, could you butter this for me?"

I reached for the butter with a wide smile on my face sharing my beneficence with everyone at the table. "Of course, James."

The mixture of kindness, confusion, politeness, and anxiety was forming a pattern that was to mark almost all our connections.

I uncurled my spine as long as I was able. "You know my family is Italian."

"But no, where are they from?" Simone asked, relieved to be on ground that could only please us both.

"All of my grandparents came to America from Lucania, also known as Basilicata, one town called Tolve and the other is called Avigliano, both about twenty kilometers from Potenza." I'm proud that I can say Aviglianese, Tolvese, that I can use kilometer, that I can say *dalla regione di Basilicata* or alternately *sono Lucana* with the right penultimate accent, even if my Italian is mostly only good enough to travel with.

"Oh," hesitantly, then, "really." Simone looked down and away to her left. "When did they come?"

"Well, they came during the great immigrant wave at the turn of the century. First, my grandfather, who went back and married my grandmother and then left. She had a baby, Arcangela. She built her own house and waited for my grandfather to come home. But he didn't come home."

"My mother's family had been cheese makers. My father's family had been blacksmiths and then ironworkers." Artisanal skills were the pride of these parts of our family. I pictured my grandmother's arthritic hands deep in hot salty water, kneading the fresh cheese, stretching it into long plaits above the water, twisting it, squeezing the water from it, then submerging it again to knead it again. I could taste the fresh, fresh still-wet cheese, crisscrossed with hatching from the twigs woven into its basket. I could see her hands molding the cheese into little birds, pigs, cows.

Our mothers' stories: "You know we had no toys. Not like you girls have," Mama used to make us dolls and animals out of cheese. You can't imagine. To have a doll. Then one night she said to me, " '*Port' la' bambol*,'" my mother laughs when she tells this story. She dumped my baby into *'a minestra*. Someone once gave my Aunt Archangela a real doll, and one of our uncles took the doll out of her hands and smashed it to the ground. "You don't need that thing. What do you need a doll for?" When those women grew up their children were given dolls and toys in abundance.

On Amsterdam Avenue, sitting with Simone, Federico, and Chiara at Popovers, our food had arrived while I thought about my grandmother's dark spotted hands submerged underwater "to work the cheese." Then my eyes found Simone's manicured nails elegantly poised to cut Chiara's hamburger into bite-sized pieces.

I chatted on, determined to make Simone see my pride. "Most of the family stayed in the south, although much later on, in the sixties, some of my cousins went to Torino to work at Fiat."

"Oh," Simone said in her flat certain tones. "That was a terrible time, really terrible. Before that Torino was so small and everyone knew each other. But that really changed Torino when those people came.

"Your people ruined our city. Our city was pure before they came. We were all Piemontese. We were all the same. There weren't others. It was so wonderful before they came." She looked at me directly, clear, without apology.

My prattling stopped. The loud hum of vibration inside began.

"Mom, I don't like this hamburger. It's no good." James clamored for my attention. "I want more bread."

"But he hasn't really eaten," Simone said to me, very concerned. "What will you do?"

How do I document all the endless tiny details of the day that left me certain that I had failed? To be a proper hostess, a good guide, a proper mother. Most importantly, that I had failed to be Joanna, while she was Simone. There were many episodes that trapped me between her values, between her bourgeois Italy, and my Waterbury peasant world I had tried so hard to leave. Instead, I found myself stranded, wanting to meet Simone on her ground, and wanting to stand my own.

Later that day we arrived at the Metropolitan Museum of Art, where James decided that he, at any rate, would be a good host. He got a floor plan for Chiara and himself. He intended to lead Chiara to something he thought worthy of her attention. We always gave him his wishes in the Met, which at nine, he knew pretty well. We did this so that he would love going to museums and not see them as places of duty, but rather of adventure. He loved maps and finding his way around with them. And he did lead me to things that I would never have found alone. Museums were not dull, quiet places for him. They were exciting, crazy.

Simone and Federico thought it was unusual at least that James should appoint himself guide in a serious museum. It was clear that what Simone saw as a day for the children was not the day I saw. By then I had begun to understand each tiny wince of Simone's and to see that I would indeed not get to be Joanna, while she definitely *would* be Simone.

When I realized how stunned she was, I explained that James was trying to show off for Chiara's sake. Simone and Federico found this curious, even interesting, but definitely wrong. In a jerky way, sometimes James leading, sometimes me steering, we started around the museum. James would run ahead to show how well he knew the floor plan, and then I would pull him back to show my son wasn't completely out of control. I have always been able to walk through the Met blindfolded—I know its turns that well—but James and I both misled our party to each of the galleries we wanted to see. In these situations, my husband usually thinks me paranoid and foolish, and that all is going swimmingly, saying what a jolly time we're having. It apparently seems so to him.

We were in the American Wing courtyard when James, I could see, had had enough. Simone and Federico, who collect Japanese art, wanted to go to the Japanese rooms. I suggested that perhaps I would stay in the garden with the children, playing some quiet kind of game. I thought it would give everyone a moment of relief. Simone and Federico could proceed as adults and really look. The children could be children and relax, and I could be briefly off the hook.

Simone seemed even more stunned by my idea than she was by my son and said firmly, "No, Chiara must come and look with us." I had lost whatever ground I might have started the day with. I crumpled into the sureness of my failure. Her child knew how to behave in a museum and mine, apparently, did not.

By now I had swung my pendulum to the furthest point of anguish. James was a bad child, out of control. I was his feckless mother. At each restless gesture that he made I said no, no, no, he could not walk quickly, could not race ahead of us, he could not, not. Not. Needless to say he got worse and worse, and I was in despair. Mercifully, the museum finally closed, and I insisted that we go, at least briefly, to the playground nearby. I knew that if James didn't run soon he would burst, and I would disintegrate further. So, though it was dark by now, we went and sat on the cold benches and let the children climb and jump. I was pleased to see that Chiara's long legs were not used to running much, and I could happily think to myself that, well, there is at least something they are clearly not doing well by her, a miserable sort of satisfaction. Just then, as we sat on the cold benches, in the dark, while the children ran, Federico said in his kind voice, "It's tiring being the guides."

All I wanted at that moment was to go home and sink into the certainty that the our journey to Torino was sure to be rocky going.

By the time we were headed to the American Museum of Natural History, I really wanted a drink. I thought we could stop at some nearby restaurant, but each place said it was dinner hour. My desperation made me feel more and more foolish for needing a drink. They could see how tense I was, and that I didn't even know the customs of my own neighborhood. By the time we were sitting in the 3D movie at the Museum of Natural History, all tired and James moaning out loud about how hungry he was—"I'm starving Mommy, I can't wait"—I had fallen under a small cloud of grief.

We all made the best of it, got through dinner and went home. I had a scotch before dinner. Simone and Federico reminded me that scotch was meant for after dinner. "You really should only drink light drinks before dinner, like vermouth. You'll get sick. Scotch before dinner will make you sick."

For several days after there was a heavy silence on both of our parts, until Bill confessed to me one morning that he was now apprehensive about what our experience in Torino was likely going to be, given what happened with the Novarres that day. He's the one who always says, wasn't it jolly? isn't it nice to spend the day with friends? whenever I am convinced things are going bad for us socially. His confession made it clear we really were in trouble. All hope of being Joanna had faded. My mother was lost to me once again.

But we had been getting ready to go for months. I had given notice at my job. There was really no way to back out. I merely expressed my worries to my closest friends and tried to think about how joyous our life in Paris had been when Bill was a visiting professor there.

IN TORINO

We took our stay in Torino as an opportunity to drive down from Paris, stopping to visit friends and seeing places we hadn't been to before. The night before we were to arrive, Bill spent a great deal of time trying to phone Simone from Switzerland.

This was long before cell phones, and every phone call left you standing in some small box that was badly lit, trying to discern what those enigmatic symbols on the front of the phone meant. There were heavy brass tokens to be bought at the *tabac*, but when you were in an extremely busy café, bar, or hotel, they weren't even going to take our order, much less going to help us with the phone.

All through dinner Bill jumped up to race to the phone booth out in the hall to have another go at it. Finally, when you do figure it out, you realize that it is all perfectly clear and perfectly easy. When you travel to places where you don't know the customs of the country, it's a wonderful kind of regression. You get to visit the time of your childhood when you learned to master all kinds of ordinary activities, like using the phone, going to the store, going to the post office to mail a package—the simplest activities become moments of triumph.

Bill finally reached Simone and he came back to dessert pleased to have accomplished his task, laughing, happy. "She says that they've been waiting for us for two days, because I said we'd be there around the twentieth. The landlady has been frantically getting everything ready for us. She's very fussy apparently."

My face doesn't go into a miserable wince, it tightens. I look old, and tired, when I am worried.

"It's all right. Everything's all right. She was very jolly." This kind of reassurance from Bill is the equivalent of saying to a child, "Don't cry, everything will be all right," when a favorite doll has just been run over by a car. Get over this so I can move on to other matters. I began to breathe shallowly for the next few hours, which is as close as I can come to holding my breath and still stay alive. "The landlady's very fussy," made many a round trip in my brain that night. What am I going to do about James? The one conclusion I had come to during the two weeks between our day in New York with Simone, Federico, and Chiara and our leaving was that my son was *not* going to be sacrificed to this situation. I had burdened him with enough already. I couldn't add on the conflicts of the new world and the old. I had to find some way to deal with this, and now I had another element to deal with as well, our landlady, Signora Frari whom my family always called La Signora.

The idea of protecting James as a lively, curious, inventive child with all of his natural speed and flashes of humor and playfulness, has been my mission from the time I understood that I had had a child just like myself. This plan for being James's mother was that he wasn't going to be sacrificed, as I had been, to my mother's ancient gods of strict manners, excessive gift giving, and all rigid rules and customs.

Now there was the mad, wonderful La Signora in our lives. When I first met her I wanted very much to call her Madame. She was just that, a large woman of heft and presence, a matron in charge of all that comes under her purview. Eventually I settled on La Signora, because it gave me what I needed, a title for her. Perhaps *padrona*, chief, or boss, would have been better suited to her, but she was La Signora to us.

The day we arrived in Torino, Simone met us at the apartment. Bill and James were out looking for milk when Chiara appeared in the bedroom where I was unpacking. I was so surprised and pleased to see my little friend there in front of me. "Chiara," I said and hugged her. It was obvious to her, and to her parents who stood watching, how much I liked her.

We had been traveling for ten days. We were scruffy, wrinkled, and tired, but we were happy too. Simply arriving in Italy is always reason for celebration.

We had come to the home of nurturance, the nurturance you get from good food, kind people, from looking at things of great beauty every day. Italy's a country that comforts you. It's a place that makes you happy. Each time I cross the border I feel an inner lift of spirits. "I'm in Italy," my body says, thrilled. "I am home." The apartment that Simone had spent weeks looking for was wonderful. It was in an old building. It was charming, clean, nicely furnished, beautifully laid out. It had a large kitchen, larger than I had ever had, with an enormous kitchen table. I was more than indebted to her. So when Federico asked how I was, I could answer truthfully, "I am tired, but very happy."

Simone seemed very relaxed, happy. The kids were off playing in the living room. They had brought us bags of goodies: many bottles of wine and a large bottle of scotch, "When I told the Signora that you like to drink," Simone said, "she wanted to bring you something, but I said that we would do that." And then many bags of food, pasta, pizza that her mother had made, and salad and bread and butter and oil and cheese. There were beautiful new heavy linens that looked like wedding presents she hadn't ever dared use. Now they were here for us. It was overwhelming. "Well, everything is closed. You won't find anything to eat. We had assumed you would eat with us."

I could only wonder what they might have been thinking about us in the short time we arrived. But they were certainly being kind, generous, and helpful. Why are they doing all this for us? But I realized the deeper question about her generosity was, what would I have to do to reciprocate? My worry meant that I had lost my way enough that I no longer had any ruler to use, no way to gauge myself or anyone else.

Over the next few days I kept thinking about how my mother would handle this. She would have anticipated every nuance of Simone's behavior. She would have come with the right gifts, greetings, and her impeccable manners. There was never any dilemma for her about these kinds of situations. In fact they were her métier. She might have been briefly thrown by her encounter with Mrs. Squibb, but she had been prepared to deal with it. There was never uncertainty in her about what to do. Facing Simone and La Signora, I thought of her often, that she would know just what to do. She's never at a loss where obligations and ceremony are concerned. You do. You do a lot. You do as much as you can think of. And then you do more. You become the best in the gift game of manners, hospitality, and customs.

In my America, in New York City, this kind of behavior is extended only to people you love dearly or to those whom you are greatly indebted. Not for those who are indebted to you. Perhaps this was why I was unable to calculate either her or my own behavior.

Bill and Simone began to do business. Federico and I helped the children across the language barrier. They were playing a game. James let Chiara win one round of the game he was teaching her, but when she teased him at the end it became too much for him, and he beat her royally in the next. Federico said, "He's very bossy isn't he?" I laughed and said yes, but my heart sank.

"Now, Joanna, let me tell you where the markets are and which ones are the best," Simone said. I love food, marketing, cooking. Still the fact that this was instantly assigned to me seemed for a moment odd, until I realized that this was probably exactly Simone's province. Along with everything else, it seemed.

Simone began to explain about La Signora and how she was very worried that everything should be just so for us and left us fruit and juice and soda and beer. Where now to begin? I had just arrived and I had already incurred enough social debts to keep me panicked the whole of my visit here—in the country of my origins. But then Torino is and isn't Italy. It wasn't my Italy, not the version of Italian village in which I had been raised nor the rest of Italy I had traveled in extensively, and certainly not my family's Italy.

Simone began to go over things about the apartment that the Signora had asked her to tell us about. One was not to move the drain in the shower, "Not that you would. I don't know why she thinks that you would?" We were not to go out and leave the windows open. No we wouldn't. We were to make sure that the shutters were secured by their hooks. We would. She, the Signora, would show us how to use the washing machine. Fine. As Simone explained things to us, Federico turned to us to explain, "I asked Simone if she's the kind of woman who will be up here all the time?" No, no, Simone said with a shake of her head, not at all.

Federico had to leave. He had a business engagement, just now. He was most apologetic, we must forgive him, business called. "Simone, could I have some money. I haven't any on me."

Simone laughed, "He's like Agnelli, the president of Fiat," she explained. "He goes out without anything in his pockets. Just like that."

Simone seemed to be a woman who took care of everything. Still, she was more relaxed here than in New York. When she instructed James that "when you see Signora Frari you must stand very still," she mimicked a stiff soldier, with humor and playfulness. I could hear though, her concern about how James would behave was serious.

This was the bedrock of our relationship. What does she think of us? How are we seen? Was I right to think she sees James as difficult? But then didn't I, too? Yes, but I adore him too. Had she said something, however discreet, for one could always count on Simone's manners, to La Signora?

SETTLING IN?

That was Sunday. On Monday Bill had to go to Milan to pick up the luggage we had shipped, and James and I spent the day exploring Torino together. We found a place to change some money and go to the *mercato* to buy some food. I felt adventurous and ready. James's natural way of walking down the street is to whistle as he runs, then turn back to us to shout something, then perhaps to hop over whatever obstacle he found nearby to serve his gymnastic purposes. Even as he goes he sings favorite songs from American musical comedies. Mostly I accept this. When he began to climb the traffic poles in New York, I insisted he stop, but he was never going to be a child who could sit still easily. For that matter, he didn't become an adult who could sit still easily, either. I understand him too well, having so much of the same restlessness in me. If only had I understood him less, perhaps I would have mothered him better.

But here in Torino, the great city that my poor relatives had ruined, his delightful, intense boyish ways worried me. I suddenly felt a new grasp of something my grandmother used to say frequently, "What are the people going to think?" We once laughed at those anonymous people out there always haunting the byways of her life. But in Torino I knew just why and to what end she used to say that all the time. The Torinesi might dismiss my illiterate grandmother, but I could see how very much they had both come from the same world.

What would people think of my son here in Torino? And what would they think of me as his mother. James was on edge himself. "I don't want to go out there. I don't like it when people stare at us," he said letting me know just how anxious he was. Mostly he had lived in a world that he knew, that loved him for his charming and curious self. The doormen on every street we lived always smiled when he walked down the street. I had never seen him shrink from new situations, but once in a great while there could suddenly be a flash of very real discomfort. This was one of those times. In Torino, just walking down the street made him uncomfortable, and he'd balk completely. I waited awhile, then used my ultimate bait.

"I bet we could find at least one game of Shinobi along the way."

"I don't care Mom, I'm not going out there. "For him to resist his favorite video game told me how miserable he was feeling. We had found it in Paris, and it became his treat at the end of sightseeing expeditions. It gave us the balance between his needs and ours

"I'll stay here by myself. You go Mom." But I was right to count on video magic, and after a while the pull was too strong. "Well, how many games would I be allowed to play?"

We left the house to find our way to Porta Nuova, the train station, peering in many small bars to see if there were video machines inside. James began in his usual manner. He was at this time very involved in learning the words from the musical *Gypsy*, so he began to sing, "Some people can get a thrill, knitting sweaters and sitting still, that's okay for some people . . . " in his usually loud, kid, uneven tones. There were two old women holding onto one another, as they walked to the *mercato*. They looked around, not so much as with disapproval, as with total sober surprise.

"James you can't sing on the street here. People will think we're odd."

"Mom, see, I told you people look at us," he said to me annoyed and righteous.

"Well, if we act like them they won't look at us." So we proceeded. He went rushing past the two women to look in the window of a bar to see if they had videos.

"James, James," I rushed round them in a wide berth, "you can't rush by people, you'll push them." There were no videos in that bar. Off we went again. But along the way, each gesture and stance he took seemed untoward, noisy, full of too much haste. I corrected him with rising annoyance. And for a long time he was in such a good mood about looking for Shinobi that it didn't matter. We did find several places where we found games, none of them "his games," but he played at each of them. I got to look around.

I noticed though, that he was right. People *were* looking at us. Because of our English and because he was playing video games. In Europe, video games seemed to be for young men and bad teenagers, associated with drugs, idleness, generally unacceptable ways.

I was so hard on him, which even I began to wonder how he was staying so cheerful through all my admonitions. He did all right for most of our outing, but by the end his mood had turned, and I felt as if I had done exactly what I had vowed not to, turned on him.

La Signora and Simone were mirrors of where I would see my inadequacies. But Torino mirrored them both.

When Bill and I met at City College, where I had gone to get a master's degree, I had begun to despair of getting married. Worst was the possibility of not having children. If you are brought up in an Italian American family, children are more central to life than even food is. There were always babies around me, several each year, and always the joyous focus on the newest ones. Not just by the women and girls whose care these babies were entrusted to, but by old men and teenage boys alike. Babies were simply the most important thing that could happen to anyone, and without them is not a way to live.

But Bill was a catch-22. He was lovely, smart, warm, friendly, and clearly wrong for me. He is seventeen years older than I am, and at the time that I met him he had two older teenage daughters from a previous marriage. Moreover, he made it clear that he didn't want to have more children. So I promptly took him up. He was perfect for me. Lots of trouble.

Even more so because we are really supremely well matched. There's a similar hysteria of large gestures, operatic longings, a love of literature. There's an appetite for noisy goings on. We were both so lonely we could hardly breathe. So what with the goods that lay between us, and the rather complete impossibility of the situation, we took each other up with a vengeance. And we spent the next three years squandering our time and energy fighting about having children. He wanted none, but would concede to one. I wanted many, but would concede to two. It was the perfect state of stasis if you both want and are afraid of proceeding with your life.

I was thirty-five when James was born. He was, from the moment of conception, what I cared about most. The morning that he was born, when I reached down to pull him from me, when I took his little wet, red body from inside my own, the words that came from as deep inside as he had been, unbidden were, "Honey, I've waited for you for so long." Perhaps too long. Because I am still in awe that I have him with me.

Mothering him has been fraught with worry that I am too involved with him, not involved enough. That I ask too little, that I ask too much. That I let him down, that I hold him up. Despite this, he is lively, smart, with an interesting turn of brain, a strong body, a strong mind, and a generous nature. He has been nothing if not a lively companion. He began to climb out of his crib before he was a year. He spoke early and well. And his senses are keen. Once, when we moved from one part of town to another and left some friends behind, walking down the street he said to me, "Lizzie," his much beloved babysitter, "is near, I smell her." He was two then. A woman passing by was wearing Lizzie's perfume. He was also difficult, demanding, self-involved, and as Federico pointed out, bossy. All this was true.

There were several reasons why it was difficult for me to mother him as I had wanted to—without worry, in a calm and confident way. My mother had no trouble with the certainty of her rules, what she would teach us, and how we were to behave. She only had trouble with me. As a result, I hate rules and convention utterly. On the other hand, there was enough trouble between us that I came to be convinced that I was a bad type, so often disobedient. Caught between two poles of bad and bad, you don't come out with a good sense of how to proceed. Both ways damn you.

On the other hand, my obsession with how I am perceived makes me the goodest bad girl anyone has ever known.

I thought when I started with James that I would make sure that he knew his liveliness and energy were good qualities, to be cherished by both of us. I know that I passed on all of my inner divisions, and who but a child, can intuit such things better in a mother?

Simone and Torino locked onto my confusions perfectly. I bring them with me wherever I go. Perhaps the crux of our problem was in my not only admiring, but really liking Simone, and wanting her good opinion of me.

LA SIGNORA

Bill had met La Signora first. And as he told it, he was so taken with her kindness and warmth that at his very first meeting, on that very first day, he had announced to all of us, Simone, Federico, the children, and me, that he had kissed her. "She's wonderful. She's so kind." I looked at Simone when he said that, and she just put her head back and laughed. Of course, this is exactly this that I most love about my Bill, but I asked myself what the rest of Torino would think.

Over the next few days Margarita, La Signora's lovely daughter, would appear with a message from her mother. "Please to let me tell you how to use the dishwashing machine." Or, "Please not to use the clothes washing machine. I don't know how, and my mother will come tonight to show you." Then a few days would pass. "Do you have enough blankets because we can give more to you. I will take this one," she said, "because it is belonging to my niece." A few nights later. "Please be very careful with the kitchen sink faucet because last year it sent water down through the ceiling, use it but be careful. Please don't remove the drain from the shower." Now the sleeping bag is in her hands again. "Here you can use this for James. My mother will come tomorrow morning to show you how to wash the clothes." It was an odd mixture of concerns, about whether they were being kind enough to us, or if we knew the rules.

My anxiety rose with each of these visits. As for the washing machine lessons, we would usually wait for them for a half an hour past the appointed time, then phone and Margarita would call and say it would be later. Soon, later. And as the laundry reached mountainous heights, I grew worried about the endlessly deferred lesson on the washing machine.

I held fast to Simone's words that James should be very quiet when he met her. One day, as James and I were walking down our street, *via Belfiore*, we found a *sala di gioca,* a video game parlor, on our own block. This was enough to wipe out any anxiety James might have had about living in Italy, away from his home, friends, school, or language. "And they have Shinobi, Mommy." As we stepped away from the window of the *sala* to go home, we saw Bill in front of our building waving madly to us. Then I saw La Signora. She was large, and she had on a long large grey cape with a full fur collar, topped by the distinctive feathered cap of the Alpini, Italy's elite mountain soldiers. She stood by Bill, waving her arms, gesturing madly to us. We went to meet her. She was as full of noise and gesture as we were. Though she belabored things, and repeated and repeated, no matter how often we'd say, "*Ho capito,*" we got to know what she meant. But she had so much to say.

That day she told us in a very friendly way that she had heard James on the stairs, and she made the motion with her hands of his feet going, "*budlump budalump sulla scale.*"

All day long in Torino you heard the rumble of cars and motorcycles, but never anyone shouting on the street or even speaking loudly; no singing, no whistling.

Not that La Signora was a quiet type. Take, for example, the night she came at last to show us how to use the washing machine.

The doorbell rang. As La Signora entered with her daughter Margarita, she began to sniff the air loudly, several times as she stopped in the hallway. She didn't say anything. Was the house unaired? Did I leave the windows closed at the wrong time, open at the wrong time. Had I cooked the wrong dinner?

We proceeded to the washing machine. First she pointed to the windows. We were not to leave them open when we left the house. Fine. We were not to leave the shutters unhooked. The wind. She would first give her orders in simple clear Italian, and I would say, "*Va bene, ho capito.*" Then she would turn to Margarita and say something over again for Margarita to translate. And I would try to reassure her that I would do exactly as the Signora wished. Always, always.

She showed me how to put the clothes in. Not balled up like this, but loosely folded like that. We repeated the lesson several times. Then I took a pair of Bill's jeans and softly rolled them up and placed them gently to show her I was learning my lesson. No. I hadn't zippered the zipper. Then we went through the soap lesson. First you must put water softener in, because the water's hard. Then the soap, then the *ammorbidente*, the fabric softener. *Va bene.* Now if the clothes are *really* dirty you must use this, another box of soap. And you must use this, a bottle of bleach. She repeated its name in Italian over and over. Now the water cycle. The lesson continued. It didn't seem to matter how much I indicated that I understood. Apparently the lesson was beyond me.

Margarita rescued me by interrupting her mother, telling us to hang the clothes outside in the drying room. "*Ma dov'è la chiave?*" Do you have the key? We said we didn't have it. Mama, did you bring it? No, La Signora said, I didn't. When will you? I won't, said her mother. But why? A large Italian shrug, her eyes on her daughter as if to say I don't want to. Then they left.

For several days in a row La Signora appeared at the door to show me that the lights had been left on in the hallway. Bill was doing this unbeknownst to me. But somehow I was always home alone when she came to show me that the lights were on again. Then she might notice that I had moved a lamp and express concern that it would get broken in the place I had put it. I really began to worry about the house being ready for her. Had I opened the windows enough? Had I closed the windows enough?

She also reminded me of one of my favorite great aunts who had a reputation for being fresh, funny, full of beans. La Signora was like that too.

"I'm going right now," she told us one day as we met her leaving the building, "to get your extra key, for the apartment, for the downstairs for the mailbox." Then she rushed over to the mailbox. "I'll have them write on the keychain, Herman, Professore Herman, Dottore Professore Herman." Then she turned to us with a shake of the head, "Herr Professore Dottore Presidente Herman." You had to love her. Weeks later, only one of the keys turned up.

"My mother would know just how to handle her," I explained to Bill. "She'd have them eating out of her hand in a couple of days. She'd overwhelm her with presents, cups of coffee. La Signora would love her."

Simone called regularly. "Do you need an apron? I forgot to bring one."

"I don't normally use one, Simone. I dress very casually." How I wished she might do less for us. Maybe then I could figure out what I was supposed to do.

"I would like to have a welcome party for Bill and you, of course, and Franco (the department chair) will be returning to Genoa for the weekend, so I was thinking of Wednesday, but then I was worried about the children. Do you think that they should be there?" It would be fine for James either way.

"Well Chiara would go to bed whenever I told her of course, but . . . "

"I'm not concerned about James. But perhaps it would run rather late. Well, then I could take him home and Bill could stay on."

"Yes, perhaps that would be better. If James were here it might be difficult for Chiara to go to bed. Bill could certainly get a ride home." We circled one another as we sought some ground to stand on. But as the episodes with La Signora unfolded, I began to tease Simone.

"More tales of La Signora," I'd say cheerily.

"Oh dear," she'd reply, "What has she done now?" I felt I was being unkind to this woman who had done so much for us. Why was I doing it? I guess because she never worried about my opinion of her as I always did about hers. She helped us not necessarily because we warranted it, but because she was compelled by custom. This kind of Italian manners reflects more on the doer than on those for whom things are done. We were her obligation, worthy or not.

James had settled into the Language School for Children, where he was welcomed as an exciting student; he was American, he spoke English, and he came from New York City. The children used a pidgin English when they spoke to him. He loved all of his friends there, including a young girl whose name he insisted was Lettuce. Letizia was her name. He also insisted that they always had white sauce and dirty sauce on the pasta they were served every day. James loved them both, as he did the many food breaks they had throughout the day. He described each one with great relish.

"But how do you speak to the other children?" I asked.

"I talk to them the way they talk to me," he said.

"So they speak in English. Tell me how they talk to you," I said.

"Well Lettuce might say to me, 'De teecher weell lesson us naw.' And so I say, 'I weell sit to the lesson.' And they understand me."

Soon enough he was speaking decent Italian, enough to intercede when a street peddler came toward us on our way home to sell us sheets. I had turned him gruffly away, bur James understood the peddler's plea well enough to let me know that, "Mommy you have to buy something. He said his children are all sick at home."

We picked James up earlier than the other children who went home at five or six o'clock. That seemed to us like too long a day. "James *a casa*," they would call over the loudspeaker when we came to take him home. In Torino, children spent time together in their schools. There were no play dates or home visits. James also cherished his time at school with other children. He begged to be picked up later, as the Torinese children were.

As foreign residents, *stranieri*, we had to register at the *Questura* by a particular date or we'd be in violation of the law. La Signora had to be the one to do it with us, since she was our landlord. We came to the police station with our visas, our photocopies, the official letter from the Italian Consul in New York saying that Bill had an appointment at the Università di Torino. But this was just the beginning. We found out that we couldn't open a bank account without our Questura number, and more to the point, that we had to hand in our documents and could get registered only with La Signora alongside us. We were used to traveling independently, taking care of things on our own, always feeling competent, even cosmopolitan. The need to be accompanied everywhere was strange and confining. The pleasure of being in another place is finding your way, not being led around.

This is not the Torinese way. If you ask, "Where would we find a good toy store?" Torinesi answer with, "Oh, yes, I know the very best toy store. And I'll take you there. You'll never find it. I'll be happy to take you. And it's the best one. Tomorrow, tomorrow morning I'll take you. Maybe tomorrow evening." Here would start a series of appointments made, confirmed, then postponed. Each time we'd say we'd like to go ourselves. "But no, no, that isn't really a good idea. This Saturday for sure we'll go." This insistence on being helpful was annoying and confusing. Asking Torinesi for information or any kind of help meant they were obligated. But that didn't mean you could count on anything happening.

People often stared at us with consternation as we went about our daily business. I gradually understood why. My husband, in his sixties, wore jeans and sneakers and a leather bomber jacket. We leaned against walls while we waited for trams. James skipped down the street, and might climb a wall to walk along as if on a tightrope. Even though we always said the right greetings in the food shops, *Buona sera. Signora, Signore*. But when we shopped for a simple half-kilo of fresh pasta for dinner we'd invariably be questioned. "But how many people are you cooking for?" "Just for us." "But Signora that's too much for you. I'm not going to sell you that much."

The clerk assumed, of course, I would also be cooking a meat course and a vegetable course. She couldn't imagine that I was just cooking the pasta. And we like left-over pasta, too. She just wouldn't sell the 500 grams to me until I pretended I was having company.

On our part, *facevamo un'errore dopo l'altro. Sbagliato dopo sbagliato.* We would make one error after another, mistake after mistake. In our Torino we were confronted by the reality of bourgeois life. Not the life of the romantic Europe of literature, art, and liberation, but of an old, staid society, where manners, customs, and rules were primary. In my old world Italian family rules were equally strict, but there was a lively vitality those rules didn't dampen, as they did in this lovely, reserved, and proper northern Italian city. I had thought I knew where we were going, this was *to my* Italy, but I had landed in a very different place.

One of the rules we had come prepared for was registering as foreigners at the *Questura*, which by law had to happen within a certain time frame. Our date was set for a Monday morning with La Signora Frari.

On the ride over, she began one of her monologues. She has, "*Tre figlie,*" three, "*Sì, sì,*" I responded. "*Sì, sì,*" Bill responded. She raised three fingers, "*Tre.*" "*Sì, sì,*" again from us. "Three," she brought out proudly in English, "*Sono tre cheeldrums.*" "*Sì, sì,*" "*abbiamo capito,*" from us.

Her son has three children too, she tells us in French, German, and pidgin English. Each of his children was a daughter. Next she rambled on through the history of Catholicism, and along the way she said to Bill, Meester William, "*Lei è protestante, no?*" We were sure she knew our answer would confirm her suspicions that Bill is Jewish, *ebreo*—fine, fine—but all this somehow ended with her telling us her first grandchild was named Francesca, after St. Francis of Assisi.

"Mommy, when can I get to school?" James wanted to know. He asked why we were going, how long it would take, would I listen to him read *TinTin*, "*Sì, sì,*" I tried to assure both of them with the same "*sì, sì.*" They were equally *agita*, but the Signora won the noise battle. "James please just get through this. It shouldn't take long. It will be over in a few minutes as soon as we get to the *Questura*. It's just a matter of handing in our papers.

We drove around the *Questura* for ten minutes looking for a parking spot. There were none, so La Signora decided she would park in front of the head-quarters of Torino's Alpine Brigade, the army's elite mountain unit. There were Alpini standing around, sitting in jeeps, smoking cigarettes, charming in the traditional green *capello* spiked with its distinctive black raven feather. She pulled into a place clearly illegal, got out of her small Fiat, her long wool cape flying, her own feathered capello in place, her arm raised. "It's all right," she explained, "I know it's forbidden, I am going to park here anyway." No, the soldiers explained to her, she wasn't. It was the captain's spot. Anyway, it was forbidden. It didn't matter. She stood there explaining we were foreigners she had to take to the Questura. There are no parking spots, it's important. It's the law that they be registered. "*Sì, sì, Signora*," but you can't park here.

"I'll give you my keys, you can watch it for me." They were buying none of this, of course. Everyone knew. Then she spotted an opening down the street, mostly on the sidewalk. She got us back into the car and we landed the spot. She handed me the papers and her pocketbook, grabbed James's school bag and threw his books in the trunk while talking nonstop about trunks of cars, thieves, and parking spaces.

In the *Questura* we were deposited in front of a young handsome fellow with a three-day beard standing behind the counter. Signora Frari explained what we were doing there. "Yes," he said, "but where are the *bolle*, the official seals, and the other photographs, and this letter is in English, not Italian,"

"But the letter has the official stamp, they are foreigners, they have to sign," La Signora countered. He calmly explained that our papers were incomplete. We needed photocopies of our passports and visas, we needed more official seals and the letter from the University needed to be in Italian.

Ma we were *stranieri*, Meester William was *uno professore*, we had to get our papers, it was essential. "*Sì, sì, sì,*" he said, but it wouldn't do. Bill was getting more and more desperate. James, too, was tired of looking at soldiers with guns. "I want to go to school, Mommy, I'll miss gym."

Signora finally decided she would sit down and fill out the papers she had to sign on our behalf. At least that part would be complete.

Nearby there was a cluster of Yugoslavs looking bewildered. They had been asking timid questions of the *poliziotti* standing around talking and smoking and looking friendly. The policemen had been talking to James, so I liked them. They were sorry, they told the Yugoslavs, but they were only to guard the *Questura*. They didn't actually work there. They couldn't help them.

Bill and I stepped to one side to figure out how to handle our situation. We'd get the letter tomorrow, the bank account the next day. Why not at least get James to school. We turned to find Signora deep in conversation with the Yugoslavs. Their eyebrows were raised, foreheads furrowed, looking to her with worry and fear. She was talking to them the way she talked to us, slowly, helpfully, repeatedly. They did not speak Italian, but she patiently signed and talked. She was examining their papers.

Bill and I looked at each other. When we turned again, she was filling out their papers. A little more relaxed, the Yugoslavs surrounded her at the counter as she worked one set of papers at a time. Perhaps she was going to save them. She looked up at us briefly to say, "They don't know what to do. I have to help them." The Yugoslavs were barely groomed, hair badly cut, wearing ill fitting, stained clothes on thick lumpy bodies made of hard, peasant work. They smelled of cooking and sweat.

We waited for an opening in the Yugoslavian exchange. None came. We decided to risk our standing with the Signora. We were going to retrieve James's book bag and get him to school, we announced. "Take the car," she commanded. "No, no," I said, *sotto voce*, "let's just get the bag and let's get out of here."

I knew that in Italy everything took weeks longer than we were told, and I was furious with La Signora for wasting our time by helping the Yugoslavians. Because they smelled of oil, of food, of dirt, of sweat, because their clothes were stained. Because I realized they seemed so inept, so exactly as my grandparents may have seemed when they arrived in America, so exactly as my relatives must have seemed when they arrived in Torino. But I was most furious of all for having my own deeply hypocritical self revealed to me succinctly. I was impressed with and furious at La Signora. "They have no one to help them," she pleaded in Italian. "I have to help them." She said it only once.

The longer this detour continued, the more I found myself in a state of horrible revulsion at this group of people. I found myself holding my breath against the smell of sweat and food on them, horrified by their terrified hunched bodies, by their intense, obvious fear, by images of how my own family might have appeared when they were immigrants arriving in America. Now I just wanted to get my own business done and I didn't want to be under La Signora's control. I recognized the ghastly prejudice I was experiencing. What she was doing was exactly right. And I hated her for it.

I had completed almost two full stints with psychotherapists for exactly this very moment. I had lived with my family for eighteen years in fact, and for forty-five years emotionally. We *would* leave the *Questura*, with our papers, with our son. We got James's book bag from the car and brought the keys back to Signora, still deeply involved with the Yugoslavs.

"Stasera ci vedremo a casa, ma adesso andiamo alla scuola di James, Giacomo." We'll see you at home tonight, but now we were going to bring James to school. She turned to the Yugoslavs surrounding her. She offered us the keys again. We pushed her hand away and left.

Simone called that night to say that she had settled on Wednesday for the party because Franco was free then. And there was one more thing.

"Signora Frari was looking for you at James's school today. She was supposed to meet you there to go to the *Questura*." After we left and Signora had finished with the Yugoslavs, she called Simone's home, and since Simone wasn't home she reached Federico to ask where James's school was. Federico thought he was somehow supposed to know who she was and what this was about.

"She's quite eccentric you know," I took a stab at explaining to Simone what might have happened.

"Well, I suppose she is," Simone said with some discomfort in her voice, "but I thought she would at least be kind."

"Oh, she is, and we are amused by her too and I like her, but really I promise you we were not supposed to meet her at James's school."

I didn't try to explain everything to Simone. I just said, "She gets things very mixed up. We were supposed to meet her at home." There must have been an edge in my voice. I felt bad that I was making Simone feel bad, but La Signora had burst into our home with her own key once too often.

I paid Simone back for thinking badly of James, and for thinking badly of me, but I thought how worried each of us was, Simone about fulfilling her duty, La Signora too, in her own way, wanting to take us, show us, explain to us, make us behave. So worried about how we will be seen by each other. Is that what we women, so worried about manners and seemliness, are about: What will people think about us?

Caught between the two of them and their manners, I was in a permanent state of miserable gratitude. Simply being Joanna had of course long since faded from my dreams. Now I wanted merely not to be seen as horribly ill mannered. Or perhaps, better yet, to get it over with and accept being un'Americana *scustumade e mal'educata*, boorish and ignorant. That was all I hoped for now. To relax and take what pleasure I could from this old old world. "I don't want to be the kind of person who travels to China only to constantly be thinking about what's wrong with China," I kept saying to Bill.

It was exactly this endless parsing of manners that had driven me away from my family in Waterbury. I fled, not wanting my mind to be occupied by whether or not I had purchased the correct greeting card. Only cleanliness was more important in my mother's home than proper manners. My grandparents had brought an old world of manners with them, and an obsession with hospitality. My mother loved to talk about how, when she was a child, having guests was their great entertainment. Hers was a hard, physical life from another century. But pleasures came from the fact that people came to visit them all the time. For dinner, for the week, for the summer, sometimes even for years. "And this was our fun," my mother said, "to wait on them." It meant a time of her parents laughing and telling stories, of having other children around her.

Often when we were children our family would plan to take a ride on a summer night with the prospect of an ice cream cone on the way to the drive-in movie. But if someone dropped by, even as we were in the act of getting in the car to leave, all plans were suspended. You must always welcome guests. The coffee would be put on, and food laid out. So although my people had ruined Torino when they arrived to work in Fiat, were thought to be so different, they still shared these rules for living with the Torinese—a tightly interlocked, excruciatingly detailed handbook of obligations, written on their DNA and reinforced at their mother's breasts. My situation turned entirely on this: whose obligation was to whom, and for what purpose or reason?

I began to feel small inklings of discomfort from the small victory I achieved in getting Simone to see that the Signora could really be quite difficult. I tried to convince Simone that she should not worry about us so much. I reminded her how much Bill and I had traveled, how we had lived in Paris, how we loved exploring on our own. Perhaps that might alleviate some of the pressure I felt. I found at least a bit of a way to calm her anxiety.

"When shall I bring you the baking pans that I promised? I could drop them off tomorrow." Always she seemed worried about what she hadn't done for us. Always I tried to convince her that she had done enough, really too much already.

"Please Simone, don't worry about us. We are thriving. We'll get the pans whenever it's convenient." But always my response was somehow wrong. Over and over the tone of her voice seemed disappointed.

"The party is set for this Wednesday. We'll have a lovely time. Perhaps you could take the pans then. The other members of the department will join us. And you'll bring James. We'll start early. Will that be all right?" To really enjoy the pleasures of being a guest I believe you have to feel worthy of the attention you're given. Because I didn't, each of these phone calls made me feel worse.

"One night, I should really come and show you around Torino, to the squares and so forth." I didn't quite know how to reassure her that I was a member of the female tribe, that I liked being a doer and a caretaker myself.

"Oh we are doing really very well. We've tried almost all the markets. And today we walked up along the Po into Piazza Veneto, then we walked into Piazza Castello for a coffee, and finally to San Carlo to the Café Luxemburg. It was thrilling. We love Torino. I think it is vastly underrated for its beauty."

From the other end of the phone I heard something like a gurgle in her throat, one, I thought, of pleasure. She laughed and said, "Ah, do you think so?"

After I got off the phone that I realized that for once I didn't feel quite as bad as I usually did. I had made her happy. I had only to tell her that she didn't always have to take us by the hand, and that we loved her home.

That was what she must have wanted all along. I had been focused on how I was being perceived. All I had to do was to look up and smile.

I didn't tell Simone how at the *Questura* on one of our many return visits, La Signora had spent a great deal of time explaining to the clerks that we were taking our son to these video game parlors where drugs are sold. And that she couldn't get us to understand why we shouldn't. In return, I managed to suggest to one of the clerks, in my pidgin Italian, that *La Signora è molto preoccupato*. Very worried. The clerk gave back a wry smile of recognition.

FATE TAKES A TURN

The older I get, the more I am convinced there are two factors that determine how our lives proceed—fate and our own unconscious. It is often easy to tell, usually after the fact, which part the one, and which part the other, took. So fate came to take its turn.

Simone's voice on the phone was somber. "I'm afraid we'll have to postpone the party. Something has happened. I'm really terribly, terribly sorry."

My immediate impulse was to reassure her that surely she didn't owe us more. "Simone, really it is all right. You've done too much already. You mustn't do more."

"But really, I feel so bad that we can't do it. You will see why." Her voice was filled with deep apology. "You see I never go to the doctor. I haven't been, I am very much ashamed to say, practically since Chiara was born. You know how we strong people are. Never worrying about ourselves. Always getting on. And I went because my arm was bothering me for a long time now. So finally I went and it seems my arm is fine, but there are other problems. So this is why I can't make the party on Wednesday. I went to the gynecologist today and he says there are things I must look into."

I didn't know if I had the right to ask. "Is it your breasts?"

"No it's the other, not the uterus, but the other part—there are fibrous things growing. So I am so sorry to tell you that we will have to postpone your party."

"Simone, please stop thinking about this party. Please you must take care of yourself. This is important."

"Well, I am not used to this; to things like this. I am always strong. I am never weak about health. I have so many friends who run to the doctor all the time. And I think that they are silly, but now . . . "

"You are used to taking care of everyone else," I said, "not yourself. Now you must."

"Yes," she agreed quietly. "That is my way. But I will be fine. It's nothing I am sure. I will have some tests tomorrow then I will know more. Why don't you come to lunch on Sunday since we can't have the party on Wednesday."

"Please Simone, we can see you some other time. Just have your tests done and we'll be here for months, plenty of time to have dinner."

"No you must come. This is not really a problem. It will only be a little lunch—the children can play in the garden. Will it be all right for you to come at two? Unless you are busy, of course. Then you can see how out of control my life is, my house is not organized you know. I don't believe one should waste one's time on that. Then my life is so complicated. You'll see. But I am fine. You mustn't worry about me. It's not my habit to do so."

Was it for me to press upon her the seriousness of what she faced? I agreed that we would go to lunch just to get her to stop talking about it. I felt so worried, so sad for her. I knew what having fibroids in the uterus meant. It could be nothing or quite serious. Cancer, particularly reproductive cancer, runs a river through my family.

How deeply felt were these Torinese manners, if even in the face of serious health issues, a woman still feels she must fulfill a lunch invitation? I was to manners and customs born. Nothing is more sacred in my family than manners, nothing more a mark of one's humanity than hospitality.

It was exactly this recognition that had so frightened me when we'd arrived to so much ceremony. Baskets of food waiting for us. Greeting parties. Parties planned. When we had been in Paris, it was the charm of anonymity that had freed me to discover a life of rich experience I'd never before known.

I could see that this need to be the one taking care of others, not to be the one taken care of, was at the heart of Simone's character. I saw that she had taken us on as her charges because she was strengthened by burdens. When other women and I behave like this, I call it *feminisma*, a mirror to *machismo*. We take it as central to our identity that we can handle any and everything. No load is too heavy. We are professional women, we are superb cooks, we are mothers who know exactly how important the good mother is to our lives. We're a bunch of know-it-alls and confident in our ability to solve every problem.

However, to be an obligation instead of the one obligated is a much heavier burden. I instinctively felt the press of Simone's manners on her, because although I've fled them, I am also of them. I wanted not to be her obligation but to know her in the manner of women.

The womb is the essence of being a woman, even if it's expressed by the desire to make sure the womb doesn't determine a woman's life. In my mother's perfect world, where the rules are clear and one's obligations are without doubt, a great symmetry was planned. She was to have two girls and two boys: first the girls and then the boys. It began well. My sister and I were born within several years of the consummation of her passionate marriage to my father. All was going according to schedule.

My mother loved to tell stories from her early marriage. How wildly she was in love with my father, from the very beginning.

But there were the fates too. My birth was a part of what changed her fate.

"Well, you were a breach baby, and you had to come out by forceps, and after that my womb would never stay up where it was supposed to." Dr. Lombardi had told me that he was going to pin it back up. But one day I was on the back porch hanging some clothes and a big wind came up and blew up under my skirt. "I could feel it," she told me more than a few times, "go right up inside of them through there. I could feel the cold inside me. And I got an infection after that. I went to the Dr. Lombardi and he said I needed a D and C. So I went into the hospital.

"A few weeks later he told me that he had to take out one of the ovaries. I thought I might be pregnant, because I wasn't getting my period. So I went to him and asked him, 'Did you peek inside and see if there was a baby in there?'

'No no,' he said. 'Don't worry about it.'

"Three months later he called me and your father into his office and said, 'Now I have to tell you something. You're not going to have any more children. Once I was in there, I had to do a hysterectomy. And I don't want to hear anything about you adopting a baby. And don't think you're going to go crazy either. You're not. That's the end of this.' "

In that small story hangs both my fate and my unconscious. I broke my mother's planned symmetry and all that she had built as I entered the world. I had been part of the symmetry until that operation, when the wind came and blew inside and damaged her; because of my birth, the narrative altered. "You were an easy baby. You went to sleep easily. But then I don't know what happened. You changed."

I was five years old when the wind came and blew its destruction into my mother's womb. I have had to understand what it means to no longer be "after the manner of women" like Abraham's Sarah in Genesis, no longer able to bear children.

How could a grown woman spend months recovering from a hysterectomy and not suspect a thing? How could a grown woman think that the wind flew up inside her on her back porch while she hung the wash on the clothesline and blew trouble into her?

After that, having unwittingly participated in the downfall of my mother's carefully constructed world, I was given another job in the family. I was the explanation for all that followed. Her problem child.

It was after her hysterectomy that I ceased to be of my mother's world of women and wombs. I was relegated to some other post, in my father's world, not quite a son, not quite a daughter, some kind of female *castrata*. What is the word for a woman without a womb? Why isn't there such a word, a name to go with so ordinary a procedure? If a woman has a hysterectomy, what is she? "Hysteric" has been assigned to us, for a different purpose.

For an Italian woman having children is often central to her female identity. After my mother's hysterectomy, *my* femaleness was an issue for both my mother and for me. The birth of my son was briefly an escape from this central conundrum, but by then it was extremely hard to want anything directly for myself. So this hour of triumph of the birth of my son also had to be an hour of defiance.

IN THE MANNER OF WOMEN

Simone called several days later. "Even if it is a tumor it is certainly benign, but I find after all this I am so tired. Would you mind if we canceled our lunch?"

"Of course not. Perhaps after this . . . " I searched for the right word, "small crisis I could take Chiara so that you and Federico could have some time together, say a dinner out together."

"Really, it is not a crisis, and then Chiara always has so much homework, you know. I think it's best if we didn't."

I was absorbed for days by deep concern. What could I do to show it? How could I help her? Then I bumped into La Signora on the small elevator. She looked agitated.

"Margarita," she sighed. *"Margarita è malata."* Tears sprang to her eyes. *Accidenti.* Damn. She looked so distressed; her beautiful daughter was injured. She brushed away the tears. *"Margarita nella machina, boom boom un altra macchina boom nella tram."* Now she gestured madly, Margarita jerking forward her head banging into the steering wheel. *"La colla, la colla,"* she pressed her hands to her neck show us that her daughter had to wear a brace. The tears were back in her eyes.

"Peccato, che peccato," I sympathized. I don't know if it was because I was so bereft for Simone, but tears came to my eyes, too, watching a mother so overcome for her daughter.

I wandered out to the *mercato*. It was a day glistening with hints of an early spring, cool and with that subtle shift in the air, telling you of everything hopeful to come. The flower woman on the corner was bunching the violets in small bouquets and putting them into the center of small doilies. I bought some for Margarita. But what to do for Simone?

I walked up and down past the stands of vegetables, so fresh this deep in winter, so green, and I knew what I could do. I would make soup. Our *minestra*. I would carry it to Simone as an offering. It was what I could do. Perhaps she would understand what I meant.

Minestra just means soup, or sometimes on Italian menus it indicates the first course. But for my family it is soup meant to heal wounds, comfort you, reassure you that you will be strong again. It is health, warmth, deep savories, and soothing greens.

I scoured the *mercato* for the ingredients, each slightly different than the ones I could gather at any grocery store back home in five minutes, and then take the rest of the day cooking. Finding the right ingredients here took time. And I spent the day gathering, cleaning, cooking. When I had finished, I phoned Simone and asked her if I might bring it to her.

She seemed a little surprised, but yes, I was to come up and bring it to her. Why didn't I bring James? He and Chiara could play. Did we know the way? "Now you will see how chaotically I live," she said. "You'll see I am not at all organized." I drove up twisting hills, round steep corners, till we came to her lovely large home above Torino.

At her gate a large dog was barking. Simone was standing holding his collar, looking elegant, as she always did, and worried.

"Are you afraid of dogs?" she asked James as Bill and I got out of the car. "He's okay as long as you don't show fear." James put his hand out to show him that he wasn't afraid. I turned back to get my gift of *minestra* from the car.

"Chiara's upstairs, come we'll go and find her, she said leading James toward her house. "You can see, even my dog is out of control," she said as we walked up the steps. She was protecting us from her dog. I carried my offering, James at my side, Bill behind us.

Chiara appeared in the doorway, happy to see James. It was easy to see that Chiara found James very exciting. There was sparkle in her eyes for him. They ran off to see her room and her toys.

It was a large, elegant, chaotic house. The kind of house I wish I had the temperament to live in. The stuff of life scattered everywhere. We passed a table in the hall covered with newspapers and mail, a sweater hooked over a doorknob. In the kitchen, counters were covered with baskets of fruit, some of it going bad, and there were many different bottles of wine and *aperitivi*. This was fullness and complication, many activities crowded together, a phone ringing too often, a woman's world filled with too much responsibility. I liked it very much. I liked this side of Simone, more out of control, less elegant, and richer, more varied. I turned to her to make my formal presentation. I wanted to be sure she knew what my gift meant.

"We make this soup in my family when someone is sick or has traveled a long way—when you need strength."

"Ah," she said with a sigh, "I need it." Standing next to her kitchen counter, tears sprang into her eyes.

"You know, the doctor said I will have to have it off. I can't bear it. Not that I intended to have any more children, still I don't want it."

I felt so helpless. I wanted to change it for her.

"You know, he said to me today, when he told me. 'You are an educated woman. You must have known that it was very serious.' But I didn't. Truly I didn't. I just don't think of myself that way. Today after the doctor, I met my sister in the street quite by chance, you know, and she said to me, 'Not you Simone, we never think of you as being ill or weak.' She was so surprised."

"You'll be okay, Simone, though it may not seem so now," I attempted. "You'll be fine. Once it's over and you recover, you'll regain your strength. You'll be your usual self." I was thinking of my mother who had very much had the life she had hoped for except for my two spectral brothers. Simone blinked back her tears, they stilled. She wiped at her face.

Immediately I regretted my words. Why hadn't I let her say her words of sadness? Why hadn't I let her tears come instead of intruding my clumsy consolation? I had lost my chance to allow us to be after the manner of women together.

How could I have betrayed us? Both?

Simone wiped at her face a last time, lifted her chin. "Yes, I'll be fine." She turned to lift the cover to the pot. "This looks marvelous. It was so kind of you. It's not really a soup is it, all this meat."

Then, "Let me show you this house." She turned and led me through a large rambling set of comfortable rooms. There was a large salon, with high ceilings, filled with light from immense windows, enormous easy chairs, and a huge table for a formal dinner. "This was where we meant to have your party. It's a lovely room for parties." It had high ceilings. It was filled with a sense of beauty and generosity.

"Chiara's room is ridiculous of course," she announced, next on the tour. "More mess. You know she's so nervous, feels everything too intensely. She seems so smart usually, and then she can be so stupid, all of a sudden. I've tried to explain to her that this won't do, won't help her to succeed in life. That she must control these feelings inside, to learn to have hold of herself, in order to get on in the world, to accomplish anything. So I let her keep her room just as she wished, her haven, but it's absurd."

But it wasn't a mess. It was merely a child's room filled with toys and the disorder of little girl's things. James and Chiara were playing with a small computer, using sign language, and getting on pretty well.

Simone's study was her nest. There were papers and books on her desk and on a small table. It looked as if there were a few projects, maybe more in midstream. "Here is where all my papers are. I keep thinking I should burn them now, in case. God forbid anyone should have to deal with them. What a mess. Or try to publish them, worse. I couldn't leave them behind. Last night I couldn't sleep all night, even though I didn't expect what he said. I kept thinking about these papers—what would I do with them?

"But now I don't know. My life is so complicated. My parents can't know about this, you know, if I must go ahead. They need me so much, for everything. They depend on me for everything, even their shopping."

Here, I thought, was Simone's attention to duty and obligation. Her endless need to be the one responsible. Her generosity.

"But what about your sisters. Can't they help you?"

"Oh, they are very nice people, but you know everyone counts on me. I am the eldest. It's always my opinion my parents need. It's just that way in my family. And then there is Chiara. I don't think I can give into this. I don't want to. I don't want people looking at me, worrying about me. If I have to do it, I'll see if I can go to Switzerland and do it over the holiday." It was as if there was shame involved. "I want to see what else I can do?" Her face was determined and worried. Sad.

Each of her next sentences came, staccato, insistent, telling.

"Federico said to me last night in the middle of the night, 'When will you have wisdom?'"

"I won't ever, I told him. It's not me. I am really a wild person. I don't act rationally. I know I don't seem like that on the outside, but those who know me well they say, 'Ah, Simone, you are really wild.'" She laughed now, pleased with herself.

"You mean that the outside is only your beginning, your facade. You depend on emotion to guide you. Good for you," I said, wishing I had known this Simone all along.

Briefly, there in her study, we stood and talked as friends, the one being intimate, revealing, the other praising her revelation. I felt so happy and proud of Simone for her wild insides. I was so moved by her revelations, her confiding in me. We had found our way past ourselves to this moment of intimacy—this way between women.

"I won't give into this so easily," she said. "I will see what I can do. I'm still fiddling." Her head was held high, she was brave and confident. "I don't want it off."

I had never liked Simone more than at that moment; with her great complications, her chaos, her dependent parents, her immature sisters, her home, her work, all spread out around her, she seemed a richer, finer, more generous person than all her manners and helpfulness and gifts had rendered her.

Before we left she thrust several baking pans, some beautiful books on Torino, and several games of Chiara's for James to borrow.

"I will touch iron for you," I said. Simone had told me that was what Italians say for luck instead of knock on wood.

Several days later she called Bill and told him that a doctor in Switzerland said she might wait and monitor herself. It wasn't necessary for an operation yet.

I was so pleased that the fortunes had turned in her favor, so that she could carry on with her responsibilities freely, as she liked.

Although my sister never married into the Squibb family—and my mother never had to face inviting Mrs. Squibb to her house for dinner—she did marry into another American family. Perhaps her rehearsal with the Squibb's had prepared her. My parents, an ironworker and a housewife, and my brother-in-law's parents, a research scientist and a professor, got on extremely well.

My mother told the end of her story. "And you know, it's so funny because when Lucia married John, my son-in-law, I was worried all over again. Before the wedding I was so nervous about meeting them. But they were so friendly, and now they stop by on their way to New Hampshire all the time and stay with us. They could stay wherever they liked, but they insist on staying with us."

It's true. Each time the Mudd's drove from their great house on the Main Line in Philadelphia to their small compound in New Hampshire, they stopped by my mother's one-bedroom garden apartment. They ate the food my mother had been preparing for a week. They made a great fuss over her and how wonderful she was. She even had fans on the Main Line. I had to hand it to her. My mother knew how to be Rose.

The day Simone called Bill to share her good news, I went for a long walk along the Po. I went up into Piazza Veneto, that great Baroque square, which, when approached from the river, extends two enormous arcaded arms out as if to embrace you, to guide you into the heart of Torino where you could have a coffee, buy a book, and watch the parade of young men and women out strutting for one another. I entered its embrace and walked along a stretch of arcades. Bill was at the university. James was at school, and I was on my own.

I turned off into the smaller more intimate Piazza Carignano, where the Palazzo Carignano sat on one side and the beautifully grand and old restaurant, Del Cambio, sat on the other, while I sat in the circle of benches in the sun. I was restless, with no appointments, no obligations, and no friend to meet. I didn't know what to do with the hours of freedom that stretched in front of me. But they were mine.

A few weeks later before we left to drive south to visit my people in Basilicata, I phoned Simone to thank her for everything. I found out that Simone's dog had died. She told me that her neighbor poisoned it because it barked so much when in heat. "I found it stiff the day I got back from Switzerland. I had just learned that I could wait to have the operation." Her voice, sober and quiet, spoke of all she had endured. But I will tell you this: though the dog had died; though her house was filled with the chaos of life lived; though her daughter sometimes acted stupid and intense; though she might even eventually have to have her operation, she, Simone, will, for a long time—quivering between anxiety and arrogance—continue to live on. I can't imagine Torino getting on without her.

The Grief Estate

Do not separate yourself from your dead.

If the Italian way with the dead is to regularly visit the grave sites, weed, plant flowers, wash the grave stone, sit with our lost people, perhaps in this way I'm no longer a real Italian. Instead, as an aging, somewhat secular, somewhat modern, but still southern Italian woman, I visit my dead in my writing. I polish and clean my encomiums as my grandmother and mother visited and washed the grave stones in our family. I count my dead over and over in my writing. Here I commune with them.

Visiting Our Dead

DEATH IS THE GREAT ABSENCE MAKER. SOMEONE WE LOVE IS WITH US, here. Then, there they aren't. Not here! A whole continent in our lives has ceased to be. How can we possibly have any other response than a wild animal screech: *No!*

At some point as an adult, long after I had abandoned my Catholic idea of an afterlife, I came to accept the received truths about grief: that there are stages to it, that we proceed from one stage to another, and that over time, acceptance comes. But faced with real deaths of people I loved, that idea made no sense to me.

This simply isn't how I experience death or mourning. Stages? Gradual acceptance? Death is the great irrational other, the feral opposite of reason. A nerve obliterating *no!*

When I finally owned up to what I actually believe about death and grief, I felt an immense surge of release; this idea about stages of grief is too neatly packaged in a series of containers. Death is a cataclysmic shock, then a planet-covering flood of sadness.

The acceptance of death is the ultimate paradox, which we have no choice but to live with. If we're alive to think about our own annihilation, it means we still have time to postpone its arrival. Because death can't be fully comprehended, there's nothing to do but push it away.

As I age, I am less and less afraid of death and dying. I've been lucky enough to have done a lot of living. I've always liked wakes, funerals, sitting shiva, as these rituals set communion in our midst where we gather to take good care of one another. But accept death? Neither my mind nor my body knows how to do that.

As my father would say, *Nah!*

This frozen *No!* I assume, goes back to that original shock I felt when I came to understand that everybody dies: me too, I would die.

In the dusk of a late summer day, sitting on the front step of our 1950s ranch home, I was picking at one of the permanent half-dollar-sized scabs on my knee. My father, in his sleeveless undershirt, was sitting in his chair on the front porch just to my left reading the *Waterbury Republican American.* It was after dinner, when the insect buzz of quiet comes.

I worked up the nerve to ask my father: "Is it true that everybody has to die?"

He took in a short, sharp breath, then quickly gathered his reluctance. "We do all die," he said. "It's true," he said with a short nod of his cleft chin.

"Am I going to die?" "Yes, you will too," he said, drawing in the air around him.

"I'm afraid of dying." I was waiting for him to tell me I was wrong.

In the air between he took a long slow breath and then said, "Well it's not as bad as it seems to you.

"Let me put it this way," he said as gently as he could. By now I was leaning into his knee. "I'm so much older than you are and I'm going to die before you do. And I'm not afraid of dying." His voice was quiet and convincing.

He was about thirty-three years old at the time. He was in the fullness of his strength. While what I think about death has changed a few times over the course of my life, that moment on the porch with my father was the first location of relief and comfort. My father loved his job as a father.

What he said that summer evening relocated me *enough*, shifted the earth's surface almost back to where it had been before I pushed out that dreaded question. He created a continent between me and death that was his own life.

When our father died at eighty-one, my sister, Lucia, and I were sent into a downward spiral of grief. A cosmic rent opened up in front of us. Our continent was gone—but much, much worse, he was gone, this mass of male love and protection. Where would we place our feet now as we tried to go forward? Would we forever have to circumnavigate this absence to move in any direction at all?

As a former Catholic, the myths and stories of the church are familiar and even dear to me. Once, as I was explaining to my Jewish friend exactly what the Holy Trinity is, it came to me in a flash of recognition that the Holy Ghost is the dead grandfather, or our ancestors, the generations that are lost to us, that came before us. We have the present, the future, and, in the Holy Ghost, our beloved dead.

My father has become our Holy Ghost. He is the one my sister and I turn to when we need unbroken ground beneath our feet. Our dad isn't here. His spirit or residue or dissolved matter might be somewhere, which I sometimes believe in completely and sometimes not. I float about in clouds of unknowing.

My own visits with my father go like this. I begin to think about him, his large spirit, his complexity and his great good fathering. I call him to me. I see him in front of me, always standing not on our ground but slightly up and off, near. Sometimes I simply visit with this man who has been one of my great influences. I think about how much I loved and love him, about how much he loved and loves us. Sometimes I turn to him with greater purpose. When I need help. I begin to talk to him about something that is on my mind. Dad, I have to take care of this and I'm not sure how to do it. Turning to him immediately brings me calm. I speak directly to him. "I need you to stand with me, to help me find a way to deal with this. Help me figure this out."

At those times I see his large physical presence; he's in his gray work pants, his sleeveless undershirt, and I feel spectral presence as a fullness, rather than an absence. Please stay with me now. I place the responsibility of finding a solution between us at those times—we'll deal with this together. I think about him quietly and soberly, and I leave my concerns resting there between us, knowing that something will occur to me in the next hours, days, weeks, or months, and that this will happen because I have just laid before my Holy Ghost. He will help me with this problem. Whenever something comes as a solution to my problem it feels if he has delivered it.

My father's visits with my sister are different from his with me. Lucia and my father visit each other in ways, which are in and of this world. These visits are substantial, based in the everyday. In these visits, he is represented by living creatures or by the matter of earth. The gift of these signs is a powerful presence in her life.

Lucia has a gentle nature, kind and sweet in a way that one imagines St. Francis probably was. People are drawn to her as soon as they meet her. In an earlier time she could have been a holy person—a monk or a nun. But she is a wife, a mother, a grandmother, and a teacher. She loves to take care of the vulnerable, the aging, the beset. Perhaps her numinous radiance gives credibility to the experiences she has had with our father. I believe her.

Here is my sister, Lucia Mudd, writing about her visits with our father.

I was standing in the new, flat, open, treeless cemetery, where we go to choose a resting place for our father, we look around, and say, "How can we leave him here?" Then I say to him in my head, "Dad, help us out here, we can't leave you in this barren place." Then the fellow taking us around says, "Unless you'd like to go up to the old cemetery where we have pulled up some roads to make more places. The stones are already in place, so you won't get to choose a stone." We go. It's beautiful! And it's under a tree, surrounded by grass and beautiful gravestones with angels and St. Anthonys. It overlooks our town with many of the sites where Dad has done ironwork.

His next visit to me came the first time I come back to visit the cemetery. I think, as I approach his stone, "If you're here, let me see the hawk when I look up." (The hawk had been circling when we laid him to rest in the cemetery.) Before I can look up, I hear the hawk's cry, which I had never heard before. But there he was.

Another piece of my Dad making himself known to me happened this way. Shortly after Dad died my husband John and I decided to sell the house in upstate New York that my father had loved so much. We invited the neighbors in to take things and pack the rest in the truck we had rented. The house was empty but I was roaming around, feeling that I was leaving something. I go into the cellar still feeling I'm leaving something important. I say, "Dad, what is it? What do you want me to find?" I look up and there in the rafters is the star he made when we were kids to hang outside our house at Christmas. It has blue lights.

Once while I was walking on York Beach in Maine, I suddenly thought, "Are you here, Dad?" I reached down and picked up a smooth black stone, which exactly fit in my thumb and hand like a handholding.

After Mom died, and she was buried in the same plot just above him vertically, we planted a yellow lily, a true lily, not a daylily. Next time I went to visit them at the cemetery the lily had so many blossoms I couldn't believe it. I decided to count them: forty-one. When I told a friend, she said, "Does that number have any significance?" Significance? Oh my goodness. 1941 … that was the year Mom and Dad were married.

My father came to me again in this way after Mom died. I was leaving the cemetery, I got into the car, turned on the ignition. I was not tuned to a music station but NPR. They were doing some series about great American singers. Nat King Cole's mellifluous voice was singing, "*They try to tell us we're too young*

/ *Too young to really be in love.*" This was one of my father's favorite songs. He sang it all the time.

When my first grandchild, Leo Isaac Mudd, was born to my son Peter and his mother, Lisa Hickey, my daughter Anna and I went to the cemetery. We're standing there and I was saying to my father in my head, "How I wish I knew if you know about Peter's new family."

Then Anna says, "Mom, Look!" She's pointing to a stone diagonal to Mom and Dad's stone on which is written *Leo*. And directly behind it is another stone that says *Hickey*.

This summer it was the fifteenth anniversary of Dad's passing over. I was outside in the hammock when a paper fell out of the book I had taken with me. It was the lyrics, which I had copied a long time ago, to the song dad sang over and over in the weeks before he died, "Let the Rest of the World Go By": "*We'll build a sweet little nest somewhere out in the west / And let the rest of the world go by.*"

I was amazed. I said, "Okay, is there anything else you want to tell us?" I looked up and see a giant, sky-sized X (a kiss!) in the sky made by two planes crossing.

You might say that what I sometimes believe, and what my sister, Lucia, always believes, are gifts of her unconscious. But I think that the cosmos is so huge and unknowable that it's too easy to believe in only what is before our senses. Our senses are feeble instruments before the universe. I surrender that work to the dead.

My Father's Bones

MY FATHER'S BONES ARE A VERSION OF HIM, THE STRUCTURING GROUND inside, a connecting architecture. Light in weight, strong, dense, his bones protected his heart, his lungs, held up his belly, and all the rest. Bones bind and support, connect us to ourselves. They allow us to move, go forward, to change. My father's bones grew under the crushing weight of a terrible early life: innumerable blows from his father's large blacksmith hands, the loss of his mother to insanity, and two brothers dying early and tragic deaths. But somehow from those weighted burdens, came an architecture that made a man that held a good life. This was the scaffolding for this tall, sturdy, agile man.

His bones, flesh, and blood allowed him to climb up high away onto rocks, trees, towers, telephone poles and onto the high iron he worked. His bones were as sturdy as the iron his family had worked as blacksmiths, at least for centuries, more likely for millennia, in the deep south of Italy. The Claps men worked that abundant substance, which comes from Gaia, mother earth. Iron ore lies deep in the planet's core and also makes up much of its crust. Iron was in stars, before they collapsed as supernovas.

Iron is deep in the earth. It's also on the surface and it's made from bursting stars. My father's bones were made of similar stuff: structural, strong, and malleable and from the *fated* universe. They allowed him to climb iron and get away from the grinding miseries in which he had grown.

My father was also a man of the flesh. When he was young he was lean, muscular, even sculptural, in his beauty. This was the result of a time and place where fruit was an occasion, where hard physical work was daily life, and where using the body to play was as natural as using the body to do brutal work twelve hours a day. His body was shaped by the sweat of ironwork: from hefting long, large, heavy pieces of metal to setting them into the planes and corners of the buildings he was helping to raise. As he lifted and carried, held and welded, an exchange of sorts took place: a dialogue between structures, his own and those he helped build for others. Doing construction gave his body the strength to make more buildings, a conversation built over time.

To walk across eight-inch I-beams ten or twenty stories off the ground, you have to have muscles that are so sure, so agile, they can only carry you with casual grace. The confidence that comes from this physical strength and balance is almost automatic. Only a special few can lift heavy things with such self-assurance, move them at will, climb heights, walk lightly across dangerous spaces. My father was one of those creatures, moving with the pleasure a strong body gives, easily, playfully, unselfconsciously, without arrogance or pride, but a kind of delight that your body always does what you want it to, as if ordered by your character or nature.

He loved heights. They called to my father often and early—his body pulling him inexorably up. Rocks, roofs, quarries, and trees lifted him first as a boy toward the sky, up telephone poles toward the high voltage wires. Later, on the iron, and over time, up every tower, turret, or steep stairs he came upon, he was as if compelled to go above his confining earth.

"When we were kids, we loved nothing better than to dive from the highest rock down into the quarry to swim. We'd do anything, anything at all, to impress each other, climb up onto a roof and jump off. We'd see who could climb to the top of a tree faster than the other guy, and of course we'd climb up the telephone poles. Up we'd go, vying for who got to be the first one up there. Naturally there are live wires up there, the currents are bad. But we didn't think—we just had to, had to, had to, get to the top of the pole, and I can remember vividly Charlie saying 'I'm not going up there.' And me—now here, he's my best, best friend—thinking how jerky can you be? It just could not, would not be tolerated.

"It is just natural for young boys to be drawn to these things. We thought he was embarrassing. It was so wrong from the way we looked at things from, I should say, our limited and foolish way of looking at things. Actually he was right. Those wires could kill you instantly, but in our youth, in our reckless high spirits, we had no use for that kind of thinking. Nothing needs must do but we had to get up that pole. We simply weren't afraid. Oh, those glorious days."

Later, just as he finally began to escape his father's crushing reach, he met my mother. She helped him find another height, another way out of the primordial harshness that he was raised in.

On my parents' first date my father drove out to the Hanging Hills of Connecticut. "I had no idea where he was taking me," my mother loved to say. They climbed the long curving path through the thick woods, past the forest streams and flowers that would bring them up to the lookout tower on the top of the hill.

The sun filtered through the verdant woods. "That was the first time he held my hand. I wasn't used to that, with a fella. I was so shy. He was so handsome and strong. I just went along with him." The excitement of this first touch stayed in my mother's voice all her life. When they reached the lookout tower they began their climb up the stairs inside. Young lean limbs used to hard work would make light of such ascent. Did they slip lightly up, holding hands one in front of the other, suspecting, hoping, what waited for them up there?

Up there in the soft Connecticut hills, her heart caught and ready, his large hands around her tiny waist drawing her to him, his heart pounding, they were taken away from the ancient rules of constraint, the rules of their people that young men and women must be kept separate and supervised, because their bodies would be pulled to each other in a place apart. They would be. And were. Their people were right.

All the limits of their world were tight and confining. How could you expect the young to ever come together to create the most essential of fabrications, a family, from within those boundaries?

"That was my first kiss. Oh, we went there many times after that. That was our place. I knew I loved him right away. I was just head over heels in love with him."

This was the housing our handsome, dark haired father's large and wild spirit inhabited when my sister and I were children. The flesh, bone, and spirit that held and carried us, my sister and me. At the end of a long summer night playing with our cousins up the farm, he'd pick up the two dead weights of his sleeping children out of the back of the car, as if we were two large paper bags of groceries, one in each arm, and climb the stairs to our attic rent on the top floor of the Pagano's house. He'd deposit us in our bed, brushing back sweaty bangs from our foreheads, pulling the cotton covers up and around, and then bending down and kissing our soft skin with the pleasure of one who has escaped.

The pleasures of heights were passed on to us so early, that they were no more visible than the air. As my father climbed we climbed too, up monkey bars, up the trees to the highest limbs, up the long New England hills on bicycles, up to the highest diving boards where he taught us to take a three-step run out to the tip of the board, bounce hard with all our force, to spring high into the air, hang there light, gravity suspended with just enough time to bring the body into the tight shape it must be, legs straight, toes pointed, hands touching the toes, then out into a long straight point to knife deep into the water.

Up all the steps of any and all towers he could find, up clock towers, the Empire State Building (where you used to walk the last floors to get to the viewing deck), on bridges to walk high over waters. Up.

One day, the Statue of Liberty. After the long climb up the dark stone stairwell, there was a shock of blinding sunlight, then disorientation. It was unnerving up there. There was no feeling that we were standing in her torch—only one of being on a round veranda, a bizarre topography. Her face was too close, her nose was too big; it wasn't the face we'd seen from afar so many times. We'd arrived on another plane where, instead of looking down on things made tiny, as if they belonged to you, the things we'd come to see so close to us, were without shape and meaning. But I did know that day, standing next to my father, that he was handing over his great passion, going as high as possible, to be above, looking out, here at the edge of celestial life

His father, my Grandpa Clapps, was the opposite; his life was lived low, close to the ground, embedded in the earthly core of iron and flesh, iron for work, and flesh for women and bed. The one elevation he sought each night was from the enormous amount of wine he made and drank every night. He gathered with his friends to drink, sing, and play cards at the table where he held court in his kitchen. He was a man without a wife. His wife, my grandmother, had come undone and was locked away in a facility. But his drinking pushed him above the earth for short hours before it turned into a stupor of drunken forgetting.

The single elevating *gioia* that my grandfather and my father did share was that they both loved to sing. They loved to breathe deep of the air, sending it into their earthly cores, where it gathered force to climb out. From those large centers their big breaths rose up, into throat and mouth, shaped there by tongue and glottal, twisting, turning, and holding; then sending out, sound and voice, on the breath, on the tongue, of the mouth, of the lips, this thing of music, this thing of love. Singing was their ascension, gave them calm, and imbued them with joy and consolation, comfort and ecstasy, every day. The only ascension father and son shared. The rest was difference.

Each of them inhaled and released his voice with the same joy. But they rarely sang together. We've been there for dinner where my grandfather has drunk an ordinary amount of wine. We've visited with Uncle Paul and Aunt Dora too when my grandfather's cronies arrived. They sat around his table, drank their wine and began to sing. Soon they'd play cards.

My father stood at the head of the kitchen table where my grandfather held court each night and joined his father in song for a few verses, one of the old time, a drinking song, too, "Non sono più la sveglia." Their voices rose together, but as soon as one or two songs were over, despite Grandpa's urging to stay and sing with them, my father insisted, "Okay, girls it's time to go." Did these lovely old Italian songs signal that his father was about to descend into too much drink and who knew what else? My father had witnessed too many of these nights. We kissed and left. *Scappati.*

But song was the one element he took from his father. It was a part of his coming to consciousness every morning. It was a part of being awake, alive, a part of being a living creature, calling into the air around him. His legs swung over the side of the bed and as he pushed off into the day he might begin by humming a little to himself, which soon rose into melody and words. He stood in front of the bathroom sink lathering the soap, reaching for his double-edged razor, twisting his mouth up and to one side to shave in those tight corners around the mouth, spreading the skin under his lip and going into the indentation of his dimpled chin, while melodies and some words found their way through his turning and twisting lips out of the side of his mouth. *I'll be loving you Always / With a love that's true Always.*

He reached for his comb on top of the medicine chest, made a clear straight part, then as he swept his hair to one side, and might move into "Somewhere over the Rainbow." He sang through each of these daily routines. He'd go back into the bedroom to get dressed for work. By now he might be whistling. Then into the kitchen where he drank his coffee.

He sang or whistled as he dressed, as he drove, as he loaded iron onto his truck, and as he gathered up his tools—the metal of the tools and iron clanging, his voice rising as he worked iron. Up from his belly, resonating in his chest and mouth, surrounding him with air to walk in.

When he got up from his afternoon nap he might begin with a few whistled bars, blowing them into a string, gradually into full lyric whistling, "*They try to tell us we're too young / Too young to really be in love.*" Music was as much

Joanna Clapps Herman   233

a part of him as his heartbeat, the pulse of his blood, the cells in his marrow; music and song in his blood and along his bones.

On Saturday mornings as the light cracked, my father often rose to deal with whatever hadn't gone well on the job during the week. I was an early riser, too. And I trailed him wherever and whenever I could, so I'd sit at the kitchen table while he put on his socks waiting for him to say, "Can you get dressed quick?" He was loading the iron truck down at the shop before we get on the road to the construction site. He was singing, "If I Loved You" all day. He picked up a twelve-foot I-beam, hoisting it up onto his right shoulder, shifting it into balance, and walked across the yard over to the truck. The sheer strength of this jolted me: Even then I knew this wasn't what the human body was made for. Yet I could see that it was for him. He walked one beam then another over to the truck, lifted them onto his truck. Had he traded in the burdens of misery of his early life to carry these extraordinary weights instead? Did hauling those I-beams eventually tilt his body to one side, a list to the right, a slightly lowered shoulder, a downward hint in his gait that was so distinctly his?

Later on my father thickened, accumulating the solidity of an ancient Greek column, a man who could support weight, burdens. He was a man you could lean into. I can lean into him and feel his profound sturdiness still. This was the simple comfort that came to me after his death. I can still feel his body's weight and heft, its space and stability. It's the sensation of him, of his presence, which lives inside my own body. I know how much weight there is for me to lean into. I can feel how much it would take to push that body off center. More than I have. For all the complications he faced having come from violence, madness, death, and misery, he stood this body against it all, to hold as much from my sister and me as he could. I still find great comfort in leaning into the large column that his memory is. I find the strength I need there.

When he died it was ten weeks from diagnosis to burial. His strength hid all the sickness he bore until it was too late to treat him. He was eighty. But he still had "the pulse of a thirty-year-old," the doctors had said. But he was weeks from death, the cancer was everywhere inside. We just didn't know it yet. His strength had disguised what was happening inside of him.

While we waited to be told this treatment or that treatment could be tried, each of his grandchildren went to visit him. Each time he took them to climb the tower where he first kissed their grandmother. The first few times he climbed with us up to the top to view where a piece of their lives had come from. By the last two visits he couldn't climb it, so he drove us and we climbed up without him. We were still sure we could find a way.

There had been so many heights in his life, so many trees and rocks, diving boards, towers and stairs, and iron scaffolds along his path, and now one more height to climb. The last day was one of torturing pain. He woke with such pain that he asked my sister to find a drug dealer, anyone, to buy something anything, heroin, to help stop it. It was a Fourth of July weekend—a holiday—and a dangerous time to be in the hospital. The nurse continued to dismiss his request for stronger pain medication. "You're just postoperative. You have to expect some pain," she said in ill-disguised condescension.

That morning my mother was shaving him—probably for the only time in their long years together—when his nurse came in again. "What are you doing?" she asked, furious. She took the razor from my mother's hand and handed it to my father. "He can shave himself." And he did, sitting up in bed, singing a Willie Nelson song he sang often in those last weeks, "I'd like to leave it all behind and go and find / A place that's known to God alone just a spot we could call our own."

When his medical records arrived after his death, there was one clear, impossibly beautiful image of my father, a full-body X-ray—all his bones stretched long for us to see. The length is there, the heft, the strength too. There was such a shock of recognition. These were our father's bones. The list is there too—the slight downward tilt of the right shoulder, from all the heavy iron lifted, all the I-beams lifted, carried into place, all of the weight and wear pressed deep into his bones.

It was seeing that our father's bones laid bare that tilt that made my sister and I weep.

Here was the frame, the understructure, his architecture. His bones laid long.

Within that sturdy frame and easy body, all his life, his untamed spirit sometimes had little control of itself. The memories of those early years were deep inside him, and although he tried to hold them there, they'd force their way out and the storms would blow and we all knew where they came from. But the storms were spent now, and the bones are quiet when he lay for this final X-ray. He wouldn't get up to sing again.

After he died, in rare moments for mere seconds, I have allowed myself to peer into the ground and imagine his bones peeling back into just themselves as they rest in the gaia—that strong scaffolding taken down, not having to climb or build or hold or carry finally, but in deep repose in the solid earth. My own grief for my father lies down there next to his bones.

One night of the first snowstorm, my father insists that we all bundle up and go out while the rest of the city is hidden inside. He wants to pull my mother, my sister, and me on the back of our sled up the center of deserted streets, running and laughing out of the powerful center of his charmed vitality. The snow feathers against our faces as he runs all the way from the bottom of Division Street to the top of Long Hill Road. His body is a wild horse of an engine, each leg rising high to the gallop, each stroke of a leg lightly grabbing the snowy ground and pushing it behind him, his thick-soled work shoes churning down in through the thick white blanket to find the crunch of ground below, pulling us up the hill out of reality into this astonishing night. Midgallop, midflight, lengths from the top of the street, he flings a look over his shoulder, throwing back to us the ecstatic light this labor creates in him. A rupture of the light escapes, cracking through him from his aboriginal core, flinging phosphorescence out over the quiescent night. Chains on cars on tires, clanking, slowing slowly through the snow three streets away are not in the same universe with us. My father can carry his girls through this snow, up steep hills, in a night that belongs only to him, only to us. We three, his girls, ride on wooden slats. There at the other end of the rope he pulls his weighted cargo, the clay to his fire, just barely holding him down to earth.

Voglio bene

I

IN EARLY JUNE ON HUMID DAYS I HAVE OFTEN FOUND MYSELF WANDERING in a loose confusion—drifting through rooms, peering into drawers, fingering the folds of my nylon underthings, then feeling along the back edges of closet shelves—what did I do with my blue fan? Where can I have put it? I've always had my blue fan, always loved it, but it vanished in the ordinary disarrangements of domestic life so long ago that it might well be laying under a landfill in Staten Island, or behind the bottom drawer of a dresser that no longer belongs to me. Sadly, I am capable of giving away, or even throwing away, a beloved object in a fit of clearing out, which years later I predictably regret. At those moments I am disturbed in the way only humidity and loss can elicit.

The search for my blue fan marks those two weeks before the annual installation of the window air-conditioner, blocking the ever-quavering Hudson and the wide light from the sky above. In that late spring, I can't accept machinery as the solution to discomfort, especially since one day is perfect—high seventies with a breeze—and the next is subcontinental heat. Instead of going to talk to my super, I go looking for my blue fan.

My mother brought me the fan from Italy—Naples, I think—when she went for the first time to visit our Tolve. She also gave me a gold necklace she bought on the Ponte Vecchio in Florence. I have the necklace; a simple eighteen inches that sits across my breastbone as if my mother herself had personally tattooed it there. But the fan seems to have vanished.

My fan used to resurface seasonally on just the right occasions. I used it one blazingly hot summer night at an open-air opera in Rome. Its fine dark-blue silk spread up along its thin wood slats just the exact good number of inches beyond the curl of my hand around the pivot, making—as any good implement should—an extension of the hand in order to provide a small, almost silent sweep of air.

The light brush of air—whoa, whoa, past my face and neck—has the hint of incantation about it, evaporating the droplets of sweat on my face, neck, and breastbone where the gold chain is glued to my skin by perspiration. The breeze I create frees the chain from my skin. A perfect match between hand and instrument, the fan fits my hand as if a thirteenth-century Neapolitan craftsman had measured me for it. My fan made the perfect breeze, the best of weathers in a kind of self-induced paradise.

But the fan was gone for so long that I had to accept that fact, though I've asked myself again and again, why would I get rid of something so small, so unobtrusive, so loved? It created an ache of longing in me.

There were other thoughtful and generous gifts my mother gave me: a substantial sewing machine, a dainty silver thimble that fit my fingertip as if it had been molded to it. But it's the lost gifts that are surprisingly perfect in their absence.

A small, powerful pair of theater glasses that came in a leather case—easy enough to carry in an evening bag, strong enough to see the stage from far away—went missing too, just like my fan. Here in my top drawer with my jewelry, then not there. Where can I have put them?

II

Although my mother's father, Vito Becce, prospered in America beyond all of the dreams he carried with him as a young man from deep southern Italy, my mother and her family lived like the frugal peasants they had been in that ancient place. There was abundance of food and of land. And work. The rest was carefully husbanded. Clothes were worn until they frayed, brooms swept until they were small hard knobs of worn straw. Fences were made from bedsprings.

My grandfather carried with him anger against priests and their church because when the church loaned money to the peasants to purchase seed after a bad crop, the church then confiscated whatever parcels of land these *contadini* had managed to acquire if the crop failed again. It was usury. And the Catholic Church too was just another oppressive institution. But my grandfather's daughters had Italian friends who loved the church, and influenced his daughters. One by one, they were baptized and were married in the church my grandfather hated. Perhaps the luxury of candles and flowers, the flowing sheen of embroidered garments, were as appealing to his daughters as belonging to their larger community.

When my grandfather's four daughters became wives and mothers—controlling their own money, but still smartly frugal—they all acquired crosses, as if to mark their arrival into full ripeness. The crosses were substantial in design and weight—lovely pieces on good gold chains. Not overly ornate. The crosses became a part of them, resting just below their clavicles. While they carefully removed their engagement rings and wedding bands, placing them in small dishes or on shelves near their sinks when they washed dishes, I don't remember any of these women ever taking off their crosses, not even for bathing or showering, swimming or gardening. I can see my mother's hand pushing the towel underneath the cross and chain to dry herself, where water clung to skin and gold. The crosses seemed to come with being a grownup woman in my family.

As girls we were given or bought (with allowances, babysitting money, earnings from painting the back porch) medals with images of St. Christopher and the other saints we looked to for protection, guidance, hope in the face of hopelessness—St. Jude for lost causes, St. Anthony for lost objects, St. Christopher for travel. Saints' medals were objects of our contemplation for weeks at the tiny store in St. Lucy's Church, after Sunday Mass or Saturday confession. "I think I'll buy St. Anne, the mother of Mary . . . so beautiful the way she holds Mary in her arms." Already we were imagining ourselves as young mothers, beatific with our babies in our arms. I would marry, it seemed apparent to me, the dark-haired boy I looked at longingly for years during mass, but with whom I never spoke, whose name I never knew. The blond boy would be with my cousin Linda; our friend Mary would be with the sandy-haired boy.

The medals bore our earnest religiosity, containing in their exquisitely crafted details tiny worlds of hope and desire. One day the boys we longed for but could never speak to would kiss us in some dark place and long for us too. It was all iconic and real in those careful ovals stamped with saints and animals, winged creatures, churches on the back.

Once my father, out of his large and ample spirit, gave my sister and me five dollars each. This was an untold amount for girls like us, when weekly allowances were twenty-five cents or fifty cents at best. I went the very next day to buy the medal I had been looking at in our church store, where the glass cases were filled with shining objects of perfect miniature worlds. I had loitered after mass on Sundays, longing for that medal without hope of ever having enough money to buy it. Then suddenly I had exactly the right amount.

About a week later my father noticed me wearing my medal around my neck. "What did you do with the money I gave you?" he asked me in a friendly way.

"I bought this," I said fingering my small treasure.

"How much did it cost you?"

"Five dollars."

"Oh, you didn't," he said shaking his head. "You should always save at least some of the money you have." He had hoped we'd understand this intuitively, I wonder what might have happened if he had talked to us before giving us our shocking bounty. Would I have run to buy it just as quickly and felt guilty at that moment instead of afterward? It was a blow that my lovely father misjudged himself and me so completely. His disapproval bruised my pride and tarnished my treasure. I don't think I ever wore that medal with the same pleasure again. I know I didn't remove it. I couldn't abide the loss of its miniature perfection.

Years later, just before I graduated from high school, my mother sat me down at our Formica kitchen table. "I want to buy you something special for your graduation present," she said, elated by her own good idea. "I'm going to buy you a gold cross, and I want you to go with me downtown so that you can pick out the one you'd love." I was elated too. Gold, a cross, a jewelry store, shopping with my mother. All of it filled me up.

We took the bus from our house downtown to Bauby's Corner at Bank and West Main Streets, then crossed to stroll up Bank Street, mother and daughter, in ceremony and pleasure, in unison for this brief afternoon. I was to choose my own gold cross. My mother's instincts were right. She was buoyed with her idea and I was lifted beside her in this pleasure.

If my mother and I were often then at odds with each other, still I knew she was a model of decorum and social graces. She fit easily into her elegant suits and white gloves. She shopped downtown with a savoir-faire that could as easily have belonged in New York or Paris.

My mother stopped and chatted with several women as we walked up Bank Street toward Michael's Jewelry Store. Even I had to recognize the way these women were happy to stop and talk to my mother, her warmth and sweetness with them everything I both admired and didn't have. "This is my younger daughter." She'd turn to me as if we'd never had a bad word between us. "She's graduating Crosby High this year." None of these women were as well dressed as my mother, in her high heels and sweeping skirt; I could see they admired her elegance and sophistication. They were happy to be included in her circle.

It was the same at Michael's Jewelry, where it was, "Rose, how lovely to see you." All that day, my mother was at the height of her confidence. She was poised and benevolent. An important woman in her town.

The jeweler met her grace with his dignity, happy to lay out the crosses he carried one by one. I'm sure we looked at many before one singular cross was carefully placed on the black velvet display pad.

Crosses are made of two, narrow rectangular planes, one longer than the other, intersecting. These intersecting planes are an opportunity for all manner of designs of the imagination. Vines and lines. Jewels and draped gold.

The original was simple: the hanging body of Jesus on the cross rendered so iconically as to be almost an abstraction of the sacrificial figure. Jesus's long slender limbs are a graceful display of torture.

People who haven't grown up with the cross tell me how upsetting they find the image of a man crucified, but most of us who were raised with it see in it all the ancient narratives of sacrifice and divinity, Jesus, the sculptural embodiment of Isaac on the altar.

The crucified Jesus also evokes the ancient kouros, the slender young male at the door of maturity displaying the tenderness and beauty of his passage. The Greek kouros has a single foot forward, leading him into the future, Jesus's thin beauty is made up of all bent limbs, with one foot resting on the other in exquisite pain. Jesus's suffering has been softened on bejeweled crosses that render his sacrifice as twists of gold.

But the cross at Michael's that drew me to it was *other*.

I wasn't sure what to think when I first saw it. It was the simplest cross I had ever, or will ever, see. Its two simple flat gold arms had been turned on their sides—edges facing forward—creating two thin gold lines. This design made the cross seem almost two-dimensional.

Unembellished to the point of sheer grace, it was the one I chose. "Are you sure that's the one you want?" my mother asked. "You're sure?" I think she was ready to spend more money for something more elaborate, but she saw my instant passion for its simplicity. The purchase of that cross was a moment of détente in the long wars between us. A pause and a blessing.

III

At the end of that summer I went to Boston University and left my mother's sphere of influence. I fled the tight, confining rules she lived by with a zealotry that oddly suited the decade we were just coming into. But the cross remained my favorite piece of jewelry for a very long time. Its elegant simplicity made me feel simultaneously blessed and sophisticated whenever I wore it.

My cross went missing sometime between going to college and moving to New York. I had moved back and forth from college, been a camp counselor, driven across the country to California, and traveled to Europe a couple of times by the time I realized it had disappeared into the ether. Who knows how often my gold cross was placed in different top drawers. Then it was gone.

The house had a small, cool, modern feeling to it. The space flowed easily from one end to the other, with only two bedrooms, a living room, a decent-sized kitchen, and one bathroom. It was low and long, not deep and multistoried as so many of the other houses were on this street. In the '60s, my mother furnished it with mid-century modern Paul McCobb furniture. She no longer wore gloves and hats when she went downtown. Even she was influenced by the new.

This is where I got into trouble, played with my sister and my cousins, learned to read—to sneak off to read for hours so that no one could find me—learned to cook, clean, to be an Italian girl, and then young woman. It was at this front door that I had my first kiss.

It was that house we finally left when, after college we went out into the world. It was at that kitchen table where my father asked my mother one day after my sister and I had been working in Boston and New York, "Rose, when are the girls coming home?" My mother didn't tell us until many years later that when she said, "Peter, they're never coming back! They've left. When they went to college, they left," my father put his head down on the table and wept.

"He laughed at me for crying when we dropped you off at college. He had been waiting all this time for you both to come home."

After his heart attack, my father made clear that he wanted a smaller, quieter life. After long years as an ironworker on construction sites all over Connecticut, he had gotten his warning and he didn't want to work under constant pressure anymore. My mother wanted him to stay by her side.

The house had become a burden and what they wanted was to sell it and settle into a quieter life. They decided to sell every unnecessary thing they owned, including this house at 2279 North Main Street, and move to a one-bedroom apartment so that they'd have no strain or worry ever again.

And so the garage sale.

All of my aunts and cousins came to help. Lucia was there with her first child, Peter, who was just over a year old. I had been married and divorced all within little more than a year. We were all now in new places.

The large lawn was filled with everything that was for sale. Tables full of the hundreds of small things that came from who knows how many store counters. "Oh this is cute. I could use this when I bake Russian wedding cookies."

But there was also my father's Art Deco reading chair that had been banished to the basement, and end tables, beds, a good pale-yellow suitcase set, a gift from my mother I had used throughout college and my first trips to Europe. The basement, the closets, our attic had been emptied, and it all lay bare in the sun for strangers to gaze on, pick up, turn over, sometimes to buy.

It was a long, long day, and it was fun—like playing store when we were children. People bargained; we gave in. We helped them carry things to their cars. We worked as a team, laughing and talking. "Aunt Rose," my cousin Gilda would say, "How much do you want for this?," holding up an unpriced potato masher. I remember my father saying, "That money is gone; get whatever you can for everything. Whatever you collect today is gravy."

At the end of the day we'd made a little more than $400. My mother asked me one more time, "Jo, are you sure you don't want these beautiful suitcases? I paid so much money for them." I knew she had. A gift from my mother. But it was the '60s now, and a set of heavy suitcases just didn't belong anymore. I didn't have the space for them in my small studio apartment. And now neither would my mother. But one woman happily paid what my mother was asking. The pieces still looked brand new.

As the woman was bringing her new luggage to her car, my mother in her typical annoying way, said, "Wait, wait, let me run my hand through the side pockets inside." I turned to say to her, "For god's sake Mom, there's nothing there."

She was laughing with girlish delight when her hand came up out of the suitcase's small side-pocket. The delicate chain of my elegant gold cross was dangling from her hand. The cross. My cross.

I have had many a comeuppance with my mother—especially since she died. She had an obsessive way of keeping every single receipt for every single piece of furniture or household good she ever bought; all of the receipts turned up for the designer furniture suite that was too modern for our young taste.

Now her grandchildren love it—as well they should. It's quite smashing. After she died I found my grandfather's passport that I'm sure I would have thrown away in one of my sweeps. She held onto many things that I've come to treasure, that I had once tried to tear from her hands to discard. Thank goodness she resisted me.

I have my cross, that cross. It's the one sitting on a silver tray where I keep special pieces of jewelry. It's still elegant, still a gift from my mother.

IV

My husband Bill, the man I was with for forty years, died two-and-a-half weeks after a diagnosis. We knew he was frail, but we also knew he was not done. In his last weeks we still closed down restaurants at midnight, had friends over for long hilarious nights, went to museums and the New York Botanical Garden. Then he was gone. All of the losses in my universe were amplified.

I had to sell our apartment, buy another one, renovate it, and move—all in less than a year. It was a terrible upending but a financial necessity. But necessity can move a person forward like nothing else. I had to discard essential pieces of both of us—his desk, our Spanish table.

When it came to unpacking our dishes, our pictures, and our treasured library in my new apartment, everything was unrecognizable.

Slowly pulling our oversized morning cups out of their wrappings and placing them on strange shelves, finding out which drawers would be used for what. I knew where to store Bill's ashes and his eyeglasses and his manuscripts. I knew where to place photographs of him, but other decisions were harder to make.

And why did we have so much stuff anyway? All that stuff, which, as you unpack, you think, Why on earth did I buy this ridiculous thing? What am I keeping this for?

At the bottom of one immense box of odds and ends that I finally emptied after a month in my new apartment, I came across an old-fashioned crocheted bag my Zi'Lucia had made for my mother in the '30s. It was smart and very well made, with tight, intricately patterned stitches, but so old-fashioned that I knew I wouldn't use it again. I turned it over thinking I might pass it on to one of her granddaughters whom my sister and I had recently come to spend more time with. A bit of dust came up when I put the bag on the table, but it wouldn't lay flat. I guessed the heavy interfacing had buckled with age in a few places. Bad workmanship was not like Zi'Lucia. I unzipped the bag to see what was going on. Inside was the source of the problem. My blue fan and my opera glasses were tucked inside, waiting for me to find them—my mother's final benevolent offerings. The Italian phrase *voglio bene*, meaning "I love," is embedded in the Latin, in the word *benevolence*. A final benevolence from *madre mia.*

Somewhere My Bill

ONCE YOU LOVE SOMEONE DEEPLY AND DECIDE TO MAKE YOUR LIFE WITH that beloved, there are unspoken promises you're making, hidden from the two of you. My secret promise to Bill was that I would keep him alive. It was a promise so utterly buried I didn't know I had made it until after he died; it didn't get revealed before that because I managed to keep my promise for so long. I pulled Bill back from the brink of death—both of body and soul—so many times it seemed that I would always be able to do it.

Even though by marrying a man seventeen years older I claimed to be mindful that I'd likely lose him too early, I simply went about my job of bringing him back from the brink over and over. I got used to producing magic routinely—that was what was called for, and I was the one for that job.

Bill had a big, bright vital spirit. He was radiant in his joy, transmitting benevolent radiance to everyone he loved. It was embedded in his appreciation of all that humankind had created, whether it was a baby, a garden, a small, handmade tool, or a great masterwork, or simply whomever he happened to be talking to. Behind that, surrounding him, and deep inside Bill's fiery light, there was a large, dark, desolation that could overtake him, casting a shadow on his passionate presence. You never quite knew if incandescence, or the dread dark, would be in residence.

He was the only child born to his parents in a second marriage for both: his mother was a widow with three children from a previous marriage, his father a widower with five children. His father saw his mother through a window across his Bronx alley. When she noticed him watching her, she would draw the shade, until he paid one of her sons a nickel to lift the shade whenever she pulled it down.

Bill was the child conceived and born to heal the tragic wounds in his two families and to bring them together. Bill's much older siblings bathed him in the glow of their affection, perhaps grateful for the relief of uncomplicated love. He belonged to all of them, this adorable, love-adorned child. When they laughed and smiled at him, the ghastly stuff that had gone on, that still went on, was in those moments forgotten. Bill threw glimmers of light into the darkest corners of this complicated family. He danced and sang for them. He was the luminous center of this family for the years that his father lived.

His was a broken mess of a family. His mother was more than unkind to her stepchildren, while his father didn't defend them from her. There were two kinds of betrayal. The older siblings from each family liked each other, but they were caught in their parental divide. Although Bill was the high contrast to this mess, it was simply too much for a small child to carry. Once his father fell ill and died, the family fell apart. After that, Bill's luminescence and his darkest despair were both permanently part of him.

That early love gave this sun-glazed child a confidence, and all its attendant privileges, that the many of us couldn't imagine having. He'd talk his way in and out of situations where others would have surrendered to defeat. He *would* be allowed to use that special bathroom reserved only for members when he was not one. He *would* expect to be shown to the head of the line at a restaurant, and usually was.

At other odd, unpredictable times though, a fugue state overtook Bill; during those times he'd live in a fog. He'd barely answer when I spoke to him. Or he'd "Yes" me to death, or he'd ignore me so utterly that I came to expect it. He'd snarl when I spoke to him, so I'd go away and leave him to his misery. He expected me to understand him telepathically. Often I did. But apparently, he figured out I was never going to understand the underlying cause of these black times by either intuition or osmosis. I always thought they were random. But once, about ten years into our marriage, he explained that these moods often overcame him in the season of his father's fatal illness and death, the summer Bill was eight. His father was in bed and Bill stayed home from school pretending to be sick in order to be with his father.

One morning in September, a month before Bill's birthday, his mother sent him into the darkened bedroom to bring his father, who had been bedridden all summer, some custard for breakfast. When he tried to wake him, his father's body was cold. How had his mother left that bed only a short time earlier without realizing her husband was gone?

Bill began to wail and weep inconsolably. When he wasn't able to stop himself, his older brothers locked him in a small back bedroom where he wept by himself, looking out the window at a tree of heaven in their backyard. The dappled sun and shade from the tree sealed his grief day on that September morning. A piece of him stayed in that bedroom for most of his life, next to the iridescent child who had brought joy to his family.

Bill danced back and forth across that divide all of his life. Now exploding with energy, now certain he would never sing again.

I was twenty-nine and Bill was forty-seven when we met. Though we both had been married before, his had been a real marriage with two smart, lovely daughters. Bill loved his daughters completely, but felt he hadn't been the best father he could have been. He wasn't wrong about that. He'd slip away from them and come back when he came back to life. Not good enough for young girls.

By the time I met him, he had traveled a complicated path to his career as a professor. I was just beginning to come uncertainly into my own.

It took us a few weeks to become a couple, a few months to know there was something unusually good between us—that it wasn't just all early hot jazz—but it took three years of dating, being together, fighting, negotiating to decide that we could and would marry, despite the large age difference between us. The real stumbling block though, was the fact that Bill didn't want to raise another family. His daughters were only eighteen and nineteen. He didn't want to start over again. We both knew early in our union, and later after forty years together, that you just don't come upon what we had together so easily and so we had to find a way past our problems

There were no compromises to be made. He couldn't change his age, and you can either have a child or not have a child. There was no way around that. Either we had to give in and be with each other or walk away. We had tried the latter.

We both came back to what was so good between us; it was unique and we knew it. Neither of us had had the luck to find it before. Eventually we decided—with some joy and a lot of agonizing—to jump past the problems and enter our life together.

What was between us: We were both a couple of kids from the working class who had ridden the road out of our provincial past by reading all the time. We both loved to read and to think about literature and all forms of narrative, fiction, theater, film, television, storytelling, conversation, writing. We were both very social; we loved having friends into our homes. We loved to cook, to cook together, and to cook for our friends and family. We loved children and babies. We loved to travel. We loved living informally at home. If we were alone, we ate in our underwear when we felt like it. A great match, except for the ways we drove each other mad with frustration. He generated chaos and found it a fertile soil. My own internal chaos made it impossible to live with disorder from the outside.

We loved each other in very different ways. Beyond Bill's flamboyant brilliance, I loved how attuned he was to so many different layers of art, the humanities, history, and the broader world, how incredibly well educated he was. How extensively he had read in almost every field. He seemed to know the words to every song written in the twentieth century and could sing them all. If he didn't know the words, he'd learn them. He could call up names, places, dates, and historical trends from almost every period in Western culture. He had a phenomenal memory: he memorized my family's home addresses when he was wooing me—mostly to prove he had some pretty fancy footwork. He was a gifted mimic, an impresario, a flimflam man, a disappearing act.

He was sweet natured. *Dolcissimo.* My friends loved him. He cherished me so much. "I love the way you smell," he'd always say. "You always smell so good."

I was young and pretty and had all of my own abundant energy. He loved that and he also loved that a large family came with me. It pleased him that I wouldn't let him disappear for too long into his darkest of dark corners. He thought I was smart because I know a lot about practical life. This dazzled him. He was too easily dazzled by me.

When he was on, he'd push back his chair from the table, and as he stood up, first he'd touch his belly, then hooking his thumb over his belt he'd clear his throat. Then he'd take the room. He'd look around and launch. He'd tell stories that would have all of us mesmerized or howling with laughter. Sometimes he'd laugh so hard himself that we had no idea what he was saying. Sometimes he'd keep us laughing for hours and hours. He owned the room. Then having exhausted himself, after a bit of a pause, he's say, "Good night all. I'm going to sleep now." He might end with, "That's one in a row," and off he'd go. Slip into our bedroom and get in bed, no matter how much longer the party continued. No one minded. That was Bill. "A few laughs, you've got to have a few laughs in life," was another of his favorite sayings. He was a masterpiece of the Jewish kid from the Bronx—smart, funny, chilled too often by doubt and dark depressions underneath the humor. A classic.

Bill had a solid, sturdy body with two sculpted tree trunks for legs that was completely unearned. He did little to no exercise for most of his adult life, and enjoyed repeating endlessly, "Whenever I have the impulse to exercise, I lie down until it goes away." But he was also somewhat overweight for a good deal of his adult life, his strong body supporting a lovely *panzone*, a big belly that I loved.

Much later on, when he began to lose weight, I realized that he had a beautiful Middle Eastern face hidden under his weight. At the Metropolitan Museum of Art we came upon Bill's exact body type and facial profile in the almost-3,000-year-old friezes of the Assyrian Royal Palace Guards. There are the same bones, the same serious face with its beaked nose, the expression filled with intelligence, purpose, and intent. "Some Assyrian Royal Guard must have been messing with one of your great-great-great-grandmas," I said. These warriors were guarding their king, but although Bill looked like them, he was a lover, not a fighter.

Especially of women. It was wonderful to be *the* woman of a man who loved women. Nothing made Bill happier than hanging out with pretty women, making them laugh, telling them stories, telling them how beautiful and smart they were. Of course, women loved him back.

Early in our courtship we'd go to a double feature, then out for Chinese food, pick up the Sunday *New York Times* on Saturday night in Sheridan Square, stop by Smiler's Delicatessen for bagels and cream cheese, and settle into my tiny studio apartment for the weekend.

"Constancy," he said to me on one of the weekend nights fairly early on, lying on my trundle bed, "that's what counts in a relationship." Who says things like that? I thought. Not the younger men I had known. These details settled into me, mattered.

He defined our experiences with understanding and precision. "It's not relentlessly tasteful," he said sharply when we stayed at a quiet inn in Connecticut.

My mother didn't like Bill when she first met him. He was wearing blue jeans, a plaid shirt. He had longish hair, a big mustache, a '70s hipster.

She didn't like it when I told her I was dating an older man, but after she met him she summed up her opinion. "A man of his position dressing like that," she said with contempt. "How could he?" Suddenly I saw him the way she must have seen him—not young and handsome, way too informal. What on earth was I doing with him? I was being happy, but it unnerved me that she saw him as so wrong for me.

My father had a heart attack soon after that. Bill drove me to Waterbury to visit my father in the hospital. My mother, her sisters, my Aunt Bea all sat in the visiting room together, knitting and sewing, talking and talking. My father was allowed only one visitor every hour for about twenty minutes. My mother would wait for her turn. But I got the next turn. I went in and Bill stayed in the waiting room with the women of my family.

Visiting my father was intimate and reassuring. "When I thought I might be going," he said, "I wasn't afraid. I wasn't worried. I thought to myself, I've had a good life with your mother and you girls. I want you to know that." I stayed with him and talked and didn't mention Bill for even a minute.

"Your family is so bound together," Bill said on the drive home. "I listened to everything they said to each other. They talked and talked, about their children, about their families. 'Oh look how beautiful he looked in his communion suit.' 'You have such lovely children, Bea. They're kind and wonderful,'" I could hear their voices as he quoted them. I saw that he knew exactly who they were. "They are tribal, bound together forever," he said.

"You really don't have to worry about what they think of me, because a tribe like that has only two choices. Either they embrace me and bring me into their tribe, or they reject me. And they will never reject you. So they'll have to accept me." Bill's brilliant insight gave me a new way to see my family, to be in my family, to know them in a new way, through his eyes. In time, my family fell in love with his charm and sweetness, and he became among the most cherished members of my large Italian tribe.

One Saturday summer afternoon we were at a fancy haircutting shop on Christopher Street in the Village. As a new girlfriend, of course I thought I should take over his haircuts. Don't we love to take on grooming our new loves? I had grabbed my mail from the box on the way out of the building. Now, as the barber cut Bill's hair, I opened an envelope from my brother-in-law, John Mudd. Out of the envelope came a photo of the legs of my one-year-old nephew, Peter Mudd; the photograph stopped just below Peter's knees to show us his brand new, navy-blue, Italian leather, tie-up baby shoes that showcased his fat little calves. I was and still am, completely mad for Peter, and said, laughing, "We'd better go see these fat little legs," showing Bill the photograph. His eyes lit up and somehow in the next two days we had bought tickets, renewed his passport, and flown to Italy to see Peter and my sister and brother-in-law. It was impulsive and ridiculous. But that was how it came to be that we were in Italy soon after we met.

After our visit with my family, we went on to *fare un giro*, to tour around Tuscany. I had been in and out of Italy a few times by then, but Bill hadn't been in Italy before. Maybe almost more than anything, I wanted him to see the Piazza del Campo in Siena. I talked and talked about it as we drove there: why it was so unique, how it made you feel as you walked into it, stood in it. As we settled into our hotel watching the starlings swooping outside our window overlooking the terra-cotta roof tiles in the dusk, I talked about it some more. It's an astonishing space: spread out like a seashell, as you come to its edge, it scoops you into its medieval civic heart. In the morning we had our *cornetto* and *caffè*. I continued to talk about why I loved the Campo as we walked toward it.

Some might say that I am hyperbolic, talking high and fast about these things. As we approached the medieval tunnels that lead into the Campo, I had a flash of a revelation. Nothing could live up to what I had talked about so excessively. Bill was a few steps ahead of me and I called to him, "Bill, Bill, just a minute please." I wanted him to pause, so I could apologize, explain I had probably ruined this experience with my hyperbole. I had to call to him a few times as he walked toward the arch of light leading into the Campo.

He turned back to me, just as I was about to apologize and explain what I had done. But he had gotten his first glimpse, and now I had a glimpse of him. He looked stricken, tears were running down his face. If Bill could withstand my hyperbole, he's the man for me. I should marry this man, I thought. We walked into the Campo together as I turned this revelation over quietly inside.

Bill and I loved everything about the Mediterranean. Wherever there were old stones burning in the Mediterranean sun, we were happiest—ruins from the Greeks, from the Romans in Turkey, in France, in Italy, Crete, Greece. We loved to be there as the sun poured into those old worn blocks of what had once been buildings, theaters, squares, temples. Almost too hot to touch. That's where we were happiest. The stones had that sun glaze of Mediterranean ruins reflecting back the pleasure of our explorations.

Once in our middle years, I had a dream that Bill and I were at such a site and there was a hill ascending with a path running between two hillocks of sun-drenched rubble. I climbed and climbed to get up to the ruin I knew was at the top. At some point I realized Bill wasn't right behind me, so I turned to run back down to find him. "Bill, Bill," I called out as I ran down the hills, worried and upset. I found him at the bottom, standing outside a car gleaming in the relentless sun. "I didn't know where you were," I said, scared and breathless.

"Don't you know," he beamed at me with his sweetest smile, "I'll always be waiting for you? Always."

He was the most unconscious person I've ever known. It brought forth his brilliance from places in him about which he couldn't really talk. Writing poems that ran on scintillating electric lines—bursting out of him, or crawling up; sometimes he wrote every day for months. But then there were years of not writing at all. And he wouldn't really be able to say why. But he could wrap me up in his unconscious, too. I'm normally perceptive, even annoyingly overobservant, but there were things I missed completely because they were so deeply buried inside him—like his mourning season for his father. I think that in my deep connection to him, I helped him keep his secrets.

When we were at a body of water he'd say, "The water's too cold," after he was up to his chest in a lake that I was going to swim across. "I'm going to read on the blanket here."

Or, "Not today, Jo. I just don't feel like getting wet today. Not in the mood. You go sweetheart. I just want to keep reading here in the shade." I would. He'd be loving. He'd make a great joke, or he'd tease me. "How could I possibly keep up with you flying across the lake?" I was a reasonable swimmer and he was a reasonable man. It took me twenty years before I finally realized he couldn't swim. How could that possibly have happened? He didn't know how, and he wasn't going to reveal this. I had somehow become party to his secret by believing there was always a perfectly good reason for him not to swim on that particular day.

Reading and writing were at the center of his life as much as his family and friends were. Bill was a fine writer. I loved his work the minute I read a single piece. But when years would go by and he wouldn't write anything—not a poem, not a story, not even in his journals—the eras when he wrote nothing left him with a gaping absence.

"Why aren't you writing Bill? You're so good," I insisted year in and year out, early in our marriage.

"You leave me alone. It's none of your business. I'm not talking to you about this."

"But why can't we even talk about it?"

"That's none of your business either. Just shut up about it. And leave me alone."

He was so absolute at those times that eventually I stopped pressing him about it.

Raising James slowly began to heal the terrible mourning that lived in Bill for so long. When Bill lived beyond the age of his father's death, a darkness lifted. When James passed the age that Bill was when Bill's father died, another curtain rose to let more light inside. And slowly he worked harder at fathering his girls. He had fewer black depressions. But he still liked to dance with the dark, to linger in the shadow of misery.

Eventually I learned that I could be the witch who could bring him back from the edge where he loved to play with the idea that he might cross over. Some of his troubles were performance, some of it was genius at mourning; some of it was his Russian Jewish soul. Once he started writing again, I sat with him many times, helping him to find his way back to whatever next project was waiting in him. In those years I realized that when he didn't write, he often had terrible nightmares, physically fighting his tormentors. As he got older, he wrote always. Almost every day.

In Bill's need to dazzle and risk, dance and despair, he'd often collapse in ways that even he had almost no understanding of. Sometimes he knew but he just couldn't find a way to bring the words up. "What, what is going on with you? You're in a cloud and I have no way to find you," I might say after days of not being able to break through. "I don't know. I just don't know."

But sometimes if I badgered him enough, a clear answer would emerge, in a voice ferocious with desolation. "How could I have screamed at James that way? What's wrong with me? He's just a little boy." He'd slump down further in his chair, refuse to look at me.

This could refer to something that had happened the week before. "I'm a lousy father."

This was an easy one. "Bill, you and James adore each other. But you also drive each other crazy. That's natural. You're father and son. When he comes home from school, just tell him you wish you hadn't screamed at him last week when he lost his jacket. Give him a hug. It's okay. We have years to get this right."

He'd pick up his head. "Yeah, you think it's okay? It will be okay? I do love him so much." Now he was standing. Blood had filled his drained veins and began to roar through his body. "I was thinking, maybe I should take him on a trip across country this summer, following the baseball teams we love. You know, father and son. I'm going to look into that right now. We could do a road trip and hang out in hotels. That would be great." He'd turn to me beaming and say, "I'm going to check the schedule on the computer right now. What do you think? It's a good idea right?"

But he didn't wait for the answer. He was off and running.

"Somedays I think I'm going to live forever," he'd shout from his desk.

Cloud lifted. Problem solved. For the nonce.

As James grew up, Bill entwined his own destiny with that of James's. He was happy to pick him and all of his high school friends up at four in the morning with little more information than that they were somewhere out in Queens, a village called Glen Oaks or Laurelton. *Chissa?* James and he did seem to have something of a telepathic connection. James might walk into our apartment and take one look at his father and say, "Poppa, let's talk about it."

"What just happened? What are you talking about James?" I'd have no idea what was going on.

"Poppa's upset about what's going on with my grad school application. He thinks I'm procrastinating. He's just concerned about me." This would be something I had no idea about from either of them.

For many years, throughout his high school, college, and postcollege years James walked right past me to embrace his father and kiss him. I'd get out of his path if I were in it. It was a big romance.

Bill hated to waste his time on most practical chores. He'd yes me endlessly. "I will, I will. I promise tomorrow, I'll help you with that. In a little while." I always believed him. I had been asking him for weeks to help me move a lovely Spanish table that I was using as a desk in my study. But it was wasted under papers and books and a computer. "Let's bring it into the living room where we can see it."

"That's a great idea," he'd agree enthusiastically. "We'll definitely do it tomorrow. Happy to help you, honey." This went on for several weeks. "Of course. I'll help you with it. Give me a couple of days." Eventually I pointed out that this not very difficult task had been postponed for weeks.

He put down the book he was reading. "Okay, I'll make a date to move it. May tenth, I promise I'll help you move it on May tenth. Sitting comfortably in his reading chair, he'd look off for a few seconds, and begin to sing me a song that he was making up. "In May, in May, the tenth of May, this will be our Spanish-table moving day." This was still some days away, but given the song, the charm, the delight in having a husband who would make up a song to buy time, I accepted this con artist's trick. He sang me that song every tenth of May from then on.

I gave him the husband of the year award very often. Sometimes if I were a little annoyed I'd call him, "The very best of a bad lot," meaning men.

He'd say to me, "You're a bargain," then for emphasis in his mother's Yiddish accent, "Vat a bargain."

He loved living in the apartments I worked hard to make comfortable, functional, and as beautiful as I could on our modest budget. After he resisted every single change I suggested, he was always the one who took the most pleasure in our homes. "What a bower of bliss," he might say when I got new comforter or linens. "I love our home. You make it such a pleasure to be in."

The last ten years of our life together, we lived in an apartment that had six large windows overlooking the Hudson River. It was a dream come true that I had never even dared to hope for. We sat by those windows at the end of the day with a glass of wine, some music on, and watched the sun drift down the horizon. It had been a difficult move for Bill. I never insisted on things like that, but that time I insisted. It was something I had to do, to leave our lovely, but very dark apartment as the real-estate market went higher and higher every single week. In one three-week period it increased by such a massive amount that I knew it was a moment we had to seize. It would not last. He was seventy-seven. We were downsizing. We had to get rid of books, put stuff in storage.

We had to move three times before we could occupy apartment 8E at 315 Riverside Drive. Ordinary New York real estate stuff. All that moving was awful. But no one was happier about living in that apartment than Bill. We watched the boats and barges go up and down the river with surprise every time they came and went. "Look, look," we'd call each other to the window. We watched immense green storms come up the river. We ate dinner by the windows in our armchairs. His darkness was mostly at bay in those years.

Throughout all of our years together, at the end of each day, good or ghastly, we crawled back to our *matrimonia*, the large bed that was our home for two, where we lay side by side, reading and chatting, each of us slowly unwinding the tumult of the ordinary, so that we could to be ready for our night wanders. This was where we anchored our life.

He wrote almost every single day through the last years, despite having several terrible illnesses, including one that came very close to killing him. But we willed him back somehow, his eldest daughter Donna, our son James, and me. We went from doctor to doctor, hospital to hospital, we dragged him back from the edge again.

In October 2013 we found out that he had all kinds of cancer, but the longer term was still being figured out. He had six months to a year. We brought him to the emergency room on his eighty-seventh birthday, because his blood pressure spiked so dangerously high that he could have had a stroke. It took a full day to get him into a hospital room.

That night, as he lay on the gurney in the emergency room, he said quietly, "It's so strange. I have no desire to read at all." I should have thrown myself down on the floor and wept and wept. I should have known it meant that he'd be dead in a few days. The end came so swiftly, only seventeen days from PET scan to gone, that I never caught my breath. With each new test and revelation we were told something else, a year, or six months, then months or weeks. Probably months. It wasn't clear. It wasn't until fourteen hours before he died that a doctor finally took Donna and me aside and told us that he only had a few days to live. I counted on those days for our family to come to say goodbye. By the next morning he was gone. At the end I got everything wrong. He slipped away from us before I could protect him from anything. I wasn't able to keep him with us for even a few extra hours.

Grief is inevitably filled with regret for what you've done wrong. It's just that way. There is no other way. Because you have failed at the most basic level, as I did—to keep my beloved alive.

There is one hour of my life with Bill that is permanently alive in me. One night when James was still a toddler, we left my parents' apartment in Waterbury and drove toward Litchfield in the twilight. James had finally surrendered to sleep. Bill was talking about riding in the rumble seat of his father's car with his brother Steve's big arm around him, on a night just like this. We were in the dusk of a summer day. Peacefulness gently filled the car, the night, the air around us. It covered James asleep in the backseat. The shadows of the trees were long across the meadows as the last splashes of sun slid down behind the hills. Bill and I were alone together as the incandescent evening settled over the fields, over the hills. Alone together, in that memory, we are held in the liquid light where the time hangs loosely suspended, between day and dark, reality and dreams, between hope and fear, and I am able to keep my Bill alive. And with me. Always.

NOTES

1. My family comes from the province of Potenza, in a region in Southern Italy that has two names: Basilicata and Lucania. Lucania was the name used in ancient times by the Greeks and Roman, based on the name of the ancient tribe, the *Lucani*, who inhabited this part of Italy. I was brought up calling it Basilicata, but in the past few decades I've found that Lucane prefer to call themselves by that name, so I've adopted it too. I use both names interchangeably.

2. Waterbury, Connecticut, my ancestral village.

Wikipedia entry: Italians in Waterbury. "Connecticut has the most residents with Italian descent in the United States, with Waterbury having the largest Italian population statewide. Historically, the North End has been one of Waterbury's most heavily populated Italian neighborhoods/sections, together with Town Plot. It was the center of Italian immigration which came up the road from New York City."

3. *Pisciat*: a baby with a diaper so heavy with piss that it has an over-powering smell.

4. Claps, Clapps as an Italian name. There are many Claps families in Southern Italy, especially in our family province, Basilicata, also known as Lucania. The name Claps was originally spelled with one *p*, but my grandfather Giuseppe Clapps, for reasons we don't know, began to spell it with two *p*'s.

Claps is an Arberesh name. That means the patrilineal line of our family came to Italy from Albania. In our case it is documented to be from the fifteenth century. Church records in Naples record the Claps name in Potenza, Avigliano, from the 1480s on. We didn't keep the Eastern Orthodox dialect and customs, as many of the Arbereshe who fled Albania to live in Sicily and Southern Italy did. We didn't even know that we are what is known as Arbereshe until very recently.

Wikipedia Entry:

The Arbëreshë (Albanian pronunciation: [arˈbəreʃ], Albanian: *Arbëreshët e Italisë or Shqiptarët e Italisë*), also known as Albanians of Italy or Italo-Albanians, are an Albanian ethnic and linguistic group in Southern Italy, mostly concentrated in scattered villages in the region of Apulia, Basilicata, Calabria, Molise and Sicily. They are the descendants of mostly Tosk Albanian refugees, who fled from Albania between the fourteenth and eighteenth centuries in consequence of the Ottoman invasion of the Balkans.

During the Middle Ages, the Arbëreshë settled in Southern Italy in several waves of migration, following the establishment of the Kingdom of Albania, the death of the Albanian national hero Gjergj Kastrioti Skënderbeu and the gradual conquest of Albania and the Byzantine Empire by the Ottomans.